Ted Su
Barnacle of Baseball

Janet —

This dude pushed the blarney
like nobody else in his time.
But some of this bio
is still true.

Tom
Co

Pat O'Neill

Ted Sullivan, Barnacle of Baseball

The Life of the Prolific League Founder, Scout, Manager and Unrivaled Huckster

PAT O'NEILL AND
TOM COFFMAN

McFarland & Company, Inc., Publishers
Jefferson, North Carolina

Frontispiece: Illustration from *Nashville American*, February 14, 1893. "Ted Sullivan needs no introduction to baseball fans, for to introduce him would be to introduce baseball itself. Mr. Sullivan is so well known in the baseball world that if you should in the blissfulness of your ignorance plaintively ask 'Who is Ted Sullivan?' you would thereafter be shunned and avoided as a person of unsound mind" (*Abilene Daily Reporter*, March 25, 1920).

LIBRARY OF CONGRESS CATALOGUING-IN-PUBLICATION DATA

Names: O'Neill, Pat, 1953– author. | Coffman, Tom, author.
Title: Ted Sullivan, barnacle of baseball : the life of the prolific league founder, scout, manager and unrivaled huckster / Pat O'Neill, Tom Coffman.
Description: Jefferson, North Carolina : McFarland & Company, Inc., Publishers, 2021. | Includes bibliographical references and index.
Identifiers: LCCN 2021034552 | ISBN 9781476684789 (paperback : acid free paper) ∞
     ISBN 9781476642604 (ebook)
Subjects: LCSH: Sullivan, Timothy Paul, 1848–1929. | Baseball players—United States—Biography. | Immigrants—Ireland—Biography. | Baseball—United States—History—19th century. | Baseball—United States—History—20th century. | BISAC: SPORTS & RECREATION / Baseball / History
Classification: LCC GV865.S885 O54 2021 | DDC 796.357092 [B]—dc23
LC record available at https://lccn.loc.gov/2021034552

BRITISH LIBRARY CATALOGUING DATA ARE AVAILABLE

ISBN (print) 978-1-4766-8478-9
ISBN (ebook) 978-1-4766-4260-4

Front cover image: Ted Sullivan illustration from *Nashville American*, February 14, 1893.

Printed in the United States of America

McFarland & Company, Inc., Publishers
   Box 611, Jefferson, North Carolina 28640
   www.mcfarlandpub.com

Acknowledgments

Patti Peters and Julie O'Neill—Who want never again to hear Ted Sullivan's name spoken in their presence. God bless them for their love and patience.

James Bradley—Late of County Mayo, who channels Ted's spirit and character for us.

Karen Brown—Most patient friend and copy editor.

Mike Casey—Award-winning former reporter and editor for the *Kansas City Star*.

John Dawson—Author, researcher extraordinaire and most supportive friend.

Kevin and Karen Flynn—Who kindly shared their great knowledge of early Washington baseball.

Mike Kelley—Award-winning former reporter and editor for the *Kansas City Star* and the *Las Vegas Sun*.

Bob Kendrick—Executive director of the Negro Leagues Baseball Museum.

Mads Madsen—Talented artist and colorizer who brought to life the photos of Ted, young and old.

Milwaukee Public Library Rare Books team—who gave us access to a rare copy of *Humorous Stories of the Ball field*.

Dan Regan—Graphics designer, friend and creative counsel.

Jeff Sackman—Who transcribed *Humorous Stories of the Ball Field* in his "Summer of Jeff" blog.

Barbara Scanlon and Stacey Hodges—Genealogists who dug up Ted's lineage for us.

John Thorn—Who graciously shared St. Louis Unions memorabilia with us.

Scott Wilson—Descendant of the Sullivan clan who shared with us a most rare copy of Ted Sullivan's 1915 book, *Famous Colored Stories of the World*.

Dorothée Werner—Translator from French and speaker of that language most beautifully

Other readers, advice-givers, bugs and cranks—Chris Coffman, Bob Cox, Joe Fogarty, Carol Gonzales, Michael Gonzales, Bill Grady, Vahe Gregorian, Jenell Wallace Loschke, Mike Lynch, Mike Mahoney, Scott Marlo, Roisin Nevin, Lonnie Shalton, Tommy Wyrsch.

Thanks to the professional, gracious and helpful librarians at the Missouri Valley Room of the Kansas City (MO) Public Library, The St. Louis (MO) Public Library, the Midcontinent Library (Independence, MO), the St. Marys (KS) Public Library, the Paris (TX) Public Library, the Carnegie-Stout Public Library in Clinton (IA), the Burlington (IA) Public Library, the Chicago (IL) Public Library, the Milwaukee (WI) Public Library, the Los Angeles (CA) Public Library.

Special thanks to: Derek Gray, archivist Special Collections, Washington, D.C., Public Library; Susie Anderson-Bauer, archivist, Pius XII Memorial Library at Saint Louis University; Amy Nelson, associate director of archives and record management for the Archdiocese of Milwaukee; Peter Beirne and Brian Doyle, Clare County (Ireland) Public Library; Emily-Jane Dawson, Multnomah County (Oregon) Library; Lauren Gray, head of reference, Kansas State Historical Society.

Table of Contents

Acknowledgments   v

Preface by Pat O'Neill   1

1. A Long, Long Way from Clare to Here   7
2. Young Sullivan at Old St. Mary's: Jesuit Priests, Prairie Fires, and a Freshman Phenom   12
3. Playing for Peanuts: Ted and Charlie Take Their Game to Dubuque   18
4. In Fast Company: 1879 Dubuque Rabbits   23
5. Taking on "The Infidels"   30
6. A Sorry State of the Union   44
7. Back to the Bushes   55
8. Not Milwaukee's Best   68
9. Behind the Plate   74
10. "Senator Sullivan" Goes to Washington   77
11. Back to the "Auld" Country   90
12. Things Go South: Chattanooga and "The Dry Grins," 1892   102
13. A Tale of Two Sullivans   109
14. At Home on the Range   113
15. Ted Herds His Steers North to New Haven   121
16. Dubuque, Part II   128
17. "Same Old Trick": Southern Postscript, 1899   135
18. A Midwife of the American League   139

19. The Prodigal Hustler Returns   149
20. "The Original Gumshoe Man": Beating the Bushes
        for Prospects   154
21. Sullivan's Off-Base Humor   168
22. Baseball's Ubiquitous Ambassador   176
23. Show Him the Money   185
24. Next Stop: The World   195
25. Ted's Magic Lantern Show   218
26. Sox and Saints: Hall of Famers Slay St. Mary's   223
27. Twilight of a Colorful Career   231
28. Ted's Last Hurrah   238
29. The Third Strike   245

Sporting Editor's Notes   253
Chapter Notes   257
Bibliography   269
Index   273

Preface
by Pat O'Neill

In his day, T.P. "Ted" Sullivan was considered the best baseball mind in America. Some went so far as to call him "The Daddy" of the sport. He was early baseball's town-hopping bandleader; the ringmaster of the minor leagues; a George Washington, a Harold Hill, and a P.T. Barnum all rolled into one.

Damon Runyon dubbed him "The Barnacle of Baseball."[1]

Cunning, fast-talking, witty, charming, serious, and sober, Ted Sullivan traveled more than a million miles in the days of horse-drawn buggies, soot-spitting trains, and lumbering steamships. From the late 1860s until the day he died in 1929, Sullivan played, managed, and scouted for dozens of leagues and teams, planting the seed of his beloved sport across the breadth of the United States, Mexico, Europe, Asia, and South America.

In 1911, White Sox impresario Charles Comiskey, a.k.a. "The Old Roman," spoke for many in the early baseball world when he said: "Ted Sullivan's standing in the profession of baseball cannot be measured by modern standards. He is in a class all by himself. He is ever and always ahead of his time, with knowledge of the game and a versatility that no other baseball man of my acquaintance has ever possessed."[2]

An Illinois scribe described Ted Sullivan, in his palmy playing days of the 1870s, as "a red-cheeked, sturdy little Irishman, very much undersized for a pitcher. He was good-natured, crafty, a chatterbox when wound up, very proud of his ancestry and himself."[3]

Sullivan is, in fact, credited with discovering Comiskey in college and turning him into a crackerjack big league first baseman and, later, one of the most famous "magnates" of major league baseball. The two were the closest of friends their entire lives, with Comiskey maintaining Sullivan as the White Sox's chief talent scout and organizer of the team's annual spring training encampments.

1

Without question, in those early days no one worked harder or traveled more miles to promote baseball—and his own reputation and legacy—than Irish-born Timothy P. "Ted" Sullivan. For 50 years, from 1879 to 1929, newspapers and magazines sang his praises, genuflected to his genius, and bought his blarney by the barrel.

Yet 140-some years after he brought professional baseball to rural America, plucked future Hall of Famers from the bushes, brought them into the bigs, and introduced America's game to would-be players and fans around the globe, not one in a million baseball fans today can tell you who Ted Sullivan was, or all he did to make the game what it is today—for better and worse.

For starters, if it weren't for Ted Sullivan, you and I wouldn't even be baseball "fans." Rather, we'd still be called "bugs," "croaks," or "cranks." For it was "Sir Ted," as he was often called, who knighted us with the more genteel-sounding moniker "fans"—short and sweeter—for fanatics.

He helped pioneer ladies' days, bicycle days, newsboy days, and baseball on the Sabbath. He set trends and tinkered with baseball's evolving rules. *Sporting Life* called him "a queer genius" for suggesting that only eight players be allowed to bat, so fans could be spared having to watch the twirlers try to hit, because they were, as he said, "a lot of whippoorwill swingers."[4]

He is credited with finding and/or furthering the careers of more major league stars than any scout or manager of his day. The list of his foundlings is as long as his frequent after-dinner speeches, though many of their names have faded from baseball's memory: Arlie Latham, Billy Hamilton, Johnny Kling, Hoss Radbourn, Dave Bancroft, Charlie Comiskey, Buck Weaver, Walt Wilmot, Connie Mack, Hank O'Day, William "Dummy" Hoy, Ray Schalk, Shano Collins, Orval Overall, Dave Rowe, Jack Fournier, and George Stovall, to name just a few.

Sullivan grew up and played ball in the bungling adolescence of the sport—where batters wielded 40-ounce sticks shaved flat on one side and chose their next pitch, high or low; where "twirlers" wound up like windmills, and gnarly-fingered catchers played with no gloves, or, as Ted Sullivan once said, "without a mattress on their hand."

He cut his baseball molars in the old "dead ball" era, when the rubber-cored sphere was squishy and lopsided. When pitchers rubbed dirt, licorice, spittle, and tobacco juice into the ball to make it nearly invisible to the batter. When it took nine balls to earn a walk, and basemen routinely held onto a runner's belt to prevent a score. When ballfields were often converted farm pastures still pocked with rocks and cow patties. When whiskey, beer and other "anti-fogmatics" were sold freely in the stands. When "the plug uglies" routinely threw beer and cigar stubs at the players and at each other. When team "trainers" massaged bruised noggins and sprained ankles with doses of "Go Fast," a mix of Vaseline and Tabasco sauce.

"The players of the '80s and '90s, at least the leaders among them, were Irish, with keen wits expressed by razor tongues," wrote Al Spink, the founder of *The Sporting News* and considered the dean of sporting writers in the early days of the game. "They were charming and attractive players. They were simply fetched up in a school different from the school of today."[5]

Spink's favorite Irishman of all time was Ted Sullivan, whom he called "the best judge of a ballplayer in America, the man of widest vision in the baseball world, who predicted much for the National game years ago, and whose predictions have all come true."[6]

One innovation that Sullivan never would have allowed himself to foresee, however, was the inclusion of African Americans in America's favorite sport. Like most players, managers, owners and cranks of his day, Ted Sullivan was a dedicated adherent to the notion of American—specifically white male—exceptionalism. Blacks, in his mind, were simply inferior in intelligence, morality and physical prowess, and had no place on the ballfield alongside true athletes the likes of Ty Cobb (a virulent racist himself). Rather, to Sullivan a Negro's place was on the plantation, or on the stage as a high-stepping "yesmassah" minstrel.

The seemingly indefatigable (he liked to say he was "no gold brick") manager and scout wrote no fewer than half a dozen slapstick books and plays based on Negro folklore and perfected the "darky" dialect for his side gigs as an after-dinner speaker and comedian in the off-season. Sullivan was likable and funny to a generation or two of myopic Americans, in an era when even Blacks sometimes had to don black-face paint to get on a white-run stage and make fun of themselves for money.

The irony, of course, is that Sullivan was an Irish immigrant who came from a country where his own people were belittled, emasculated, and starved to death by a race (English) that thought itself morally and intellectually superior. To explain his insouciant racism, or at least put it in some kind of perspective, you have to look at where Sullivan came from and the times he lived in.

Baseball was the American game, and to learn it and play it was a way for Irish immigrants to, as the excellent writer and historian Jerrold I. Casway noted, "claim their place in white society after decades of alienation."[7]

Newly arrived young Irishmen, who were largely uneducated and unskilled—but white and English-speaking—feared being compared to, and treated like, African Americans. They learned early on that playing baseball and belittling Black folks were two sure-fire ways to assimilate into the mainstream, working-class America of their day.

In his insightful tome, *The Culture and Ethnicity of Nineteenth Century*

Baseball, Casway, who pointed to Sullivan as "baseball's preeminent raconteur," wrote: "Resolved to disassociate themselves from racial occupational identities, the Irish developed deep-seated antipathy toward workers of color."[8]

Indeed, the obstructive Jim Crow laws forced into place after the Civil War and, later, the 1896 Supreme Court case *Plessy v. Ferguson,* which upheld segregation, validated for many in the baseball world the exclusion of Black players from the national game.

Ted Sullivan's slightly more ecumenical books, *Humorous Stories of the Ball Field* (1903) and *History of World's Tour—Chicago White Sox/New York Giants* (1914), along with several baseball-related sketches he wrote for vaudeville, had him giving lectures and performances in small theaters across the country in between ball games, scouting stops, league meetings, player signings, contract negotiations, and spring training preparations.[9]

Ted Sullivan's legacy in the history of America's national game was solidified by his planning and management of the famous 1913–1914 World's Tour of Baseball, for which he negotiated with monarchs, sultans, khedives, kings, and assorted world-caliber minions before being allowed to escort the White Sox and New York Giants on a barn- and castle-storming trip through major cities of Europe, Asia, Africa, and Australia.

Sullivan's numerous trips to Europe nearly always included stops in Ireland to visit family, play up baseball, "press for peace," and catch up on his people's favorite sports—hurling, soccer, rugby, and Gaelic football. One of Timothy P. Sullivan's last great schemes, in fact, was to bring Ireland's heroes, the famous Kerry footballers, to the United States in 1927 for a series of exhibition matches calculated in part to rekindle the fires for a united and fully independent Ireland … and quietly raise gun money for the IRA.

By the end, in his 80s, Timothy Paul "Ted" Sullivan was already largely forgotten. The newspaper men of his heyday were retired or dead. Young players coming up through the minor leagues had never heard of the man who was often called a Builder of Baseball. "Of all old-timers in harness," the *Los Angeles Herald* observed, "Ted Sullivan is as good as the best, or a trifle better, when it comes to reviewing the history of diamond doings of the hoary past. His memory goes back to the year one of baseball and his story of the origin of the game makes a good bit of fan literature for the off season."[10]

Indeed, in his dotage, Ted Sullivan could be spotted sitting in his lifetime seats at Comiskey Park in Chicago or Griffith Field in D.C., hoping some fans might notice him. Once in a while, a newspaper editor somewhere out in the heartland would remember him—probably because he had submitted one of his many articles about the early days of baseball—for his contributions to the growth and greatness of the game.

He was never forgotten by the builder of the iconic *Sporting News*, however. "[Sullivan's] travel and brisk acquaintance have added to his natural fund of Irish wit and made him delightful as a raconteur," wrote Spink of his old friend. "No man in the baseball world can compare with Sullivan as a storyteller."[11]

In putting together the pieces of this man's enigmatic life in and out of baseball, Tom and I rooted around in the backrooms of big and small libraries from Los Angeles to Paris (Texas), Nashville, Dubuque, Milwaukee, St. Louis, Kansas City, Chicago, and Washington, D.C., and perused more than 2,000 old newspaper and magazine articles, many from publications that have been lost to time.

Most of the tales we tell herein were gleaned from those rough, colorful, unbounded, and unrestrained sports reports of Sullivan's day. By incorporating their words into our tale of Ted Sullivan's life and career in baseball, we not only found color to match Ted's own, but tapped into the news, observations, and opinions from the very days in which he lived.

So grab a bag of peanuts and a cold anti-fogmatic and let's run down a few of the tales told by and about Timothy P. Sullivan, arguably the greatest cultivator of players— and, inarguably, the best purveyor of blarney in the history of baseball.

"Ted was born on March 17, 1776 and discovered baseball the following summer" (James Clarkson, *Chicago Examiner*, March 18, 1912).

◆ 1 ◆

A Long, Long Way
from Clare to Here

Ireland 1850: The Game Was Survival

Tim, T.P., Theodore, Teddy, and Ted were all born at the same time, an amalgamation of identities, personalities and ambitions in one pale little body that would grow up to make multiple and lasting contributions to a game his parents had likely never heard of prior to arriving in America.

His hatching came about in 1848, somewhere in County Clare, Ireland, at a time when the only sport worth engaging in was called "survival." The island's potato crops had become blighted and poisonous to eat. The people of Clare, most of whom lived in one-room, mud-walled cabins and relied on the bland but nutritious potato for sustenance, were dying in droves from disease and starvation.

The Sullivans—"ma" Mary (née Blakeney), "da" Timothy Sr., and children Daniel, Timothy Jr. (called Teddy), and John—lived through the worst years of "An Gorta Mor" (the great hunger), and around 1855, like so many of their neighbors, escaped to America in the steerage of an old passenger tub.

Among the Muskrats

Milwaukee's old Third Ward, with its immigrant shanties and Irish- and German-owned saloons and shipping warehouses built over landfilled lowlands between Lake Michigan and the Milwaukee River, must have seemed almost civilized to famine survivors like the Sullivans. Never mind the fumes that coughed from the nearby gasworks or the constant rumble of railcars and dock-bound freighters coming to and from the lake. In spite of the city's preponderance of residents from the Rhineland, Milwaukee

The boy named Tim but called Ted was born in Ireland in 1848, as blighted potato crops spread famine and disease across the island. Absentee English landlords evicted hundreds of thousands of Irish sharecropper tenants, who could no longer afford to pay rent for their tiny stone houses and minuscule gardens. Like tens of thousands of other poor Irish families, the Sullivans fled to America. "Emigrants Arrival at Cork," from the cover of *The Illustrated London News*, May 10, 1851.

was tolerant, even accepting of the newly arrived Irish. The consensus was that somebody had to carry the beer kegs and bring fair play and callused fists to City Hall and the Police Department.

The 1860 census shows Timothy Sullivan, Sr., 46, and Mary Sullivan, 38, living in a $300 home in the Third Ward, and sheltering Daniel, 14; Theodore, 11; and John, 8, all born in Ireland; and brothers Denis, 5, and Eugene (wrongly identified as female on the census), 3, both born in Wisconsin.

It was the second child, Timothy Jr., a.k.a. T.P., Theodore, Ted, and Teddy, who embraced the abundance of America with the biggest hug— then happily stuck his hands in its pockets for the next six decades.

Schoolyards and Sandlots

When not reading, ciphering, or making up stories at St. Gall's School, Timothy Paul "Ted" Sullivan reveled in sandlot baseball, coercing his schoolmates onto rival teams and scheduling games after school.

The one book young Ted Sullivan read without the padres or penguins standing over him with a pointer was Henry Chadwick's seminal *American Base Ball Manual.* A popular baseball reporter, columnist, and author, Chadwick—thought of by many as "The Father of Baseball"— explained the game in a way working class men and boys could relate to. "At 10 years old I began reading the venerable old man's advice to the rulers of the great pastime," Sullivan would one day recall, in what had become his signature bloviated style. "He discovered the little foundling called baseball in its swaddling clothes on the Elysian Fields, Hoboken, N.J., took it up in his arms and cared for it, nursed it, suggested advice for it, until the game entered the state of manhood and was able to take care of itself."[1]

Decades later, Sullivan would regale story-needy reporters with tales of his youthful exploits and his own manly impact on the game.

In one article that appeared in newspapers all across the country in late 1911 and early 1912, it was said, under the headline TED SULLIVAN— LEAGUE MAKER: "Ted Sullivan cut his infantile teeth on a baseball and when he was old enough to play with toy soldiers, he whipped out his jack-knife and altered the make-believe bayonets so that they looked like bats … and once, when his father said of a neighbor, 'He's a Democrat,' young T. S. corrected his parent: 'He ain't neither, pop,' said Master Sullivan, 'He's an outfielder.'"[2]

Ted Sullivan claimed that his first sport involved tossing a rooster, not a baseball, over the fence so that the flustered fowl could engage in cock fights with a spurred warrior belonging to the boy next door.

"When I was a boy I was quite a rooster fighter but the laws of refined evolution put me out of that barbaric sport and into base ball," he recalled wistfully.[3]

The Days of "Pure Amateur Baseball"

Sometime in the late 1860s, teenaged Tim—now going by "Teddy"— found a ball and a stick and began to play, and not just read about, "base ball."

Not long before heading off to St. Marys, Kansas, to crack the college books and play ball, Ted Sullivan got to witness the amazing play of baseball's first superstar, "short fielder" George Wright, who flawlessly scooped up hot shots through the infield with his bare hands (he could throw equally well with either hand) and notched base hits in more than 60 percent of his at-bats.

Young Sullivan was infatuated with Wright's athleticism, discipline, and style of play (e.g., Wright pioneered the strategy of covering second base to turn double plays).

"I saw George first when I was a mere boy," Sullivan wrote some 34 years later. "He was brain and nothing but brain in all his movements. When a whole infield was going to pieces in the face of a tornado of hitting, Wright was cool as an iceberg."[4]

About that time, there was one dominant amateur ball team that he and his pals followed from park to park—"The Cream Citys," named not for Wisconsin's historic and copious dairy production, but for the color of brick used in much of the early construction in and around downtown Milwaukee.

Young Sullivan and his pals watched the local heroes take on—and get creamed by—visiting "Professionals of the east," teams such as the Unions of Morrisania (historical name for the South Bronx), New York, the Atlantics of Brooklyn, and Wright's Cincinnati Red Stockings.

His First "League"

Ted Sullivan used his better-heeled and well-connected contacts from grade school and high school to form a junior league. His own team, which

Ted and his teenaged friends followed and aspired to play for—and once challenged—Milwaukee's local amateur team, the Cream Citys, before forming a junior league of their own in 1869.

he modestly called "The Stars," was made up of "FFM's"—young men from the "First Families of Milwaukee." Sullivan served as team captain of the squad that, after defeating all other junior clubs, boldly challenged the Cream Citys of the senior league to a state championship. When the Cream Citys refused, a pick-up team consisting of a few Cream City players and players from a social club called "The West Ends" was put together, calling themselves "The Athletics," and a game was played. The game took place at Cream City Park, and at least as Sullivan remembered it, The Stars won 22–2.

He would one day write: "Never in all my life, of the many clubs I handled and of the games I took part in, did I ever relish a victory or fight harder for it, than I did for those boys of my youth, The Stars of Milwaukee."[5]

Ted Sullivan would eventually pop up in dozens of cities and towns across the United States, to play ball, start a team, manage a team, form a league, scout players for any number of major league teams, or simply promote the game.

As he told a reporter many years later: "I played ball from the age of 12 years on, so I may say I grew up with the game, or in a certain sense the game grew up with me in many parts of America."[6]

Throughout his baseball life, Sullivan even did his share of umpiring at all levels of the sport, dating back to an 11–1 victory by the visiting Chicago White Stockings over Milwaukee's West Ends in June of 1876.

Ted Sullivan attended Saint Louis University (high school division) for at least one school year, 1865–1866, but no school would prove more important to his life and legacy than little old St. Mary's College, in rural St. Marys, Kansas.

◆ 2 ◆

Young Sullivan
at Old St. Mary's

Jesuit Priests, Prairie Fires,
and a Freshman Phenom

The lives of Timothy P. "Ted" Sullivan and Charles A. Comiskey converging at tiny St. Mary's College in St. Marys, Kansas, hundreds of miles from their respective homes in Milwaukee and Chicago, was a coincidence of fate. Likely, their respective Irish Catholic immigrant parents took stock in the belief of the school's Jesuit founders that the college's rural location would promote innocence in morals and religious vocations.

Admittance to the newly founded college in the early 1870s was limited to students of excellent character who could present unimpeachable testimonials, and whose character had to be approved by his parish priest. The academics were rigorous, with instruction in Latin, German, and Greek as well as math, world history, the natural sciences, rhetoric, elocution, and religion.

Ted Sullivan was never going to become a priest, but he was a whip-smart student and, at about 5'7" and 140 pounds, he could throw a pill over the plate. As captain of the varsity baseball team, the red-headed Irish boy ruled the school's ballfield roost. He pitched and played shortstop his senior year, in 1874, when he took the 15-year-old freshman Comiskey under his wing—a friendship that would one day take them both around the world.

Besides hunting strawberries along Pawnee Creek, there weren't many places to go or things to do if you ditched school in St. Marys. But the call of next-level baseball once led Sullivan to play hooky and hop a train to Topeka, 25 miles away, in order to suit up with the amateur Topekas for an important game with a rival nine from nearby Lawrence. "The faculty held me in high esteem, as I was paying my own tuition," he recalled. "The rector personally was willing to grant me any privilege that was consistent with college rules; still he could not make an exception in my case."[1]

So Ted Sullivan left St. Marys the way he would exit many a city and town in the future—he disappeared in a cloud of smoke—only in this case, literally.

Fires were regular and problematic on the often-parched grass prairies surrounding St. Marys, and the college boys were often given water-soaked bags and sent to help farmers save their crops, cattle, and buildings.

Gave Priests the Slip

"On this particular day, I remember, I was solving a problem in equations of unknown quantities, when the college bell set up the alarm of a prairie fire," Sullivan remembered. He proceeded to leave the campus with about 20 other boys, then slipped into the tall grass and hightailed it for the depot in nearby Silver Lake, where he took a Union Pacific train to Topeka and the next day helped the locals beat the club from Lawrence.[2]

He later wrote:

COMISKEY— 1ᵉ Base ST. LOUIS.

I then traversed my steps back to where we put out the prairie fire, over the hill and back to the campus. When the boys caught sight of me coming over the hill, cheer after cheer went up, the lost was found. I had the whole college shaking hands with me. Professors gathered around me to hear my story of how I found my way back to the college. I told them I went through the high grass, thinking I was coming towards the college and kept walking and walking until I was on the verge of despair, ready to throw myself on

Young Charlie Comiskey showed up at St. Mary's as a "freshie" in 1874 (the year of "the great grasshopper invasion" in Kansas). His father sent the boy to the remote little Catholic college to cure him of his "baseballitis," and was miffed when Ted Sullivan took the boy under his wing and placed him on the school's varsity ball team. Souvenir card, Allen & Ginter's Cigarettes, 1887 (Library of Congress).

the grass, when I saw the lights of Topeka. I then knew I was safe from the terrible fate of being eaten by wolves. When I got into the city, by accident I met a friend from Kansas City, and told him my tale ... he insisted I should play in the game of ball the next day. I consented and here I am. That settled it; I was back in old St. Mary's.[3]

"Smartest Kid on the Team"

"Honest John" Comiskey, the powerful Chicago alderman, had no high regard for the game of baseball. The Irish-born president of Chicago's Sons of Erin wanted his sons, Jim and Charles, to concentrate on the more obtuse problems of mathematics at college, then take on respectable professions as plumbers or carpenters.

The alderman abhorred idleness and frowned on frivolous play. He attempted to keep his younger son occupied and away from the temptations of baseball by arranging for him to spend summers apprenticing with a family friend and plumber named Joe Hogan. When Charles' mother passed away, the Comiskey boys were shipped off to distant St. Mary's, where the Jesuit scholastic regimen was solid and where many of the young boarders were not even acquainted with the national game.

"Students came to St. Mary's from all parts of the world," Charles told George Robbins of *The Sporting News* many years later, "and I had an opportunity to study different nationalities as well as books, but I put most of my time on baseball."[4]

Charles Comiskey would later recall "It was at St. Mary's that I first met Ted Sullivan, who was one of the most enthusiastic baseball men I had known up to that time."[5]

Out of sight of the folks in Chicago, Comiskey immediately joined the freshman team and was elected its captain. His older brother, Jim, was reportedly a "corking" good catcher on the school's varsity team.

In his 1919 biography, *Commy, The Life Story of Charles A. Comiskey,* Gustaf Axelson wrote: "One Ted Sullivan seems to have cut the biggest swath on the St. Mary's grounds ... the Ted who later in life became the greatest organizer of baseball clubs and leagues in the history of the game."[6]

Sullivan would recall the young Comiskey as being an awkward-looking kid with some speed and an obvious passion for baseball. In his own book of memories, Sullivan wrote that he picked Comiskey to mentor because the kid was the smartest player on the freshman team ... if not the brightest light in the classroom.[7] "If I remember right, he took more to the bat than the book," Sullivan once quipped. "(I) took him out of the freshman team and placed him in the senior—his first promotion, and I dare say his most cherished one."[8]

"There was quite a schoolboy riot when Sullivan promoted Comiskey, a mere child, to the college baseball team," read one later account of the Comiskey-Sullivan collaboration.[9]

Both men in their later years liked to recall their first interaction on the ballfield at old St. Mary's in 1874, the year of the great grasshopper invasion, when billions of "Rocky Mountain Locusts" blanketed the Midwestern prairies and ate everything green in sight—including infields and outfields. That was the year when the players at St. Mary's had to dodge grasshoppers running bases and dig the ball out of banks of the hoppers, which had accumulated in the outfield.[10]

Normally a shortstop, Sullivan occasionally took a fling at pitching for the St. Mary's Saints, and when he was pitching, he wanted young Charles Comiskey as his battery mate.

In one close contest, with a runner on third (at least one version of the story had Charles' older brother, Jim, the base runner) Sullivan animatedly refused catcher Comiskey's signs and angrily summoned the freshman backstop to the mound. Unobserved, he slipped the ball into Comiskey's glove and returned to the mound. Comiskey soon whipped the ball to third, catching the runner ten feet off the base.[11]

Like a lot of city-bred Irish boys, Sullivan was infatuated with the manly art of pugilism—a sport dominated in those days by Celtic-American warriors like Paddy Ryan and the great John L. Sullivan. While at St. Mary's, Sullivan sent to Kansas City for a couple of pairs of boxing gloves and proceeded to box the ears of his fellow college boys.

"Sullivan could put it over on all the boys with whom he boxed," wrote George Robbins in the *Chicago Daily News*, some 37 years later. "But he hadn't tackled Jim Comiskey, Charlie's big brother. The challenge finally came and the boys put on the gloves and went at it. At last Ted met his master."[12]

Jim Comiskey proceeded to "flatten out" Sullivan, who, according to the younger Comiskey, "was good natured about his drubbing," but reluctant to put the gloves back on again.[13]

At the end of the school year in 1874, Sullivan headed back home to Milwaukee, where he put together a ticket- and snack-selling amateur baseball team called "The Alerts."

Ted Sullivan and Charlie Comiskey would not only stay in touch after St. Mary's, but for the next 50 years they would be a team of their own, influencing the game of baseball in countless ways.

The nomadic Sullivan would return often to St. Mary's as a guest of the faculty. He sometimes gave his popular history-of-baseball lectures to the students. In 1913, he offered a gold medal to the student at St. Mary's who wrote the best paper on Irish-American history. In the spring of 1916, he and Comiskey brought their White Sox to St. Mary's and gave the young Saints the stunning privilege of playing the soon-to-be world champions in a pick-up game.

On to the School of Hard Knocks

A college diploma clearly not in his future, the teenaged Comiskey went back to Chicago to practice his work ethic. The story goes that he was the teamster on a wagon load of bricks bound for the rebuilding of Chicago's City Hall when he eyed a sandlot ball game between a couple of amateur teams, the Libertys and the NeverSweats. Sensing that the Libertys could use some help on the mound, he dropped the reins and talked his way into the game.[14]

In retelling the incident decades later, Bozeman Bulger, one of the deans of sportswriters, claimed the Liberty team was led by none other than a very young Hank O'Day. O'Day would one day end up pitching for Ted Sullivan at Washington. "All the NeverSweats heard for the next two hours was a baseball whizzing by them," Bulger waxed.[15]

With the game winding down, Comiskey's father, the alderman, happened onto the abandoned wagon and, choking back his anger, picked up the reins and drove the team to the City Hall job site.

Meanwhile, up in Milwaukee, Ted Sullivan wasn't breaking any bricks or striking out many opponents with his fast-fading pitching arm. As much as the man who would come to be known as "hustling Ted" yearned to be the ringmaster at the center of any and all shows, he knew his days as a twirler were numbered. On the QT, he offered young Comiskey, who was glumly looking at a future of fixing leaky pipes, 50 bucks cash to bring his curve ball up to Milwaukee.

In a bit of thimble-rigging, Sullivan told his old elementary school pal, Tom Shaugnessy—the financial supporter who bankrolled uniforms and equipment for the Alerts—that the team urgently needed $50 for fence repairs. Shaugnessy made good on the request, and Sullivan in turn slipped the cash to his recruit from Chicago.

Shaugnessy, son of an Irish Catholic immigrant cop, later became president of the Canadian Pacific Railway, but in 1876 he was just a Milwaukee city councilman representing the Sullivans and their Third Ward neighbors. When he later asked about that $50 for the still-unrepaired fence, Shaugnessy was neither surprised nor upset when Sullivan admitted that he used the cash for an under-the-table payment to the "amateur" Comiskey.

"That $50 for a month's work was really the first money I ever earned as a ball player," Comiskey later recalled.[16]

The tension between Charles Comiskey and his alderman father over the younger man's choice of careers had been tightening ever since Charlie met Ted Sullivan at St. Mary's. According to a story published years later in the *Buffalo Enquirer,*

> The thought of becoming a real professional dazzled Charlie's brain. When Charlie broached the subject of going away, and told his father what a nice fellow Ted was and what a great friend he was, his father acknowledged the qualities, but to play baseball professionally? Never.
>
> Ted wanted to see Charlie's father, and talk with him, but Charlie would not have it, fearing Ted would weaken when he heard what his father had to say. Well, when Comiskey's father found out that the boy had left, great was his indignation and Ted Sullivan would catch it, and would more than catch it if he ever saw him in Chicago again.[17]

Charlie Comiskey spent the following off-season laboring in Chicago to appease his father, before angering the old man further by slipping off to Elgin, Illinois, to play the 1877 season for the Elgin Watch Factory team—where he won every game he pitched.

♦ 3 ♦

Playing for Peanuts

Ted and Charlie
Take Their Game to Dubuque

After college, the industrious Ted Sullivan snagged a job as a news agent serving the Illinois Central Railroad on a route between Chicago and Dubuque, Iowa, and set about putting together and captaining an amateur baseball club in the latter city.

His nine were comprised of Irish boys from "the lower end of the city," i.e., the boggy flood plain, who proved good enough to win the river town's championships in 1876 and 1877.[1]

In 1878, Sullivan lured his friend Charlie Comiskey out of Chicago again, offering him $50 a month to play ball, plus a chance to earn 20 percent commissions working as a "peanut butcher" hawking newspapers, magazines, cigars, and prize packages containing cheap jewelry, playing cards, loaded dice, and chewing tobacco to railroad passengers. "The amusing part of his coming to Dubuque," said Sullivan, "was that his father still considered it to be a disgrace to be a professional ball player, and he made threats to report me."[2]

Sullivan put several of his ball-playing recruits to work as "butcher boys," assigning them to shifts on passenger rail routes in and around Dubuque and Chicago. He arranged their work schedules so that his best ball-playing butchers would be back in town on game days.

Always competitive, the young Comiskey proved to be good at hustling magazines, books, puzzles, snacks, and cigars on the trains. "I bet I sold more papers on that railroad than any other boys ever did," Comiskey said, looking back.[3]

The future big-league magnate proved to be even more aggressive on the ballfield. "That new player of mine will fight the butcher if he doesn't win every one of his games," Sullivan told a reporter. "One of these days he'll bite the cover off the ball when he isn't going right."[4]

Sullivan said his young pitcher delivered a mean fast ball, one that would leave a welt on a sluggish batter, whether thrown high or low. "The distance from the pitcher's mound to the batter was 45 feet," he explained, "and at that distance his [Comiskey's] long arms used to send balls across the plate that the country clubs around Dubuque were afraid to face. Many of the members of those clubs returned home with fractured ribs and blackened shins from Comiskey's rifle-shot delivery."[5]

In later years, Sullivan liked to remind young reporters "we didn't have any gloves then, and we caught the ball with our hands half-crossed. The infielders wore nets on their feet to snare the pellet when it slipped through their mitts."[6]

Ted Sullivan, Player/Manager/News Agent/ Billiard Parlor Operator. Dubuque, Iowa, 1878.

A Sullivan Experiment

In his free time, Sullivan helped the young utility player hone his fielding skills by hitting him grounders in a hollow alongside the rail yard. Comiskey would take a brick and pretend it was first base. Sullivan would gradually drill grounders farther and farther away from the base. As the *Dubuque Telegraph-Herald* told it, "He [Comiskey] would catch the sphere and spring back to first, endeavoring to beat the imaginary runner."[7]

"Panting switch engines passed and repassed, throwing cinders and smoke in their faces," is how another old newspaper described the scene. "They paid no attention to this discomfort, nor did they heed the shouts of the engineers, firemen and yard hands who lined the embankment laughing and kidding the players ... They were unaware at the time they were watching baseball history in the making."[8]

In their endless talks about practices and techniques, Sullivan and Comiskey had concluded that first basemen (sportswriters often called them "supervisors of the initial sack" or "keepers of the keystone station") were losing many chances by standing on the bag and waiting for the ball to be thrown to them. Why not, they figured, let the first baseman also be the fielder? He doesn't have to be on the bag until the ball is thrown.

Looking back, Comiskey would say: "In those days the first baseman was just a dub, a hitching post. All he did was to stand up and be thrown at. When you got too slow for the infield, they sent you to the outfield, and when you couldn't chase a fly on your poor old legs, they'd put you at first."[9]

The first time the young Comiskey took the field and stood well away from the bag, opposing players laughed and pointed, thinking the kid had lost his marbles. "Great was the astonishment of the opposing batters to find their usual hits being gobbled up by the young Comiskey," wrote one sporting scribe. "And their chagrin waxed still deeper when the daring youth went even further and took his stand not only 10 or 15 feet away from the sack, but in a line several yards behind it."[10]

"The audience was electrified to see this new and unknown newcomer dash out into territory that was never trespassed on before by a first baseman," Sullivan would boast. "They cheered and cheered."[11]

Comiskey became the prototype "keeper of the keystone station," one who could also "swing the willow." Sullivan joked that Commy's only weakness was his self-made superstition that he couldn't hit left-handed pitchers with mustaches.

Ted Chased with Hot Kettles

Recruiting players for his Dubuque lineup caused more than just Honest John Comiskey to take up arms.

"For a year or so in Dubuque I had a hard time dodging old women who were chasing me with hot kettles

Alderman Comiskey wasn't the only parent upset that Ted Sullivan had lured their son into the ungentlemanly world of baseball. Sullivan claimed he "had a hard time dodging old women who were chasing me with hot kettles." Illustration *Kansas City Star*, May 7, 1905 for making their sons professional baseball players," Sullivan said. "But years afterward, when their sons came home and lifted the mortgages or bought them a farm or two, those same kettles were heated to brew me a pot of tea."[12]

Sullivan's Dubuque nines shared a feature common to Sullivan teams throughout the ages—the roster read like names scratched on the inside of a New York paddy wagon, which played well with the hundreds of working-class Irish living in Dubuque's Little Dublin neighborhood. Throughout his life, Sullivan waxed eloquently about the superiority of the Irish player in America's great game, and a random lineup from an 1878 game against nearby Davenport's nine reflected his preference:

O'Rourke—First base
Colford—Shortstop
Comiskey—Catcher
Dolan—Right Field
Farrell—Left Field
Brady—Center Field
Sullivan—Third Base
Phelan—Second Base
Ross—Pitcher

In late June, the Dubuque Base-Ball Association was formed, with Sullivan named as manager. The group's avowed goal was to lure proven players from nearby Davenport and from across the river in Illinois. The Dubuque nine had had their troubles with the Reds squad from over in Peoria, a team of real pros that actually beat the NL champion Boston team that year. But in a stroke of good fortune, Hustling Ted was able to lure Charles Gardner Radbourn away from the rival Reds to become the pitching centerpiece of his young Dubuque club.

The team busked around the region in 1878, with Sullivan frequently playing the field. Along the way, he methodically strengthened his roster by swapping out local amateurs for professional players.

Before Radbourn came on board, the youthful Comiskey was still Dubuque's hot-shot twirler and thought of himself as a giant-killer. He would always remember the day he had the powerful Peoria nine tied up in knots with his high and low offerings. "The Peoria sluggers couldn't do a thing with me," he told a reporter nearly 20 years later. "Didn't I feel big when I thought I had the game cinched? There was a magnificent audience looking on me as the master spirit of the occasion."[13]

But then his manager and mentor, who was covering third base, flubbed a pair of grounders and Peoria came from behind to win the game, 3–2. "It broke my heart," Comiskey said. "The first thought that came to my mind was to assassinate Ted, as it was his errors that lost the game, but on second thought I concluded to let him live."[14]

"Commy had cyclonic speed," said Sullivan, "but was wild as a hawk and hit so many batters that he became a terror to his opponents."[15] Whereas Comiskey would take his skills to the "initial sack," as he called it, Ted Sullivan took more and more to the sidelines, managing and signal-calling.

◆ 4 ◆

In Fast Company

1879 Dubuque Rabbits

Ted Sullivan didn't know it at the time, but his actions following the 1878 season would alter his life, Comiskey's life, and baseball's history in ways that would have been unimaginable to a pair of young bucks living in rented rooms and hanging out in Ted's and Tom Loftus's billiard hall in Dubuque.

With the backing of U.S. Senator William Allison and David Henderson, who later served as Speaker of the United States House of Representatives, Sullivan set about establishing the first of several baseball leagues he would create over the ensuing five decades.

He met with potential supporters from the Dubuque business community and with baseball clubs across the region, and the Northwestern League was formally organized in October 1878 at the Burtis House Hotel in Davenport, Iowa. Clubs from Davenport, Dubuque, Omaha, and Rockford adopted a formal salary structure and created what would become a legendary minor league. A blueprint was created that boosters in smaller cities would attempt to replicate for years to come.

"Dubuque aimed high," Sullivan recalled. "The backers tossed aside their semi-professional swaddling clothes and told me to go forth and give them an out-and-out professional baseball team. The result was that we organized the first Northwestern League, with Jim McKee, of Rockford, Illinois, and myself as the real promoters."[1]

Sullivan hustled to line up investors and players for the Dubuque club. The Rockford club had already purchased virtually the entire roster of the defunct 1878 Milwaukee major league franchise and was expected to run away with the Northwestern League title in 1879. Sullivan stacked his own roster with players he picked off from the Peoria Reds, including infielders John and William Gleason, brothers from St. Louis who went on to have decorated major league careers; Tom Loftus, also of St. Louis, who later earned respect and fame as a player, manager and owner; and Irish-born

=LOFTUS= RADBOURN. =COMISKEY= =LAPHAM=

CHAMPIONS *1879* NORTH WEST.

SULLIVAN. REIS.

=ALVERETTA= W.GLEASON. =J.GLEASON= =TAYLOR=

The photograph reproduced here is in the possession of T. H. Merriam of La Grange and is chiefly interesting to Chicago fandom because it shows two men, who have been most prominently before the baseball public here, in the earliest days of their careers on the diamond. These are Charles A. Comiskey, owner of the White Stockings, and T. J. Loftus, until last year manager of the Chicago National league team and slated for the leadership of the New York American league club the coming season. The lifelong friendship which exists between them is explained by the fact they broke into the game together on the team which was famous enough to remain prominent in diamond history for nearly a quarter of a century.

Sullivan's mighty Dubuquers—he called them his "Rabbits"—of the minor Northwestern League were nearly unbeatable during the 1879 season. His "stalwarts," as he touted them, caught the attention of National League officials when they whipped Cap Anson's Chicago nine in an exhibition contest (*Chicago Tribune*, February 15, 1903).

catcher Thomas "Sleeper" Sullivan (aka "Old Iron Hands"), who served as Dubuque's backstop prior to a solid major league career. W. B. Lapham, Henry Alverreta, William Taylor, and Comiskey rounded out the position players, while Lawrence P. "Laurie" Reis and future Hall of Famer "Old Hoss" Radbourn served as the team's pitching staff.

Admittedly not able to keep up with his newly-gathered fast company, Sullivan gave up playing and concentrated on managing, only donning a glove or grabbing a bat when necessary. According to a *Dubuque Daily Times* retrospective published on Aug. 5, 1906, "Ted made a record as a short stop of .823 fielding and .229 batting average before quitting the active service in 1879."

Few thought Ted Sullivan's patched-together aggregation could compete with the powerful Rockford team. As Comiskey would say: "We were a lot of youngsters who looked good only to ourselves and our manager, Ted Sullivan."[2]

Sullivan's Secret Weapon

After spending 1878 with Peoria's barnstorming team as a pitcher and right fielder, Radbourn had moved to Dubuque and joined Ted Sullivan's Northwestern League club for the 1879 season. Radbourn, of course, went on to become the most dominating pitcher of his era, with a record of eye-popping statistics that likely will never be matched.

Radbourn's fastball was lively, but his success never relied on speed. In an era when the overhand pitch was banned, Radbourn's arsenal included a screwball, a sinker, a changeup, curves, spitters, and scuffed balls, all coming from various angles.

In an exhibition game against the Prairie Du Chien

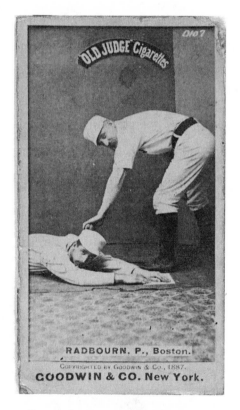

Sullivan's 1879 Dubuque Rabbits were propelled to dominance by future Hall of Fame pitcher Charles "Old Hoss" Radbourn. Photo Boston Red Stockings, 1889 (National Baseball Hall of Fame Library, public domain).

College team, Radbourn was accused of throwing "a crooked ball" that curved, dropped and faded. The college coach insisted on a new ball. After Dubuque won the game, 25–0, fans asked to see Radbourn's fingers—to see if they were crooked, too.

According to Sullivan, Radbourn threw "a perplexing slow ball that was never duplicated on the ballfield" and "a drop ball that he did not have to spit on, and called it a 'spit ball.'" Sullivan also told the story of one of Radbourn's outings when an umpire refused to call strikes during an exhibition game against a local team. Radbourn's curve ball, it seems, aroused the suspicions of the umpire, who exclaimed: "You're pitching with a trick ball! The ball ain't official! Every time it leaves yer hand it ducks in and out so that our boys can't hit it. If yer can't pitch the ball straight or get a new one that ain't a trick ball I'll give the game to our team, b'gosh."[3]

The Dubuque Rabbits (ginger-headed Sullivan also referred to the team as his "Red Stockings") sent a strong message when they opened the 1879 season with an 8–0 shutout at rival Rockford. Despite Radbourn's performance, the vaunted Rockford nine were dismissive of the Rabbits, and specifically Radbourn. After hearing the cocky Rockford team's comments, Sullivan agreed to let Radbourn pitch every game against Rockford, and the "Old Hoss" shut down the Rockfords every time.

In fact, Sullivan's nine were nearly unbeatable during the 1879 season. They never reached double digits in the loss column, and Dubuque's dominance ultimately crippled fan interest across the Northwestern League.

All the teams in the fledgling league struggled financially, but Ted Sullivan's Rabbits enjoyed a big and loyal following at home and, on the road, folks bought tickets just to see Radbourn convey those curious, "crooked pitches" of his.

> "Our town thought we were the greatest in the country,
> and we agreed with them."—Charles Comiskey[4]

To save money, the frugal manager gave free tickets to young "fence-hangers" in return for their running after and retrieving precious baseballs hit out of the stadium, and he arranged for his local heroes to eat free meals at the homes of admiring fans.[5]

"We managed to eat now and then," recalled Comiskey. "But none of us had any coin to speak of. I remember when we all went to this place for a drink, there were just nine of us on the team and Ted Sullivan was a stickler on training and wouldn't let any of us touch alcoholic drinks. So he laid 50 cents on the bar and said: 'Give us 10 drinks of buttermilk.' He was the only one who had a cent."[6]

As the other league teams struggled, Dubuque's share of gate receipts at away games became meager and were sometimes withheld. Before summer's end, both the Omaha and Davenport teams had disbanded, and Dubuque and Rockford were left to square off in a championship series as the only two teams left in the league. Sullivan's squad won the series, and the Northwest League—considered by some to be the first modern-style minor league—was out of business. Ted Sullivan and his Rabbits were forced to take to the road as an independent club in search of opponents.

Ted's Ringers Fall Off a Turnip Wagon

In the early days of the game, nothing was more fun for small-town baseball cranks than a good grudge match with the next town over.

Sullivan's 1879 Dubuque team was, as he put it, "resting on their oars" after winning the Northwest League championship that year, when a pair of nearby Iowa burgs, Cresco and Decorah, challenged one another to a contest for local bragging rights.

Cresco's town fathers proceeded to quietly recruit catcher Billy Taylor and crooked-fingered Radbourn (who the next season would debut in the National League). As Sullivan said, "Rad was ready for any scheme where there was fun and a little pay."

Radbourn and Taylor were slipped onto a farm outside of Cresco and were passed off as itinerant farm hands. "Their line of business," recalled Sullivan, "was to watch the other farm hands toss hay."

Radbourn and Taylor purposely stayed on the farm and didn't play in the big game, and the Decorah nine prevailed. Cresco, naturally, demanded a rematch and set to plotting revenge. As Sullivan told it, Cresco's town fathers "went deep and ingenious into their scheme to get even with Decorah."[7]

The Rematch

The Decorah manager slipped over to Chicago to recruit a few ringers of his own, and inter-town betting and boasting resumed fast and furious. On the day of the rematch, wagon- and buggy-loads of farmers and townies poured into Cresco. An excursion train brought throngs of cocky fans from Decorah. Before the game was to start, Decorah's players put on a "dress parade," showing off their fielding skills, followed by warm-up drills among what Sullivan described as "the awkward and ungainly oaks of Cresco—minus their battery."

Cresco's manager explained that his pitcher and catcher had to work that day and would be a little late arriving. After waiting some time, the crowd began to call for the game to start. But still no sign of Cresco's pitcher and catcher. "Cry and cry was set up from the impatient crowd for the game to commence," Sullivan's story went. "Finally, this old farmer who drove in with a load of hay covered with his farm hands called out, 'Say, boys, I can loan you two of my men to help you out until your two men arrive.'"

Radbourn and Taylor, dressed in overalls and chewing on straw, toppled down from the load of hay and strode toward the diamond. As they began warming up, old farmer Jenkins called out: "Don't hurt yourself, boys, you know we commence thrashing tomorrow."

And the thrashing of the cocky Decorah team began. Idle manager Sullivan observed, "Rad and Taylor threw all their ardor and jollity into this game and…. Holy Moses their [Decorah players'] hearts failed. They knew they were up against the real thing."

Taylor teased the opposing ringers by telling them where the next pitch would be, before a grinning Radbourn "shot them high and low with curves and jumps that made them seasick while they were at the plate."[8]

Cresco won the rematch, 22–0, and their fans celebrated by carrying Radbourn and Taylor off the field on their shoulders and making a bonfire out of farmer Jenkins' hay.

Radbourn Blanks Anson's Boys

On August 4, 1879, the minor Dubuque boys upset the National League's Chicago White Stockings, 1–0, and Radbourn won the praise of Chicago's manager and first baseman, Adrian "Cap" Anson, whose image would, like those of Radbourn and Comiskey, one day grace the walls of baseball's Hall of Fame. Anson recalled:

> "The great Radbourn's pitching was a revelation to us. In my fifteen years as premier batsman of the game, I never faced a pitcher who baffled me more completely with his curves than did Radbourn on the occasion of that memorable game in Dubuque. I do not hesitate to say that not one of the old school pitchers, or any of the later slabmen, could equal the famous Radbourn. He was among the earliest to curve a ball and none ever developed the curve more successfully. Every man of the Dubuque club was a star."

Anson also threw some credit to the Rabbits tender, player/manager Sullivan, saying, "We were whitewashed because of better pitching, better support and better discipline on the part of the Dubuque players."

But it was the whole Dubuque team, its youthful feeling of invincibility and the boys' joy at simply playing the game, that Sullivan would always remember. He called them "a team of stalwarts composed of witty, kindred spirits."[9]

Little did those young kindred spirits know then that they were creating baseball history.

> *"Sullivan stepped forward into baseball prominence ... having organized the St. Louis Browns; it was in 1883. He pulled together a team of youngsters and created a sensation by the way he handled them. The young team won twenty-three out of twenty-five game The work of this team stamped Sullivan at once as one of the greatest baseball generals in the business."*
> —*Atlanta Constitution,* January 1, 1894

Taking on "The Infidels"

Chris Von der Ahe was everything but dull. He was colorful, eccentric, a sentimentalist, and a sucker. But no one can argue Von der Ahe's role as a founder of the American Association and the champion of working-class baseball fans.

Von der Ahe was born in 1851 in Hille, Westphalia, Germany, and the Prussian's American success story grew to include a grocery, a tavern, and political influence in St. Louis's German community.

He moved his Golden Lion tavern to a site across the street from the downtrodden Grand Avenue Grounds, which showed Von der Ahe the marketable connection between beer and baseball.

Von der Ahe stepped into the local baseball scene and in 1880 created the Sportsman's Park and Club Association (SPCA), serving as the organization's president and largest shareholder. He quickly set about rebuilding the deteriorating Grand Avenue ballpark, and during the 1881 season fans packed his renamed Sportsman's Park to watch the competitive Brown Stockings club play strong visiting teams from New York, Philadelphia, Cincinnati, Chicago, and other major markets.

The established pro circuit—dubbed "the infidels of the National League" by Ted Sullivan—had little interest in catering to working-class fans. In contrast to the National League's 50-cent admission, ban on alcohol, and outlawing of Sunday games, Von der Ahe provided the people of St. Louis with a competitive team, a 25-cent admission, Sunday games, and a festive stadium with as much beer and spirits as patrons cared to buy. St. Louis baseball fans took notice, as did traveling independent teams who flocked to the newly refurbished Sportsman's Park to play before huge crowds.

Player/manager Ted Sullivan's barnstorming, independent Dubuque nine popped up again in the sports columns of the national birdcage liners in 1880 when they whipped the semi—but mostly professional—St. Louis Red Stockings, 4–1. By then, many of the boys from the 1879 Dubuques had gone on, or were on their way, to careers in the major leagues.

The Gleason brothers were already playing for the St. Louis Reds. Hoss Radbourn was playing for the Buffalo Bisons, and Loftus, Sleeper Sullivan, and Comiskey were starting to get looks from the National League.

Come the winter of 1881, it was reported that Ted Sullivan was still in Dubuque, working his railroad news and snack business, but not affiliated with any club—although he claimed to have received many "'splendid' inducements from other cities." Future Hall of Famer Radbourn was said to be back in Bloomington, Illinois, living with his parents; the Gleason brothers were working as firemen in St. Louis, and Charlie Comiskey was still in town, working for Sullivan, "and has not played with any club since '79."[1]

With no baseball to play, sport-loving Sullivan was teaching locals an ancient Irish game.

VON DER AHE - PRESIDENT ST. LOUIS

Sullivan's extraordinary success as manager of the minor league Rabbits led to him being recruited by beer baron Chris Von der Ahe, owner of the major league St. Louis Browns. Buchner Gold Coin souvenir card, 1887 (Library of Congress).

He introduced the game of hurling to the Irish American boys of "the lower part of the city," offering them apples and cigars as inducements for them to do their best at the game.[2]

In 1881, Comiskey took over as manager of Dubuque's still-independent club, and it was another exhibition game against St. Louis—this time against Chris Von der Ahe's newly-minted Brown Stockings—in July of that year that changed the fortunes for both him and his mentor, Sullivan.

The small-town Dubuques drew smirks and second looks when they stepped off a rail coach on a stiflingly hot day at St. Louis, wearing straw hats and long linen dusters, and carrying their bats. In charge of getting the Dubuquers a place to stay and a wagon ride to the ball park, Al Spink recalled that Ted Sullivan and his boys were put up for three days in an "ancient hostelry" at Fourth and

Locust streets called the Everett House, but went back to Iowa "happy as larks."[3]

According to Spink, "It was the first time Comiskey had ever played baseball in a regular enclosure. Ted Sullivan appeared as the pitcher for Dubuque in this famous game, but after six innings, on account of fearful heat, he retired. When Sullivan quit the score stood 2 to 1 in favor of the Browns. But after his departure St. Louis had a walkover and won by a score of 9 to 1."[4]

Still, the *St. Louis Globe-Democrat* was impressed, noting that "Sullivan, who pitches for the Dubuquers, Loftus, their second baseman, and Comiskey, who guards the first bag, are a little team in themselves. They play a grand game."[5]

While the Dubuques got drubbed by the Browns, Comiskey's athletic, off-the-bag style of defense caught the attention of the locals, and he was offered a contract to join the Browns for the 1882 season at $75 per month. Sullivan, who had been quietly touting Comiskey's abilities to various teams, advised his old schoolie to take a pay cut and head to St. Louis. Comiskey took Sullivan's advice, and Von der Ahe soon more than made up for Comiskey's lost railroad wages.

Following is Sullivan's version of the negotiations with the St. Louis beer baron: "Charles held out for $125. 'That's my price,' he told Chris. 'I can't afford to take less.'

'Vait a minute,' cried Von der Ahe, who needed a first baseman sorely. 'My, how queevk you Irishers are to quid. I tell you vot I do. I give you vot you ask if you manach it, Hein?'"[6]

There's no mention in the record books of a rematch of sorts between the Rabbits and the Browns that took place in Dubuque on September 29 the following year. That was the day Sullivan's protégé, Mr. Charles Comiskey, married Miss Nan Kelley of The Key City.

Married to Baseball

Much to the surprise and amusement of the sporting press, Comiskey, to celebrate his wedding, brought his pals from the St. Louis Browns to Dubuque to play a ball game.

Sullivan and his billiards hall partner, Tom Loftus, got together a nine of groomsmen and friends, and the boys went out after the nuptials at Dubuque's St. Patrick's Catholic Church and played in the dirt. Loftus and Sullivan acted quite serious, barking out instructions in meaningless code words that mystified and irritated the Browns players.

According to a story in the *Cincinnati Enquirer*, "As the game progressed and the Dubuquers began to pile up the runs, Bill and Jack [the Gleason brothers] grew warm in the collar. The Dubuquers whipped the Browns and Bill Gleason was so mad that he would not bid Loftus good-by after the game."[7]

A typical Irish wedding reception, some would say, except nobody got in a fight.

It has been often reported, but not substantiated, that Ted Sullivan married Nan Kelley's sister, Nellie Kelley. If he did, the betrothal didn't last long enough for Ted to take off his traveling shoes.

Coincidentally, he liked to say, "The three things that inspire the most profanity are an alarm clock, a fountain pen and a wife."[8]

Beer Man Turns to Ted

After his Browns finished the inaugural American Association season in fifth place in the six-team major league in 1882, Von der Ahe was in the

Manager Sullivan led the 1883 St. Louis Browns to a brilliant 53–26 record before clashing with the oft-meddling owner, Chris Von der Ahe (the fellow in street clothes at center).

market for a new manager. As part of his hunt, he sought the opinions of some of his players and leading figures of the game. Source after source recommended the Dubuque-based railroad news agent as the next manager of the Browns, and eventually Von der Ahe took that advice and set up a meeting with Ted Sullivan.

> *"The old boys I had in Dubuque kept telling Chris about me. I met him by appointment in Chicago. He perfumed my atmosphere with the fragrance of the many bouquets he threw at me. I was his long-looked-for Moses, as he said. The bargain was made and I was bound to enter the gilded cavern of professional baseball."*
>
> —Ted Sullivan[9]

To the shock and chagrin of the local sporting press (one scribe sneered that Sullivan was nothing but "a bib rube from corn country"), Sullivan was named manager of the Browns on October 16, barely two weeks after Comiskey's betrothal (and the wedding reception drubbing) in Dubuque.

In St. Louis, Ted Sullivan was reunited with a host of his former Dubuque players, including the Gleason brothers, Tom "Sleeper" Sullivan, Tom Loftus, and Comiskey. His management style continued to be one of friendly but firm discipline.

The *Times-Picayune* of November 11, 1883, noted, "Ted's principal duty is to look after the financial interests and moral welfare of his nine, both of which he is generally successful in doing."

As Al Spink later put it, the press and bugs of St. Louis soon found that "the only Ted wasn't raised on a load of hay," but they had engaged a master who was "always full of good nature but terribly positive and earnest when giving orders on the ball field."[10]

Ted Sullivan loved telling the story:

When I went to St. Louis to take charge of the Browns, Chris took me into the dressing-room, introduced me to the players, and made a speech. The speech ran about like this: "Fellers, this is Tet Sullivan, ond he has a mint of his own in his head, and that is vat I like in a manacher. Ted vill haf the vatch out for you fellers. I von't be in it. Dot is, I vill be in it, ond I von't be in it. I vill pay you your selleries, ond Tet vill tell you vot is which ond tat from cat. Ven I meet you on the street I vill bow to you but not talk vit you. I vill know you and not know you. As Tet says himself in Union there is strength, so do all the chimnasium work you can, but no crooking the elbow over stines of beer goes. Ond look to Mr. Sullifan first, last and altogether."[11]

Early in the 1883 season, Von der Ahe enraged his new manager by impetuously releasing Loftus. In response, Sullivan named Comiskey to replace

Loftus as captain and ordered Von der Ahe to bump Comiskey's salary by $500. The owner complied, but the relationship between "der Poss Bresident of der Browns" and his hot-headed Irish manager was doomed—at least for the balance of the 1883 season.

A series of outrages cascaded through the season, and Sullivan increasingly chafed as Von der Ahe dictated player moves, second-guessed game decisions, wailed about unremarkable losses, erupted over curfew issues, and levied fines (which were never paid) for scores of ridiculous reasons.

Whereas he frustrated and confused his players and managers, the press loved writing about and quoting the meddling, language-mashing owner. Laughed Sullivan: "Chris in trying to keep his name out of the newspapers was as novel as it was amusing. He was like the elephant that was supposed to get out of the way of vehicles; he was always backing into them."[12]

Earned Runs and Run-ins

Despite the growing tension between manager and owner, the Brown Stockings piled up the wins. The team that finished six games below .500 the previous season was playing Sullivan's aggressive brand of baseball, particularly in the field and on the base paths.

Even Sullivan—who the local press conceded was "no spring chicken"—pitched a hot streak in exhibitions, holding the Springfields, the Quincys, the Toledos, and the Bay Citys to a total of just one earned run.[13]

Hugh Nicol, a young Scottish outfielder, and loudmouthed Arlie Latham, "The Freshest Man in Baseball," were added to the 1883 roster and brought a new level of energy and intensity. The Browns also excelled at Sullivan's favorite tactics, including umpire baiting, physical intimidation, and profane exchanges with opponents.

Position players weren't alone in creating the team's ferocious reputation. Another new addition to the roster, Tony Mullane, "The Apollo of the Box," was a dominant pitcher in the American Association. A native of County Cork, the ambidextrous pitcher posted a 35–15 record for St. Louis, while fellow pitcher Jumbo McGinnis went 28–16. But it was Mullane's nasty demeanor, along with a trail of message pitches and hit batsmen, that added a hint of menace to the team's reputation. That menace spilled over into Mullane's personal life, and in 1893 his wife filed for divorce, saying that he viciously assaulted her and threatened to cut her throat. Mullane set records for seven teams across 13 major league seasons, was inducted into the Cincinnati Reds Hall of Fame, and retired as a Chicago cop.

From a fan's perspective, the 1883 season was steamrolling along enter-tainingly, but behind the scenes Sullivan was barreling toward a fateful con-frontation with his checked-suit-wearing, English-language-butchering team owner.

The Boomerang Watch

The relationship between the manager and the owner reached an explosive conclusion following a September game between the Browns and the New York Metropolitans. As Sullivan told a *St. Louis Globe-Democrat* reporter shortly after his fiery resignation, his departure from the Browns "was the result of a misunderstanding with President Von der Ahe." Frus-trated at watching McGinnis giving up hit after hit to New York batters, the owner demanded that Sullivan replace the starter with Mullane, who was scheduled to start the next day's game. Sullivan ignored Von der Ahe's order, which led to "some warm words" and Sullivan's heated resignation immediately after the game.

Sullivan told a more colorful version of the story in his 1903 book, *Humorous Stories of the Ball Field*:

> On a quiet sunny April morning, at Sportsman's Park, St. Louis, Chris whis-pered in my ear that he thought there was something in a plush box for me at his office. I hastened to find out what it was. When I opened the box there was a handsome gold watch and chain contained therein. I opened it and inside was the following inscription, "C. Von der Ahe to T.P. Sullivan, April 4th, 1883." This watch had another presentation, at the Broadway Central Hotel in New York on a September morning of that same year in which the writer hurled it back at him after his disagreement with the famous Chris.[14]

And just like that, Sullivan was done as manager of the St. Louis jug-gernaut. The team boasted a 53–26 record at Sullivan's departure, and the club didn't skip a beat, remaining an American Association force through the rest of the decade. Comiskey was named manager for the final 19 games of the 1883 season, pulling together a 12–7 record and leading the Browns to a second-place finish, just one game behind Philadelphia. The Sullivan-built turnaround from the 1882 season was complete.

Comiskey's transition to a "respectable" career as a big league player and manager was complete as well. According to an 1899 retrospective on his career, "Commy made his father a present of a piece of property, and the old gentleman did not then think of killing Sullivan for putting his son into baseball."[15]

While both Sullivan and Comiskey would go on to forge successful careers in the national game, Von der Ahe's life took a sad trajectory that most reports attribute to a combination of his personal habits as well as a series of financial and on-field misfortunes. Eventually, in an effort to remain afloat, he was forced to sell his best players, which led to more losses and, in turn, falling gate revenues. Throw in divorces and other costs associated with his womanizing ways, gambling losses, settlements connected to a tragic stadium fire, and his lifelong generous nature, overall the 1890s were not kind to Chris Von der Ahe. His humiliation reached a nadir in 1898 when he was abducted in St. Louis by a Pittsburgh detective, forced onto a train, and imprisoned in a Steel City jail cell in connection with the floundering Prussian's refusal to pay a civil judgment owed to a former player.

Eventually, the genial and generous "der Poss President of der Browns" was forced by court action to sell his beloved franchise in 1898 for $38,000—all of which went to creditors.

Chris Von der Ahe died in humble circumstances on June 7, 1913. Charles Comiskey—by then one of the wealthiest men in American sports—had helped keep his old owner financially afloat in those final years. When the time came to escort the brash Prussian who created a new baseball culture to his final resting place, he was accompanied by a group of pallbearers from his groundbreaking 1883 club, his friends and biggest "fans": Charlie Comiskey, Ban Johnson, C. C. Spink, "Big Jim" Davis, Bill and Jack Gleason, George "Jumbo" McGinnis, and Ted Sullivan.

"Mr. Von der Ahe was never given credit for what he did," lamented Sullivan. "In his days of success he was lavish in his generosity to needy people, and many times I have seen him help broken down ballplayers by getting them transportation to their homes. Great kindness of the past should never be forgotten."[16]

Cranky Manager Comes Up with a Name to Describe "Over Effusive Advice-Givers"[17]

Same old rooters! Same old cranks
Holding down the blistered planks,
Same old rubberneck sports
Giving vent to angry snorts
—from "Batter Up" by James Barton Adams,
Denver Post, April 1905

Despite its immense popularity, baseball didn't have "fans" in the early decades of the sport. The game had "rooters," "croakers," "bugs," and "cranks," but it didn't have "fans"—at least not until an irritated Ted Sullivan said something out of the side of his mouth in 1883.

From its earliest days, baseball had spawned groups of rooters who evolved into formal organizations that levied dues, held events, paraded to

Tired of a know-it-all citizen constantly giving him advice on how to better run his St. Louis ball club, Sullivan is said to have coined the term "fan," short for "fanatic" (vintage illustration reimagined by Dan Regan 2020).

games with marching bands, and often brought a mob mentality to their seating (and standing) sections.

Individual enthusiasts were generally called bugs and cranks—particularly the partisans who talked too often and in too much indelicate detail about teams, players, strategies, and game situations. Perceived as crackpots, they offered their advice freely from the stands and the sidewalks, but their insights were either ridiculed or ignored by players, managers and sportswriters of the day.

The opening of a 1911 piece by Cincinnati-based sports columnist Ren Mulford Jr. was indicative of the attitude toward cranks: "Down at the Bug Club the other afternoon one of the charter members—a 33rd degree fan from Fantown—was insistent along one line. 'Put me down as a prophet,' said he, 'and if what I say doesn't come true I'll give you a luncheon next Fall and will eat your old straw hat as a salad, served with mayonnaise dressing.'"[18]

The origin of the move from *crank* to *fan* is pretty much universally attributed to Ted Sullivan, who shortened fanatic to "fan" during his 1883 managerial stint in St. Louis. But Ted, being Ted, over the years offered up multiple and variant versions of the origin event. In one telling, Sullivan told team owner Chris Von der Ahe that the club's board of directors was overrun with meddlesome cranks and "I did not propose to be run by a lot of fanatics."

In another version, Sullivan said that he was with Comiskey and a group of other players when they became annoyed at the bloviating of a know-it-all crank. After the offending party departed, Comiskey described the crank as a "fanatic," which Sullivan said he immediately shortened to "fan."

Four years later, Tom Sullivan confirmed in *Sporting Life* that Ted Sullivan was acknowledged around baseball as the father of the now ubiquitous sobriquet: "It was Ted who gave the nickname of 'fans' to base ball cranks. You never hear a man called a 'fiend' out in the Western League cities. 'Fan' is the word that is invariably used. It is a quick way of saying 'fanatic.'"[19]

But not all "fan" origin stories are tied to Sullivan's time in St. Louis. According to a piece in the May 20, 1911, edition of the *Boston Globe*, the abbreviation of "fanatic" dated back to Sullivan's history-making 1879 Dubuque Rabbits.

The *Globe's* source (likely Sullivan himself) recalled that "whiskered farmers" from across the state of Iowa routinely descended on Dubuque to watch the mighty Rabbits. Not satisfied to just watch the games, the baseball bugs would gather in hotel lobbies, where "the grangers, lost in admiration, would sit up close and blow tobacco smoke and baseball dope into the faces of Ted Sullivan and the players."

The story went that, when Sullivan would talk of "the hayseeds ... fanning us with that hot air," it was a short jump to "fanning bees" and ultimately "fans." Within a few years, Sullivan said, the use of the words "fan" and "fanning" had spread to players across the country.

When telling the story—as he did at least 100 times—Sullivan liked to say there were three kinds of fans: The Ironclad Fan; The Persevering Fan, and The Heart Rending Fan.

> "A 'fan' is a man, normal in most respects, who is afflicted with a mental aberration that is manifested in a highly intense emotional passion for any one form of sport. Thus, he who sits on the 'bleachers' coaching the players and roaring maledictions at the umpire is a 'fan.'"
> —*Boston Globe,* May 20, 1911

Regardless of the conflicting origin stories, columnist Ren Mulford laid out the accepted source of the term, noting that "Bug-itis" had become epidemic among Reds rooters: "The Ohio man who claims to have invented the name 'fan' is reaching out for a distinction which Ted Sullivan has had copper-riveted and nailed down for years. 'Fan,' according to the long-accepted Sullivanesque interpretation, is a 'boil down' of 'Fanatic.'"[20]

As the *Nashville Tennessean* noted in 1907 when it attributed the coining of the phrase to "that versatile character, Ted Sullivan" ... "it ('fan') has crept into the vernacular of pen-pushers of baseball history with an abandon."[21]

Not one to quit with a story while he was ahead, Sullivan claimed that in 1909 he actually ran into the original St. Louis crank turned "fan," who was working as a floorwalker at the Chicago Fair.[22]

Ted Takes Boston Strong Boy from Ring to Diamond

It has been said that, in his early youth, the great pugilist John L. Sullivan was something of a ball player, playing a little semi-pro around Boston, and was once offered a tryout with the Cincinnati Red Stockings. Perhaps and maybe. But what Ted Sullivan knew for sure was that putting the biggest name in boxing on a ballfield, any ballfield, on the Sabbath Day, would punch a lot of tickets and bring in a big stack of greenbacks.

JOHN L. SULLIVAN'S COLORS.

Described by Ted as having a "physical form carved out of the finest alabaster marble," the legendary fighter John L. Sullivan proved to be a bit of a palooka on the ball field (illustration 1889, publisher unknown, Library of Congress).

Although known as a bit of a softy outside the ring, "The Great John L" was not one to get suckered by a baseball promoter. Offered a $1,000 guarantee to pitch a few innings of an exhibition game, the big man pushed Sullivan for 50 percent of the gate receipts, and the irrepressible hustler had to capitulate. "While John had the faculty of throwing away his money, prompted by the warm impulse of his big heart, he had a business head on him in the mode of getting it," Sullivan remembered.[23]

"The town is in a ferment over the big man's coming," slavered the *St. Louis Post-Dispatch*. "It will show his great physique to perfect advantage, and will gratify the curiosity of thousands."[24]

Big John Not Much of a "Tosser"

ST. LOUIS GLOBE-DEMOCRAT, November 5, 1883—A crowd of between 4,000 and 5,000 people went to Sportsman's Park yesterday to see Sullivan, the champion pugilist, try his hand at twirling the sphere in a baseball game. The day was delightful for the sport, and had the price of admission been placed at a quarter instead of 50 cents the grounds would undoubtedly have been crowded.

The grandstand was packed with the old-time lovers of the sport, but the majority were present, not because they expected a fine game, but with a desire to see if the big pugilist could do as well in the diamond as in the prize ring. The St. Louis club, with two or three changes, was pitted against a picked nine of local semi-pro professionals.

The champion appeared on the field in a white suit with brown stockings and red cap. He made a fine appearance, and the suit displayed to his advantage his wonderful physique. The crowd appeared more intent on watching him than the game, which was nothing more than a hippodrome, and the spectators cheered more lustily at some miserable error than any fine play, of which latter, however, there were very few. As a baseball tosser Sullivan, the fighter, was not a success. His delivery was not effective and during the five innings he stood before the Brown's [sic] batters they hammered him with ease. Not much a knocker, either.

At the bat, the knocker couldn't knock at all. He popped up several flies, which were easily captured by the basemen or fielders, and his strong arms, which have been invincible in sending men to the dust, were powerless to secure him a good safe hit, and after the eighth inning Ted Sullivan, manager of the Browns, who played shortstop acceptably and sometimes brilliantly, relieved his namesake in the points. The slugger moved out to short, where he made many funny plays which brought forth the plaudits of the multitude.

It was evident before the game was half finished that the Browns were fooling with their opponents.

The large assemblage of spectators evinced the utmost good humor, and when the farce was ended boxer Sullivan was followed by an immense throng to the dressing room, and, when he emerged it was difficult for his carriage to affect [sic] a passage in the street.

The "Ted" Sullivan side prevailed, winning the farcical match, 15–3. Both the Sullivan gents went 0-for-4 at the plate.

Sure enough, the boxer-turned-baseball-player-for-a-day ended up getting more than triple the $1,000 guarantee Sullivan had offered. "He smiled and said he never carried any baseball money out of the city that he got it in," said Sullivan, and "the money should be given away to his needy friends or for charity." Before leaving St. Louis the next morning, "Big John" reportedly blew all but $130 of the more than $3,500 he made, leaving behind a bunch of old friends with new hats and hangovers.[25]

The wily baseball Sullivan came out pretty well, too, pocketing about $1,500 for himself—money he was said to have used to open a billiard hall in St. Louis.[26]

John L. Remembered "Cousin" Ted

Of all the serious and silly fundraisers the Great John L. Sullivan took part in over the years, he always remembered his first baseball gig with Ted Sullivan in St. Louis. In telling the story decades later, he said, "Ted Sullivan gives the figures and the facts in this case, so I'm not telling any romance. I squeezed into a uniform belonging to George McGinnis and pitched four innings. My side lost, but we had a good day's sport, and the crowd gave me the happy hoot every play I made. I could toss the ball over some in those days, feeling as I did like a fighting cock, and loving baseball next to fighting."[27]

The big-hearted bare-knuckle champ even remembered plowing through his $3,500 take in 24 hours. "I stood quite a few touches," he said with a smile and a shrug. "It was a thirsty place, St. Looey. Some of it went to charity.... I could never get past a Sister of Charity without emptying my pockets, and I've been told that there's a lot of good things stored up above for me—if I ever get up to collect them."

After leaving some coin with the Sisters of Charity in St. Louis, Big John L. reportedly stopped off in Independence, Missouri, to visit an old friend—the border ruffian and celebrated bank robber, Frank James.[28]

Still, the pugilist's memory of his ability to pound a baseball remained a bit hazy. "I was offered all kinds of coin to join big clubs," he said. "I turned them all down of course, for I wouldn't live under the rules of early-to-bed and so forth, not for all the coin they could roll in front of me, even if I didn't have punch engagements on hand, but I could sure play ball."[29]

Fooling the Fans

Of course, every sports fan for 500 miles around knew when and where Sullivan was scheduled to fight after leaving St. Louis. Next stop: New Orleans. Up and down the rail line from St. Louis to the Big Easy, nosy station clerks and telegraph operators followed and shared news of the famous boxer's whereabouts.

The problem was that Ted Sullivan, at the same time, was taking a team of baseball all-stars called "The St. Louis Combination" to New Orleans for some exhibition games. Whenever he and his all-stars rolled to a stop in front of a depot, throngs of boxing fans were waiting on the platform to catch a glimpse of their hero. It seemed that the telegraph tattlers were confusing their Sullivans.

Reported the *Cairo (IL) Bulletin*: "The boys had to layover. In the meantime they all took breakfast at the Halliday. Their names were Geo. McGinnis, H. C. McNair, Cliff Carroll, C. Comiskey, T. Mullane, Wm. Ewing, and T.P. Sullivan. The report was current for some time that the last named was Jno. [*sic*] L. Sullivan, and a large crowd gathered at the incline, only to be cruelly deceived."[30]

"They were cheering and calling for John L. Sullivan," recounted Ted Sullivan. "We told them he was not on the train but they would not believe us."[31]

For his baseball debut in St. Louis, John L. Sullivan had squeezed into the uniform of the Browns' biggest player, George Washington "Jumbo" McGinnis, and McGinnis was on the train with Ted Sullivan's all-stars. Since he looked a bit in girth and face like the famous John L., Ted and the other players hatched a plan to put McGinnis in an arm chair in the smoking room of the sleeper car, and told the people in the crowd they could maybe catch a glimpse of their boxing god through the smoking room window. What the people saw was Jumbo McGinnis relaxing with two boys fanning him and bringing him iced water.

Big John L.'s doppelganger, George Washington "Jumbo" McGinnis.

Ted Sullivan relished the recollection, telling interviewers:

Cigars and wine were handed into the sleeper all that day by admiring friends. Every station we passed was crowded to get a peep at John L., and McGinnis's neck was sore from bowing to admirers at the rear end of the platform.

The boys smoked all kinds of cigars that day, and enjoyed the joke along the route clear up to midnight. We arrived in New Orleans the next morning, and I suppose up to this day many people are telling their children and grandchildren that they saw the great John L. in 1883 with all his pugilists around him.[32]

◆ 6 ◆

A Sorry State
of the Union

Ted Sullivan's 1883 resuscitation of St. Louis baseball did not go unnoticed, especially locally. On St. Patrick's Day of 1884, an organizational meeting of the new Union Association was held in Cincinnati. Team representatives from Philadelphia, Baltimore, Chicago, St. Louis, Cincinnati, Washington, D.C., and Altoona (Pennsylvania) attended. The group voted to add a Boston franchise, and they selected four regular umpires and three substitutes. The schedule was expanded from 89 to 112 games, and the season was to begin April 19 and end October 15.

Henry V. Lucas, a 26-year-old heir to his family's St. Louis real estate empire, sought out Sullivan to identify potential franchises, organize the new league, and ultimately create and manage his St. Louis franchise. The Union Association was nothing less than a full-on attack on the baseball establishment by refusing to join the NL and AA as signatory to the National Agreement and its "Reserve Rule," which, in effect, kept players in contractual bondage to their teams by "reserving" their services in perpetuity.

Game Changer

Lucas was the UA's chief financier, and he professed his sympathy with the players' desire for greater bargaining power and control over their careers. He bankrolled that sympathy with his cash, and Lucas wasn't afraid of offering guaranteed, multi-year contracts at salaries well beyond those found in the two established major leagues. And while he owned the UA's St. Louis franchise, Lucas used his money to help keep afloat struggling league rivals.

Sullivan and the young magnate shared an opinion that the National

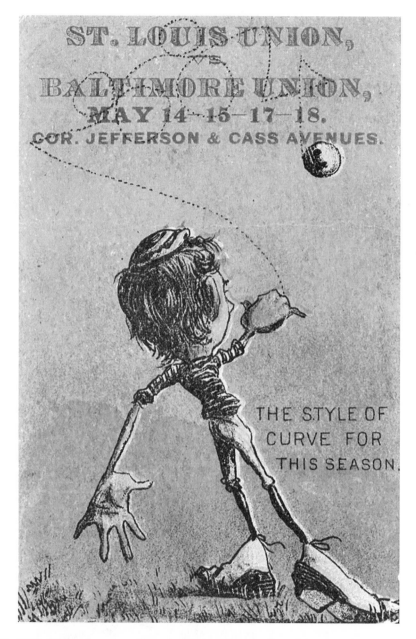

In 1884, St. Louis was on its way to becoming the fourth largest city in America. A young hometown millionaire named Henry Lucas believed there was room for a second baseball team and hired Sullivan to manage his new St. Louis Maroons of the upstart Union Association (program cover, May 14–18, 1884 series, St. Louis Unions vs. Baltimore Unions).

League's reserve rule was unjust and oppressive in its intent. Sullivan predicted the courts would one day override it.

Ultimately, Sullivan was hired on the strength of his winning results, his keen eye for talent, and his familiarity with baseball talent across the nation. "He is a straight forward gentleman whose heart is really with the cause of honest and prosperous base-ball playing," the *St. Louis Post-Dispatch* said of the new manager when he came aboard in early 1884.[1]

The scouting manager didn't disappoint, signing such talents as infielders Fred Dunlap, Joe Quinn, and David Rowe and outfielder George "Orator" Shafer, along with pitchers Billy Taylor and Charlie Sweeney, and creating a hard-to-beat nine.

> *"Joe Quinn, the Orioles great utility player was working in a lead mine around Dubuque, and he was unknown as a jewel in the bowels of the earth. Ted saw a chance to give Joe a lift, so he engaged him for the Maroons of St. Louis. Joe is now well to do in this world's goods. He is an accomplished undertaker."*
> —*Buffalo Enquirer*, March 7, 1898

Better Than Good

After his hugs-and-spit relationship with the quirky Chris Von der Ahe in 1883, Manager Sullivan had a great gig going, managing the newly minted St. Louis Maroons for the wealthy young "nobleman," Henry Lucas. As the inaugural season of the Union Association unfolded, his powerhouse nine intimidated the rest of the field, threatening to run some of their rival cities right out of the league before the season was even half finished.

The Maroons reeled off wins in their first 20 games and by late June were sitting on a record of 35 wins and only four losses. As was the case with Sullivan's dominant 1879 Dubuque team, the Maroons ran roughshod over the Union Association competition. With other affiliates struggling to field competitive teams, attendance and gate shares suffered. The Altoona squad dropped out of the association in May, after playing just 25 games. By June, the Union Association was having a tough time staying alive.

The Altoona franchise was transferred to the up-and-coming cowtown of Kansas City, Missouri, making "the Paris of the Plains" the westernmost city ever to field a so-called major league baseball team. Attendance was good in Kansas City, but the team, dubbed "The Cowboys," wasn't saddle-broke for baseball. They were lousy.

In St. Louis, the sporting press began reporting rumors of serious tension between the ballplayers and their taskmaster manager. Reportedly,

Sullivan was too much of a disciplinarian, insisting on sobriety, curfews and on-field discipline.[2]

Anxious to keep the struggling Union Association alive, Lucas brokered a deal whereby Ted Sullivan would assume partial ownership of the Kansas City franchise, move across the state, and take over management of its win-starved, mix-and-match nine.

Ted Sent to Lasso Kansas City's Cantankerous Cowboys

Dispatched from St. Louis to Kansas City to put his winning brand on the Union Association's struggling Cowboys, Sullivan stepped into a smoky, fetid milieu of stockyards, slaughterhouses and farm implement factories. The fast-growing cowtown had plenty of jobs for stock tenders, throat-slitters, beef-boners, iron puddlers and bartenders. Unfortunately for Ted Sullivan, there were not many qualified applicants for the job of "professional base ball player" (photograph circa 1885, author's collection).

Naysayers thought Lucas was really stretching his luck by gambling on such a small market as Kansas City, but the young magnate believed that the busy cattle town, with a population of 100,000 and growing, would embrace baseball if their team was any good.

Kansas City malt and grain merchant Americus McKim had paid Lucas $15,000 for the franchise, and he refurbished and expanded an old ballpark in "Cook's Pasture" just south of the city. He ordered uniforms, picked up some of Altoona's now-homeless athletes, and made a swing back east to pick up a few more players, but he was still taking applications from rock-throwing farm boys and out-of-work amateurs two days before the team's first game.

The "Kaycees," or "Cowboys," as they took to being called by their eastern rivals, presented a hodge-podge roster of mediocre veterans and young would-bes who had barely met, much less played together before they trotted onto the field to face the Chicago Unions on June 7 in what was said to be the first series of major league baseball played west of the Mississippi River and St. Louis.

Although they lost that first game, 6–5, in 12 innings, the pioneer sportswriter Al Spink later recalled that no official score was kept of the game because no one in Kansas City at that time knew how to keep a regular tabulated score.

Pitching for Chicago the following Monday, the notoriously hot-tempered and foul-mouthed pitcher "One Arm" Hugh Daily (whom Ted Sullivan had rejected from his Maroons earlier in the year) schooled the Cowboys, 12–3, and the losses started stacking up like fresh-cut Kansas City steaks.

Kansas City was a Union Association doormat, but just one of many. Ted Sullivan's St. Louis Maroons were spanking everybody. The cranks—now "fans"—in the other Union Association cities were fast losing interest, and their owners were losing lots of money.

See Ya, St. Louie!

The Missouri papers reported in mid–June that Sullivan had abruptly resigned his position with Lucas's Maroons, as "he was unable to enforce certain rules he instituted."

Sullivan stepped off the train in Kansas City to find a wide-open river bluff town teeming with unwashed cowboys from the cattle trails, reeking stock pens, belching ironworks, and block after block of noisy saloons. Work was plentiful, and more people were drifting into the city every day.

Lucas and McKim, and now Sullivan, were gambling on Kansas City's legions of blue collar workers—mostly Irish, German and Scandinavian, working as puddlers in the iron works, or throat slitters and beef boners in the expanding slaughter and meat-packing houses—to embrace and support professional baseball.

When Ted Sullivan hit town, he would have smelled manure and money—not necessarily in that order.

Ted Takes Over

Union Association players were bouncing from team to team in search of regular paychecks, but Sullivan found it wasn't easy to attract decent performers to the smoke-veiled cowtown at the edge of the American West. He did inherit or find a couple of young Turks who would, in time, prove to be keepers in the major leagues, including William "Billy" O'Brien, a first baseman who, just three years later, would lead the National League in home runs; and Emmett Seery, a reliable journeyman outfielder who would rack up nearly 1,000 games in an eight-year major league career.

The press and cranks in Kansas City were sure that the famous manager who had just led St. Louis to a record 20 straight wins would raise up their "baby" to be a winner, too. "He is fully aware that the present team is not conspicuous for its strength, either individually or collectively," reported the *Kansas City Times* of July 23, 1884. "The Union team under the management of Ted Sullivan will be compelled to report to the ball grounds at 10 a.m. each day for morning practice. If energy and judgment are of any service, he will give Kansas City a team that she need not be ashamed of."[3]

Sullivan immediately cut loose half a dozen horse-powerless Cowboys and set out in search of replacements.

Where "Canned" Came From

Ted Sullivan's managerial—and pitching—debut saw the Cowboys lose a road game to the Baltimore Monumentals, 17–5, in what the *Kansas City Journal* called a "most ignominious fashion," describing the play of KC's nine as "ridiculous."[4]

Ironically, it may have been that very ignominiously played game that spawned an American byword that has become synonymous with terminated, sacked, dismissed, axed and let go.

According to Paul Dickson's informative and entertaining book, *The Dickson Baseball Dictionary*, it was the Cowboys' klutzy catcher, Bill Dugan, who first tossed out the word "canned." Ted Sullivan's story (it varied, of course) went that poor Dugan was despondent after muffing a pair of plays that caused KC to lose both ends of a doubleheader to Baltimore.

"I quit," he told skipper Sullivan. "When a man loses two ball games in one afternoon it's time for him to get out of the game." Dugan proceeded to send a telegram to his wife back in Brooklyn: "Will be home next Monday. Shine up my dinner can, I'm going back to being a plumber. No more baseball for me."[5]

Sullivan said that after that incident, whenever he or the players heard of anyone being released, they'd say "He shined up the dinner can," or "He got canned," or the manager "attached the can to him."[6]

One of his first replacements, pitcher Peek-a-Boo Veach, later recalled that Sullivan's "famous remark" to wash-outs became "Go shine your can and take to the woods."[7]

On July 21, the Kaycee Cowboys were in dead last place in the new league, with an embarrassing record of 3–19. Kansas City's roster was so thin in talent that Sullivan was forced to put his rusty self into a couple of games to "twist the sphere" or fill holes at shortstop and in the outfield, and reportedly went 3-for-9 at the plate. The young "Mascot Manager," as the *Daily Times* called him, shuffled at least 40 different players onto the field that season, trying to find a combination that could tally a win once in a while.[8]

Despite the team's awful play and record, attendance at home games continued to be strong, with Sullivan avidly hawking promotions like Ladies-Get-In-Free Days and risking the wrath of preachers and the law by playing games on the Sabbath, which drew double and triple the number of weekday fans.

On August 11, 1884, the *Kansas City Journal* reported that 8,000 people attended a home game against Chicago, and "even a Chinaman who had overcome his religious scruples was perched upon a top seat deeply interested in the national game." Boys, including future Hall of Fame pitcher Charles "Kid" Nichols, crowded outside the outfield fences and stood atop their nags in order to see their Cowboys lose.

"In truth," the *Kansas City Times* observed after yet another August defeat, "it appeared as though our boys were rattled by the sea of faces which looked out at them from the grandstand and the outfield fences, and could neither see a football or hit a balloon.... The work of the infield was disgusting in the extreme."[9]

Despite playing consistently bum baseball, Sullivan's team was proving profitable.

Lost Balls

Even with plenty of cash coming in, "Sully's Hefties," as the *Star* took to calling the Cowboys when they occasionally won a game, still played each contest using just one ball. When a foul found its way out of the park, boys would be fetched to go get it. The paper suggested that a couple of gates be cut into the right field wall "and thereby save tedious waits on foul hits over the fence."[10]

Game balls being a precious commodity in those days, an exhibition game put a serious dent in the Cowboys' limited inventory.

Late in the 1884 season, Sullivan took his Cowboys to a small town in Kansas to take on a nine of burly, raw-boned farm boys. He insisted on pitching to the big fellows himself, and he lasted into the bottom of the ninth inning with the score tied at 2–2, and two men out.

As the hurler character Peek-a-Boo Veach later told it:

> A big chap walked up to the bat with an evident determination to do or die. Ted sailed one up to him and what a wallop he gave it. He broke the ball squarely in two, one half went over the right field fence and the fielder chased the other half and fielded it to the plate, but "Antelope Pete," the runner, made a good slide. It was a close decision, though the umpire called him safe. We argued that only half the ball was in play, and after he had taken the matter under consideration, he gave them the game 2½ to 2.[11]

> *"Whiskey, beer and other stimulants were sold in the stands and on the field. Umpire baiting was a favorite sport. It was deemed fast fun to run or rush upon the field and make the umpire take the low fence between him and the dressing room in his stride. Umpires who fled and jumped fences were known as 'timber toppers.'"*
> —Al Spink, *Spink Sports Stories*

By September the manager was as frustrated as the fans with the poor play of his team. In a match-up at Washington, the Cowboys were playing an uncharacteristically good game and tied with the Nationals, 6–6, in the ninth inning when, inexplicably, the umpire, George Seward, called the game before dusk, saying it was too dark.

The Cowboys and Sullivan felt they'd been cheated by Seward in different ways all season long. Following a bad call in a game at KC a few weeks earlier, the hometown fans had charged the field and chased Seward through a door under the grandstand and into a waiting hack with a speedy horse.[12] "It was awful," reported the *Times*, "as the bugs greeted the decision with various taunts, such as: Put him out, he's drunk; he's a thief. His [Seward's] guilty conscience needed no accuser and he sneaked away like a mangy cur caught sucking eggs."[13]

After Seward called the game in Washington, the *Star* reported that Kansas City was, again, cheated out of a victory by Seward, who "very properly beat a hasty retreat from the diamond to escape the hisses of the crowd. Manager Sullivan ordered his team to remain on the ground while he went in search of the umpire. The Nationals, however, left for their dressing room and the crowd savagely denounced the management of that club for treating the visitors in such a shameless manner."[14]

A veteran "indicator" in the American Association, Seward was known to get so sauced during games that he would halt them early and head for the nearest saloon. The local papers called him "drunk and incompetent," and predicted "If Mr. Seward appears again in Kansas City, he will probably be carried home on a stretcher."[15]

Calling the Shots

Kansas City, in fact, was not a popular destination for adjudicators. Visiting teams liked to scare first-time, $5-a-game umps with stories of cowtown fans pulling their pistols after a questionable call and shooting the covers off fly balls to keep them from being caught.

Recalled catcher Charlie Bennett: "The first time Ed Beaten umpired a game in Kansas City, he was scared as a man could possibly be. He came from Baltimore and his idea of the West was a sparsely settled country, overrun by bands of scalp-hunting Indians, cowboy desperadoes and train robbers. On the train to Kansas City, one of the boys told him to 'be ready to throw your hands up at any moment, for those cowboys are dangerous fellows.... They'd as soon shoot you as look at you.'"[16]

Bennett said another player swore to the flummoxed ump that he was once playing in Kansas City, when a Kaycee player hit a high fly to the right fielder. As the fellow chased after it, he said, "a fussilade of shots" came from the grandstand. "The cowboys were shooting at the ball. They must have hit it a dozen times. The cover was torn off the ball by their shots, and the fellow managed to catch the cover."

WHAT BEATEN EXPECTED TO SEE

Tales of Kansas City's Stetson hat-wearing, pistol-carrying fans shooting fly balls out of the air intimidated five-dollar-a-day umpires like Ed Beaten (*San Antonio Gazette*, March 23, 1906).

"He claimed an out on the catch," said Bennett, "but we disputed the claim, and the game broke up in a row. If I recall rightly, we [Kansas City] got the benefit of the doubt on all close calls that day."[17]

Sullivan was able to pick up several new "crack players" during one of the club's eastern trips—including Charlie Bastain, Pat Sullivan, and Lou Say, and he picked up a local amateur named Bill Hutchison, a right-handed pitcher who went on to be a National League wins leader and strikeout champ, which gave the low-on-bullets Cowboys a little more firepower.

When the cowpokes did manage to win a game, it was big news. Gibed one local scribe after a rare Cowboys victory in late August: "The Kansas City baseball club actually won a game last week. The city was illuminated over the unlooked for event, brass bands paraded the streets and one man blowed the gable end out of big drum."[18]

But Sullivan's boys were soon backsliding again, and when all was said and done of the Union Association's one and only season, Ted Sullivan's Unions-Kaycees-Cowboys-Onions, with a collective batting average of .199, had lost 63 of the 79 games (11–23 at home and 5–40 on the road) and finished at the bottom of the well.

	W–L
St. Louis Maroons	4–19
Milwaukee Brewers	8–4
Cincinnati Outlaw Reds	69–36
Baltimore Monumentals	58–47
Boston Reds	58–51
Chicago Browns/Pittsburgh Stogies	41–50
Washington Nationals	47–65
Philadelphia Keystones	21–46
St. Paul White Caps	2–6
Altoona Mountain Cities	6–19
Kansas City Unions/Cowboys	16–63
Wilmington Quicksteps	2–16

"The Kansas City team had the hardest kind of luck," noted a sympathetic Veach, "what he [Ted] had to contend with would have put many a manager on the faulty cranium pile."[19]

Ted Sullivan's reputation as a manager took its first arrow that season, as the Cowboys were, in the vernacular of the day, routinely and "catawamptiously chewed up," but the team's financial success gained attention from everyone in baseball. He and McKim reported an attendance of 54,000 for those 34 games at home, and they claimed a season-ending profit of $7,000, while most other Union Association affiliates were face-down in pools of red ink.

Still, the league seemed to have a future, and there was talk of "next year." But when McKim and Sullivan went to the winter meetings of the Union Association, they were the only team reps to show up so, without the benefit of good-bye or Benediction, the Union Association was declared dead.

The *Journal* blamed Kansas City fans' boisterous behavior as much as the "ignominious" play on the field for the team's and the Union Association's demise. But the truth is, the Union Association was weak, fielding a mix-and-match collection of rubes, maybes, and wannabes.[20]

Bill James, in his definitive book *The New Bill James Historical Abstract*, contends that the UA was so weak that there were several minor leagues in operation that year "could have kicked the UA's butt and stolen their lunch money," and he is probably right.[21]

Whereas a few Cowboys, like Emmett Seery, Billy O'Brien, Con Daily, and Chippy McGarr, moved on to tangible, if not illustrious careers in real major league baseball, most of Ted Sullivan's Cowboys took their dinner cans and returned to playing weekend ball with their hometown nines.

◆ 7 ◆

Back to the Bushes

"It's bad enough to be hissed and called a thief, but in the West when the local club loses, an umpire is fortunate if he escapes with his life. Of all the cities in the league Kansas City is the worst."
—Umpire Tom York upon quitting
the profession in 1886[1]

Manager-turned-entrepreneur Ted Sullivan found himself stuck in Kansas City with bats, balls, uniforms, and a few players, but no league to play in. So in the winter of 1885, he put his hustler hat back on and, once again, became the baseball version of a traveling Bible salesman.

Sullivan and other survivors of the 1884 baseball coup formed a new league—which the retributive American Association and National League insisted be strictly categorized as a "minor" league. As the new Western (minor) League's traveling representative, Sullivan was charged with organizing franchises. He spent the winter riding the rails through frigid Minnesota, Wisconsin, Indiana, Iowa, Ohio, and Nebraska, enticing small- and mid-size city chambers of commerce with visions of sunny spring days and cold lemonade.

The new league adopted the playing rules of the American Association with two exceptions: the "foul ball bound out" (any ball being struck or tipped and caught, either flying or on the first bound, was a "hand" out—per Knickerbocker Rules of 1854) was eliminated, and restrictions on a pitcher's delivery were eased, allowing for livelier and more animated challenges from the hurler's box (the "mound" wasn't introduced until 1893). Plus, Sunday games would be allowed, in hopes of boosting attendance and revenue.

Milwaukee (the Brewers), Keokuk (the Hawkeyes), Indianapolis (the Hoosiers), Omaha (the Omahogs), Cleveland (the Forest Cities), and Toledo (the Avengers) bought in to smooth-talking Ted Sullivan's new field of dreams, and the hustling manager upped his own financial stake in the Cowboys. In Kansas City, he gathered and managed a nine composed

Dressed in their stylish white and blue uniforms, Ted's rowdy Cowboys ran away with the imagination and competitive spirit of Kansas City's working-class Irish. The Cowboys earned and reveled in their reputation as minor league baseball's bat- and insult-slinging hooligans (*Missouri Valley Room*, Kansas City Public Library).

of some of his better players from the Union Association Cowboys of the year before, and added a sprinkle of untrieds, unprovens, and weren't-ever-gonna-bes. Starting to realize that good promotion was as important as good pitching when it came to selling 25-cent tickets to the working-class fan, Sullivan perfected the art of publicity, managed ticket sales, and even printed his own scorecards and advertising fliers on a small press in his office under the stands.

> "A St. Louis exchange cruelly remarks that with the Dugans, the O'Briens, the Sweeneys, and the Sullivans, Ted Sullivan will have a team fit to appear in "Muldoon's Picnic" as well as on the ball field."
> —Kansas City Star, March 25, 1885

30-Cent Pitchers

At the outset of the season, Sullivan promised that Kansas City would have no occasion to be ashamed of its club in comparison with others.

Observing Sullivan's scramble to put together a decent nine, a reporter for the *Evening Star* posted this conversation that he supposedly had with a fellow who was reading the newspaper in a hotel lobby:

"Well, this is mighty discouraging," said a young man as he looked up from his paper. "I read here that old, banged-up, broken-nosed pitchers are a drug in the market and worth only 30 cents apiece."

"What's that to you? Have you been speculating in decorative relics?" asked the reporter.

"Relics?" said the young man. "Thunder, no! I'm a base ball pitcher."[2]

Whether it was because he still had hair that was reddish in those days, or because it was the prevailing color in his Celtic complexion, in Kansas City they called Ted Sullivan "Red." On road trips he sometimes introduced the team as his "Red Lions," and even had a second set of uniforms made that were red and brown. But the Cowboys of 1885 wore blue and white uniforms, and they were sometimes referred to during games as "The Blues." Turns out, they wouldn't play enough games that year to soil either set of uniforms.[3]

Hopes in the Cowtown were high when Sullivan's Cowboys kicked off the season with a couple of exhibition victories, including a 17–6 win over the oddly-named "champion amateur club of St. Louis."

KC Takes on Prickly Ash Bitters

KANSAS CITY EVENING STAR, April 13, 1885–The Kansas Citys met the Prickly Ash nine of St. Louis yesterday in the presence of 5,000 people. The visitors, among who [sic] were many well-known professionals, were overpowered at every point, the Kansas Citys winning by 17 to 6. Tomorrow the Kansas City public will have an opportunity of seeing one of the greatest clubs in the country—the St. Louis Browns. The home club has been battling terrifically in the four games they have played, and it will be seen whether they can keep this gait up. The St. Louis Union is one of the strongest in the country and our baseball public will have a chance of witnessing two great games of ball. The games will be called at 3:45 each day to give our citizens a chance to get away from their business. The St. Louis team was the first club Manager Sullivan organized for St. Louis, and his young team will meet his old one tomorrow and Wednesday.

Note: *The Prickly Ash Bitters Company of St. Louis produced a patent medicine it claimed would cure a "torpid" liver. Its key ingredient being alcohol, it could also cure hangovers.*

The *Evening Star* predicted "a dog fight" when the Cowboys locked horns in an exhibition with Van der Ahe's Browns, which, of course, included Sullivan's old apprentice and baseball's then-rising star, Charlie Comiskey, on first base. Upon arrival, the Browns were greeted by Kanas City's "ninety-nine degree bugs" and carted to the St. James Hotel, drawn by the cowtown's finest white horses. The dominant Browns thanked the local bugs by whipping their minor leaguers, 15 to 3.[4]

The Cowboys managed to win a few games against their league rivals from Omaha, including one contest in which a player got into a hearty row with $5-a-game umpire John Brennan.

As the *Evening Star* told it, "The two fought and rolled about the street like two school boys, and at the end of that time a policeman, discerning that neither had drawn blood, separated them and walked them to the police station, where Chief Speers complimented them on their science and hard hitting qualities."[5]

Ted Sullivan's and the Cowboys' antics, if not their play, sold tickets. Attendance was surprisingly strong, with crowds of 5,000 to 10,000 not uncommon. And that wasn't counting the little bugs looking over the fence.

Sullivan's unruly but mildly talented squad held its own through May and into June, alternating places at the top of the league standings with

THE PEER·AGE

"The ball park was populated by the knothole urchins 'on the outside looking in.'" *Kansas City Star*, May 10, 1885.

the Hoosiers of Indianapolis, and paying for itself with steady gate receipts. But the business-minded manager nearly pushed his luck a bit too far at an exhibition game against the Forest Citys, played in nearby Atchison, Kansas. He boldly charged 50 cents a head for admission, causing the locals to grouse and protest. According to a reporter who was on the scene, Sullivan was able to calm the unhappy crowd by telling them they could not expect to see real live professionals for a quarter. The fans left satisfied after Billy O'Brien launched a home run to center field that knocked a ticketless young fan out of a tree, and the Cowboys won the game, 5–4.[6]

Back in Kansas City, Sullivan cranked up his little press and put out flyers hyping special promotions like "Ladies' Day." A flyer passed out on street corners proclaimed that "All ladies will be admitted free to watch the last game between the Clevelands and the Kansas Citys." Sullivan even experimented with group ticket sales, wooing organizations like the Knights Templar to help fill up the grandstand.[7]

Among the quirky characters taking the field for the Cowboys in 1885 were William Colgan, Cornelius Doyle, Ed Dugan, Fleury Sullivan, William O'Brien, Thomas O'Brien, Emmett Seery, Harry Decker, and William Walter Veach, a workhorse pitcher and outfielder who went on to play for the Pittsburgh Pirates. Sullivan and the fans in KC gave William Walter the nickname that would stick with him the rest of his life: "Peek-A-Boo."

It seems Veach, whom Sullivan brought on in August, was a solid twirler with a good assortment of pitches and a perplexing hop-skip-and-a-jump motion to the plate, but he became distracted with men on bases. One day, according to the *St. Louis Republic*, "Manager Sullivan sent him to the mound with the order: 'Keep an eye on the bench and when my hands go up, fire the ball to first.' After Veach had picked off two men, the opposing team got wise and the signal was changed for the pitcher to keep an eye on a certain post in the grandstand and throw to first whenever he saw a scorecard waved in the air. His opponent finally discovered this signal, too, but everybody began calling Veach 'Peek-a-boo,' as a result and the name stuck."[8]

"Peek-A-Boo was by no means a dummy," Sullivan remembered. "He was a bright, jovial fellow who did not require to be hit by a catapult to know what was wanted."[9]

Yup, Veach would later admit, "I was to a degree a poor hand to watch bases at that time, and Ted saw that he would have to devise some scheme to make me proficient in that important part of the game. I kept them [runners] hugging the bag and the opposition players watched me like a hawk to see where I was being tipped from. This peculiar position I took to get my tip and at the same time to shield Ted, who was hiding behind a post in the bleachers, caused them to yell 'Peek-a-Boo' at me."[10]

Fakin' It

The rules of the day allowing for no in-game substitutions of players, Manager Sullivan once had Veach, whose seemingly every pitch was getting pounded, fake a broken leg, so he could pull him out of the game and replace him with a fresh pitcher. As soon as a sharp-hit liner came in the vicinity of his leg, Veach dropped to the ground, screaming in pain. He was carried off the field and placed in the shade. With the opposing manager looking skeptical, Sullivan proceeded to search the stands for a doctor. He picked an "iron-clad" fan, a young doctor "who was so impregnated with baseball atmosphere that he would have declared all my players paralyzed standing up had I desired it."

After feeling the pitcher's injured appendage, the doctor declared that the pitcher had "snapped a tendon in his flip-maglider and would likely not be able to pitch the rest of the season, if ever."[11]

Sullivan loved telling that story, and over the years he embellished it plenty, even one-upping himself with this story, reported as gospel by small town papers across the country:

The Only Dead Man to Pitch a Game
The Appleton (Wisconsin) Post-Crescent
January 9, 1908

Apropos of the rule of the old days which forbade taking players out of the game unless they were injured, there is the story of the only dead man who ever pitched a ball game. It happened at Kansas City, and Ted Sullivan was the victim.

Ted's pitcher was getting lambasted all over the lot and Ted was figuring every way possible to get him out of the game. He didn't wish the pitcher any tough luck, but it would have been a relief if one of the many liners that whistled past had broken a leg or something like that.

Suddenly a brilliant idea struck Ted. He hastily hustled up a friendly doctor, and when the inning was over instructed the pitcher to fall dead as quickly as possible in the next inning, at least before any hits were made. On the second ball pitched the twirler threw up his hands and sank to the ground. Amidst tremendous excitement the emergency doctor rushed onto the field, felt the pitcher's heart and pronounced him dead. More excitement. The sorrowing teammates bore the pitcher off the field and Ted started to warm up his crack twirler, when the umpire stopped him.

"You can't put in another pitcher," he said.

"Why not? The man is dead!" argued Ted.

"I'm sorry for that," said the umpire, "but the rules say he must be injured. He died of heart disease, therefore he'll have to stay in."

And the dead man, who was sitting in the visiting club's dressing room smoking a cigarette while waiting for the undertaker's wagon, had to come out and finish the game.

Catching a Break

It wasn't until this season—1885, when overhand pitching was finally allowed—that a catcher for the Providence Grays started wearing a buckskin glove to help protect his already-mangled appendages. Harry Decker, a journeyman backstop who played a few games for Ted Sullivan in 1884 and 1885, began tinkering with his own version of a glove—a thumb-less leather pillow with adjustable padding that he called the "Decker Catcher's Safety Mitt." Considered an early prototype of the modern catcher's glove, Decker's design was purchased for peanuts by A. G. Spalding.

Balls and Strikes to the Head

As the season went into May, the Cowboys took to relishing their reputation in the press as baseball's wild and wooly western gunslingers, prone to verbal harangues and fistfights. Several gun incidents in Kansas City reportedly made the league's eastern investors nervous, causing them to have second thoughts about Kansas City's future as a baseball town.

Harassing and threatening the league's umpires became the Cowboys' calling card—with manager Sullivan often the first to stir up the crowd. In a losing effort against Milwaukee in early June, Sullivan accused the umpire, a fellow named Hoover, of "crookedness" and threatened to assault him in the office of the Kirby House.[12] "Hoover is physically much the inferior of the Boston slugger's namesake [Ted]," reported the *St. Louis Post-Dispatch*, "but he succeeded in parrying the vicious thrust of his antagonist and giving the latter a very hard hit."[13]

The Cowboys' reputation as the outlaws of minor league baseball grew exponentially, as pointed out in this letter planted/published in the *Kansas City Times* of May 19, 1885:

> *Dear Editor:*
>
> *I am sorry to see some of the elements of rowdyism cropping out at the Western League baseball park. At the same time I still deplore the fact that the impression has gone abroad that Kansas City has begun the oriental practice of mobbing umpires. This fellow Hoover, who pretended to umpire the games here with Indianapolis, certainly deserved a mild spanking, but it is absurd to say that he received anything more than a good deal of "back talk" from indignant persons on the grounds. I must warn Manager Ted Sullivan that a few more such instances of umpiring and evidences of loose play as characterized in a recent game will go far toward destroying the fever over baseball that has this season raged so violently in Kansas City.*
>
> *"Rose" Field*
> *The Fault Finder*

As rough and rowdy as his 1885 Cowboys were, Sullivan rarely imposed penalties on even his most incorrigible players. "Ted Sullivan is past master in the art of kidding," Veach wrote. "I played ball for Ted two seasons and I never knew him to take a cent from a ball player in fines. He would just make them ashamed by kidding them."[14]

An example Veach gave was a game in Toledo in 1884:

> While there some of us attended a circus. We played that afternoon and were doing pretty well, until Milwaukee had a man on first and second with two out. The batter hit a high one to [Joe] Visner, who was playing center. It was a cinch for Joe, but he couldn't wait for the ball to come down, but made a leap in the air after it and dropped it. The fellow on second, of course, started for third and Joe fired the ball in the grand stand. All of us then got the delirium tremens.
>
> The look on Ted's face would have done credit to a corpse and the way he shot into Joe was worth the price of admission. He told him he did not want any acrobatic ball playing on his team and if he did he would get a calcium light to throw on him when he did high and lofty tumbling, and would also get him a spring board. He cautioned Joe that if he ever heard of him going to another circus he would release him.

Cowboys "Robbed" on Train[15]

Sullivan's Cowboys relished eating almost as much as chewing on umpires. The no-frills, no-bed train cars they rode to away games became known throughout baseball as "Sullivan Sleepers," as the boys had to sleep sitting up in their seats. The young ballplayers, known for their ravenous appetites, were given a bare-bones per diem for dinner.

The manager later recalled the day the boys spotted, for the first time, a buffet car, a new concept on western trains: "They were tantalized by what they saw looking through the car window—piles of glistening grapes and copious other delicacies that looked like manna when compared to the 'meals for canary birds' that they were used to getting on the road. The novelty of eating in a buffet car dazzled them. I told them I would give them 75 cents [instead of the usual 50 cents] for dinner … then I waited with mirth for the climax."

Led by Billy O'Brien, the players stormed the buffet car. A half-hour later, O'Brien woke a pretending-to-be-sleeping Sullivan. "Say, Ted," O'Brien whispered, "did you hear about the hold-up in the biffet car? We were all robbed." O'Brien moaned that he had been charged $2.25 and was still hungry. "I believe they only gave us the photograph of that stuff they sold us." Having had his laugh and knowing he had taught the boys a lesson, manager Sullivan went ahead and fed them again at the regular dinner stop a few miles down the line.

Not on the Lord's Day!

In early June, pressure began to mount from churches and law enforcement agencies calling for an end to baseball on the Sabbath. On June 7 at Cleveland, police stopped a game between the Cowboys and the Forest Citys after just three innings of play, with Kansas City leading, 3–0.

"The authorities of the good old pious town have determined to enforce the Sunday laws," crowed the *Kansas City Evening Star* on June 8, 1885. "Ted Sullivan ... is indignant at the action taken by the ministers, and says that all the men in his club were engaged with the understanding that they would be required to play Sunday games and that if the Sunday games are prohibited, he will disband the club."

One-Armed Ump

Cleveland called it quits following the police action. The Toledo franchise also gave up, and the league began teetering on the brink of insolvency. Meanwhile, Sullivan and his support staff—including the team's treasurer, the equipment manager, a water carrier, and a one-armed back-up umpire—found themselves stranded among the smoky steel mills of Youngstown, Ohio.

"Immediately upon landing in the town, Manager Sullivan determined upon having some fun with the natives," the *Evening Star* recounted a few days later[16]:

> He solemnly challenged the boss puddler, who acted as captain and manager (of the local amateur base ball team). After consulting with the natives and discussing the ability of the famous Kansas City team, the boss puddler, with some trepidation, accepted.
>
> The funniest part of the joke was Sullivan's pitching. Sullivan never plays ball in any position, and it is difficult for his friends to believe that he even attempted to palm himself off on the Youngstowners as a pitcher. The one-armed disabled umpire, who never before had on a base ball suit, caught Sullivan's fierce delivery. The man who carries the bats and who by the way is paralyzed on one side, played first base.

According to the Kansas City paper's account, every man, woman, child, and domestic animal in Youngstown turned out to see the game. Somehow Sullivan's impostors won the match-up, 12–7, but the citizens demanded a rematch, and in that one Youngstown prevailed, 16–8. "The people of the smoky valley still think that their ball club defeated the Kansas City league team," the paper reported, "and Sullivan says he does not want them to learn of his deception until he is out of the state."

Paid in Glitter

Looking back years later, Sullivan conceded that, by early June in 1885, virtually every team in the Western League was starving for cash to survive.

In Toledo, after playing three games against his old friend, the gregarious, generous and always gambling Dan O'Leary's Avengers, Sullivan went to collect his take of the gate. He later remembered O'Leary "calling me to one side and uttering the Irish phrase 'sinn féin' [we ourselves], then whispering: 'It is this way, Ted, this backer of mine has no money.'"[17]

The backer, the owner of a jewelry store, had been paying O'Leary's creditors with jewelry. Said Sullivan: "This indeed was a new phase in baseball guarantees and for genial Dan, with his 'plámásing' (ingratiating)." Sullivan accepted jewelry and gave it to the landlord who had provided his Cowboys with three days' room and board in Toledo.

A Slugging Match

The Cowboys'—or at least Sullivan's—greatest rivals that year were Tom Loftus and his Milwaukee nine. Loftus, having played for Sullivan at Dubuque in 1879, wanted nothing more than to whip his old mentor. Sometime in the summer of 1885, the two teams reportedly battled in an exhibition contest over side bets of beer and banquets (loser pays), and harsh words. After Sullivan stood on his head on the baseline mocking Loftus, the two managers supposedly took their differences to the proverbial woodshed.

The bored scribes back in Dubuque went along with what undoubtedly was a Sullivan-contrived story of a vicious battle royal that took place between him and Loftus in the woods near Milwaukee in the early summer of 1885.

> [Sullivan] sends us a blood-curdling account of the bloodless affair, but the details are too ghastly for publication in a family paper like ours. Sullivan's colors were green, and his hair was cut like a dynamiter.... Loftus landed a left on the tip of Sullivan's bugle, and Ted responded with a rousing crack which Tom received on the breadbasket ... the bloodless battle, sad to relate, ended in a draw.[18]

In truth, Loftus and Sullivan were lifelong friends. When in Dubuque, they had played cards and polo and operated the Loftus & Sullivan billiard hall together.

Western League Whipped

The next day, on June 15, the Indianapolis club—atop the league standings with a 27–4 record—gave up the ghost, and Sullivan's Western League died with them. His Cowboys were in third place with a 17–13 record and were still profitable when the league collapsed. Billy O'Brien was leading the league in hitting (.372 over 30 games). Ernie Burch hit .361 over 26 games, and Emmett Seery hit over .300 as well. Pitcher Ed Dugan was 4–1, and Peek-A-Boo Veach finished 9–8.[19]

The baseball season being still young, Sullivan took a Sleeper to Memphis, where he signed on to manage the Reds in the fledgling minor Southern League. Billy O'Brien and some of the other Cowboys packed their saddlebags and went with him.

A Short Stop in Memphis

Where Ted Was Hit on the Head with a Chair

Hustling Ted Sullivan's Southern baseball experience—leading four different minor league franchises in five different markets across a couple of decades—would lay bare nearly all of his personal and professional traits, both charming and alarming.

At each of his stops in baseball-hungry cities across the South, initial announcements of his arrival generated great hype and enthusiasm. But it generally didn't take long for him to engender folks' animosity and be derided as a carpetbagger—and sometimes worse.

When Sullivan made his mid–June move south, he brought along many of his KC boys—he called them "Spalpeens," the Irish word for "rascals"—and the style of play that had made the Cowboys notorious across the Western League.[20]

Within weeks, his re-made Memphis Reds were the most-hated club in the Southern League.

By the Fourth of July, press accounts were touting the Memphis club as a "daisy" and a pennant contender based on Sullivan's reputation as an able scout and tactician, although the foremost tactics Sullivan brought to Memphis were what cranks called "kicking and bulldozing."

In his first month south, the bantam manager's incessant chirping—*Sporting Life* called him "uncivil, excitable and bullying"—brought him a $50 fine from umpire Ben Young. Days later, newspapers across the country detailed the relentless torrent of vitriol that Sullivan and his "pets" were routinely unleashing on Southern League umpires.[21]

It wasn't long before adjudicator Young walked away from the umpire's box. In a telegram to league officials, Young reportedly cited threats and verbal abuse from the manager, along with "daily fear of violence from Sullivan's team" as the reasons behind his resignation. Two other umpires attempted to step in for Young, but each of them worked only a single game before quitting because of threats from Memphis players and their manager.[22]

An "Unwholesome Influence"

In mid–August, Sullivan's disregard for umpires and rival clubs led to incidents of physical attacks, near-riots, and police interventions that were widely chronicled and criticized in the press. In Atlanta, the Memphis nine were pre-emptively threatened with violence by an umpire and loudly abused by a phalanx of angry toughs who were held back from the edge of a melee by a squadron of cops. Sullivan's bitching prompted a verbal altercation that led to a chair being swiped across his head.

In Macon, Sullivan assaulted an umpire and was banned from sitting on the bench. Meanwhile, catcher Tug Arundel, who was described as a player who "would rather fight than eat," was fined three times in two weeks for vulgar language and threats of violence aimed at umpires and opposing players.

> "The entire Memphis nine is achieving unenviable notoriety for ruffianism, and the Southern League should take Manager Ted Sullivan in hand and punish him for permitting such behavior. Even the Memphis papers are compelled to deplore the action of the home team. Memphis narrowly escaped expulsion once before this season, and seems to be determined to invite that fate. She is undoubtedly severely taxing the patience of her sister cities.
> —Sporting Life, August 19, 1885

Eventually, the Southern League grappled with the fate that would become common to Sullivan start-ups—insolvency. Shortly after the collapse of the Birmingham franchise, the directors of the Southern League voted to conclude their maiden season on September 17. Sullivan's crew was left in the dust, finishing with a lackluster .413 winning percentage.

While the Memphis Reds lacked on-field success, their nasty, violent and belligerent play earned them plenty of attention—almost entirely negative. Indeed, a recap of the 1885 Southern League season included the

J. ARUNDEL, C. Indianapolis
COPYRIGHTED BY GOODWIN & CO. 1887.
GOODWIN & CO. New York.

Tug Arundel—routinely described as "a man who would rather fight than eat"— was one of Ted's leading thugs in Memphis, along with future major league star, Billy O'Brien. But throughout the summer of 1885, none of the Memphis Reds would come close to out-thugging manager Sullivan. Goodwin & Co. souvenir card, 1887 (Library of Congress).

opinion that "the hostile position assumed toward Memphis since the close of the League season was due to Sullivan's unwholesome influence."[23]

By then, of course, baseball's noted nomad had moved north to more familiar terrain, working sportswriters, lobbying for several different managerial jobs, and threatening to start new leagues.

In October, the press in Washington, D.C., predicted that Sullivan (*Sporting Life* called him, "the ex-bible agent") would take over management of the Senators, who were hoping to jump from the minor Eastern League to the National League in 1886.[24]

Meanwhile, Ted Sullivan was in Dubuque with his pals Comiskey, Loftus, Quinn, and Tom Burns, organizing a polo club. That winter it was reported that he and his friend and faux enemy Tom Loftus had struck it rich selling their interest in an Iowa lead mine to some eastern capitalists for $80,000 (equivalent to a little over $2 million today).[25]

◆ 8 ◆

Not Milwaukee's Best

As he headed toward Milwaukee's Wright Street grounds in advance of a game in the fall of 1886, Ted Sullivan was in a serious slump. His Milwaukee nine had bounced along the bottom of the Northwestern League standings for much of the season, but his malaise went beyond mere wins and losses. His team's protracted slump had dragged down the two things he cared most about—his gilded reputation and his bank account.

His reputation had taken a serious beating the previous year in Memphis. Newspapers from all corners of the Southern League had branded him a thug, a bully, and a blight upon the sport. Back in February, though, he'd been back on more familiar ground, being lauded by reporters as exactly the hustler and genius needed to revitalize the Northwestern League.

When plans for the league were first announced, his hometown newspaper rightly predicted that Milwaukee would not support a minor league team. Sullivan's legendary promotional prowess and eye for talent would simply be overmatched by circumstances—inept ball players, weak fan support, and routinely meager gate receipts.

To be sure, the hustling manager wasn't met by the Welcome Wagon when he arrived in town. Milwaukee had lost out to Kansas City in the competition for the final National League slot in 1886, and their bid for American Association membership had also hit the rocks.

The local press jumped on Sullivan's case early, making fun of his coaching style and the bumbling play of his young players. "They step to the plate with a most palatable 'I'm-afraid-I-can't-hit-it' expression depicted on their countenance," gibed the *Milwaukee Sentinel*. "If manager Sullivan expects to have ball club here for another week, he must 'reorganize' and right soon."[1]

Without much to work with on the field, Sullivan could not stop the losses. Even when the talented but always angry pitcher and human novelty, "One-Arm" Hugh Daily, joined the team in late July.

When Ted came back to his hometown in the spring of 1886 to take the reins of the now minor league Brewers, Milwaukee was a cauldron brimming with unrest and violence among workers demanding eight-hour workdays. They were soon also protesting against the poor quality of play on the ballfield (promotional photo, Independent Brewing Co., Milwaukee, Wisconsin, ca. 1901).

Springs Pitcher from the Pokey

At well over six feet tall, Daily intimidated batters with his size, his practiced stink eye, and his wild, windmill wind-up. He used the leather-covered stump of his left hand to block grounders and throws from the catcher.

He also made good use of it in bar fights, brandishing it like a billy club. "He could put a man to sleep with that stump," Sullivan recalled, "and when Daily got to alternating between water and alcohol, there was no argument he would not call you down on."[2]

On a road trip in upper Wisconsin, the Irish-born Daily got drunk in a German-owned saloon and used his notorious nubbin to crack an Englishman on the jaw. On a rampage, the boozed-up pitcher broke a window and demolished a glass showcase. The German saloon looked as if a cyclone had struck it, but fortunately for Daily the town had a proud Irishman and baseball enthusiast as chief of police.

I knew it would go hard on him. The train left at 2 o'clock in the morning and I could not leave Hugh there to suffer the penalty of the law, so I hit upon a plan to get him away.

In the town was an Irish chief of police, who was a baseball enthusiast and who admired Hugh's pitching that day. He was one of those proud Irishmen, that to insult his nationality meant fight.

I accosted him in this manner: "Captain McDermott, Hugh Daily, my player, yes—a one armed man—defended himself against four who assailed the Irish race—his own blood—yet he is imprisoned like a common felon, a martyr to a race that never took an insult to anyone. Does a man of Irish blood in this broad republic of ours, the blood which has helped make it, stand by and hear his countrymen maligned … are those base Dutchmen and one Englishmen to get away with it?"

McDermott bounded to his feet—he could not hardly wait for the keys—so anxious was he to get to Hughey to shake his hand for his patriotism. The door was opened, Captain McDermott embraced Hughey, hit him on the back and told him to go.[3]

"Allegazam!"

Turning to entertainment in lieu of decent baseball, Sullivan kept things lively on the field with a "system" of secret instructions to his hapless players. When he wanted his pitcher (one of the many mediocre twirlers he tried out that season) to throw to first, he would yell "Kalamozoo." When the ball needed to be shot to third to catch a runner stealing, he'd holler "Allegazam."[4]

"Hock-a-da-sock," *St. Louis Post Dispatch* readers were informed, "is a gentle intimation to the catcher to deliver the sphere to the second baseman and also informs him that a man is endeavoring to steal that base. When on the rare occasion one of his batters got on base and rounded first, the animated manager would sing "tra-la-la-la," meaning "Go on now, ain't nobody there."[5]

By mid–July, *Sporting Life* was asking: "Has the hustler lost his grip?" And after what the *Minneapolis Tribune* called "a simply appalling" 25–9 loss to Duluth, it certainly appeared that way.[6]

Despite a series of desperate and creative diversions, nothing seemed to work. Critics excoriated Sullivan for churning his roster and signing cheap, amateur players. According to *Sporting Life*, by early August, the exasperated manager had already tried 13 pitchers (including himself on at least three disastrous occasions), seven catchers, and 12 men in other positions.[7]

A Sullied Reputation

Late in the miserable season, the *Milwaukee Journal* planted this facetious blurb in its sports notes: "The Milwaukee baseball club is in the city again: We presume it will play any club composed of boys under 15. All challenges should be addressed to Ted Sullivan."

Sullivan was known to return fire at vitriolic writers and fans. He called them "Knockers and Know-It-Alls."[8]

He would say that, whenever any team was in a slump, "the superficial and ungenerous public will commence their criticisms, which are generally ironic, caustic and insulting. One critic will say the players are drinking. Another, as he lights his cigar with one of those 'know-it-all looks,' says: 'So and so is playing for his release; this I got on the dead quiet from a particular friend of the player who took supper with me last night.' The fact is all ball clubs slump early or late."[9]

But as the losses mounted—both on the field and financially—the homegrown manager could no longer attribute his lousy team's failures to a slump.

In an effort to re-engage Milwaukee's jaded baseball fans, Sullivan helped organize a nostalgic reunion contest between alums of the old Cream City team and the amateur team of his own glory days, the Milwaukee Stars. Sullivan, of course, pitched for the Stars. The game drew a good crowd and raised a few bucks that were donated to Milwaukee's Home for the Friendless.

A Famous Play of the Game

Journeyman infielder Charlie Dougherty, who played for Sullivan in Milwaukee in 1886, swore that, despite that losing season, Ted Sullivan was the foxiest player-manager who ever trod the diamond. "He could turn a trick before the other fellows were aware that something was being attempted at all," he told syndicated columnist T.S. Andrews.

As an example, Dougherty pointed to a long-ago game in which the Milwaukees were in the final inning of a close contest with a rival nine from Duluth. The bases were full. Sullivan was next up.

Dougherty recalled that the umpire called "play," but Sullivan was a long time coming to the plate.

The rule in those days was that the batter had the privilege of calling for a high pitch or a low one.

As the story was told in many a newspaper, many a year later: "The foxy gent [Ted] had shed his own trousers and donned those of a gigantic Irishman on the team. Buckling the belt under his arm pits, Ted strode to the bat and called for high balls every time. The pitcher was up against it, and issued a walk on four balls, forcing in the winning run. That's one of the most famous plays in the game."[10]

But that good and curious deed on behalf of the friendless didn't push any more rear ends into the seats to watch Sullivan's floundering Milwaukees muddle through the rest of the season.

The newspapers and local cranks began calling for Sullivan to leave town and take his wretched team with him. In August, during a special meeting of the Northwestern League, he was given approval to move his team to West St. Paul, where he would share the West Seventh Street grounds with the rival St. Paul franchise. But Sullivan had lied to league officials about the rival St. Paul manager's agreeing to the arrangement, which led to no move, threats of expulsion, and more damage to his reputation.

Villainous Schemer

Reflecting the anger of Minnesota's baseball fans, the *St. Paul Daily Globe*, in bold-face type on the front page, called Ted Sullivan "A SCHEMER" who "for the villainy he has done should be expelled."[11]

But there Sullivan was on September 20, still stuck in Milwaukee and awaiting an afternoon game against Duluth. His team was awful, the media had turned on him, fans had long since abandoned the franchise, and here came the Duluth Jayhawks—managed by hated rival William Henry Lucas, who had previously cost Sullivan a pile of money by refusing to make up a postponed game. Suddenly, as if all the failures and frustrations of the past months had crashed over him, the son of Eire seized his opportunity for revenge. On a pretty much picture-perfect baseball day, Sullivan turned the hoses on the Wright Street grounds and flooded the field. A sudden cloudburst, he said. Too wet to play, so there could be no game today—and no gate for William Lucas.

Lucas howled when he and his team were denied access to the grounds. The league secretary imposed a deadline for Sullivan to step aside, but Sullivan was unmoved. He declared the field unplayable and announced he would not pay a guarantee to Duluth. After months of setbacks and humiliations, Ted Sullivan was finally getting his way.

Only he didn't. Not really. He ended up being forced to pay Duluth for the game that wasn't played, and the following day the league secretary proposed the expulsion of the Milwaukee franchise. Ultimately, the Northwestern League stripped Sullivan of his franchise while newspapers and their readers feverishly attacked his character. "Providing Milwaukee with a weak nine has already rendered him [Sullivan] unpopular with patrons of the game," one

Milwaukee paper trumpeted, "and his course yesterday will do a good deal towards demonstrating the utter incompetency of his management."[12]

Ted Sullivan would later admit that the "accidental" flooding was just one of the dirty tricks he played on opposing players and managers. "Saints could not live with sinners in those times," he wrote in 1910, "so I became a sinner myself."[13]

Slippery Business

As old Peek-a-boo Veach would one day note: "Half of the tricky plays practiced today are the creation of his [Sullivan's] brain. Just think of a man going out to the grounds after night and putting slippery elm on the base lines because the team we were going to play the next day had many great base runners."[14]

Shenanigans aside, the season's merciful end found Milwaukee in the cellar and T.P. Sullivan packing his ever-at-the-ready suitcase. He and his Milwaukee franchise were officially expelled from the Northwestern League on October 15.

Papers outside of Wisconsin were sympathetic and called Sullivan's attempts to build a competitive team for Milwaukee his "experiment." Sullivan moaned that the players he had had available to him in the Cream City were smellier than sour milk.

> Some of those fellows up there are pretty good ball players, but most of them are no good. You people who are used to good ball playing can't understand what we had to suffer.
> Among the pitchers I tried was a big fellow from Michigan who claimed he could break three-inch boards with the ball. He was a pretty good man, but he had a defect that ruined his prospects as a twirler. He was cross-eyed. He came very near to being the death of about seven of my eleven catchers.
> But the pitcher was not the only cross-eyed man I got. I got a fellow from the lumber region whose eyes were so mixed that he could see the four bases at one look. I thought I had struck pudding, but when the pitcher threw the ball to first base for instance, he thought it was coming right at him and he struck out so often I had to let him go, too.[15]

Within weeks of his skip-to-my-loo from Milwaukee, the ostracized manager was scouting talent for St. Louis and hunting prospects in Washington, D.C. Come Christmastime, he was warming his toes by the stove in the newsroom of *The Sporting News* in St. Louis.

"Ted is making St. Louis his home for the winter," reported the columnist known as "Muldoon on the Rampage." "Ted is always on the go and drops into the office at all hours of the day and night."[16]

◆ 9 ◆

Behind the Plate

"The first umpire I ever saw held an umbrella over his head
and stood six feet to the side of the batsman. Of course, he
had no 'curves' to squint at, for the pitcher did not have
those mystifying things in stock at that period of the game.
But still I insist his position is not complete as yet, and will
not be—until he encloses himself in a movable barbed wire
enclosure."
                                                            —Ted Sullivan[1]

Persona non-grata after that wacky and mostly winless 1886 season in
the city of his youth, Ted Sullivan found himself out in the managerial cold
again in 1887.

That was the year the prehistoric rule mandating that batters call for
either high or low pitches was eliminated, and the standard strike zone was
adopted. Without a club to preside over, the dedicated abuser of umpires
found himself a rookie-in-blue. Needing a job, the articulate and bombastic
Sullivan began umping games, one of the first being a late-summer American Association contest between Baltimore's Orioles and the Brooklyn Grays.

In one of Sullivan's first experiences as a human lightning rod for
abuse, in a contest between Baltimore and Louisville, the crowd jeered and
hooted him repeatedly for appearing to be in favor of the home team, but,
according to at least one sporting scribe, "he really did fairly well."[2]

His calls were so inexplicable in a contest between Pittsburgh and
Philadelphia that an aghast Steeltown sportswriter declared, "Sullivan, the
umpire, was the worst ever seen here."[3]

After he made a series of botched decisions in a game at Baltimore, the
Baltimore Sun said: "Ted Sullivan's umpiring yesterday was so objectionable
that at the request of the visitors [he] was substituted. He displayed poor
knowledge. His bad decisions were about equally divided…. Sullivan will
never make an umpire. He lacks judgment and knowledge. The only essen-
tial he seems to possess is good intent, and that's not enough."[4]

A few soothing sentences between umpire and umpired.

A notorious umpire baiter, in the summer of 1887, Sullivan found himself catching face and ears full of grief as a part-time adjudicator for the American Association (illustration by E.W. Kimble, 1909).

From there, things only got worse. During an August game between Boston and Detroit, the Beantown superstar, King Kelly, so obnoxiously berated the newbie umpire that the Detroit crowd booed Kelly. The next day, the *Detroit Free Press* called Sullivan "the worst selection ever made by President Young."[5]

Despite his years on the coaching line, Sullivan, as an adjudicator, displayed a poor understanding of the rules of the game. "To the surprise of every one," reported the *New York Clipper* after another August game, "umpire Ted Sullivan decided that the stoppage of the ball by the spectators was no block in consequence of the crowd being within the boundary line, and as both runners had been touched before reaching home he decided both out. The decision was illegal, as Sullivan acknowledged after the game, and it will be protested. It unquestionably prevented the Brooklyns from scoring two runs."[6]

Interesting Gossip of the Diamond
Louisville Courier-Journal,
August 19, 1887

"I see that Ted Sullivan will not umpire for the Association any longer," remarked a Chicago gentleman last evening. "I have witnessed several games that he has umpired this season, and if I had a boy that couldn't do better I'd throw him into the river. I knew Sullivan as a boy when he was peddling peanuts on trains out of Chicago. He was as close as hair on a dog, and knows more about working a train than he does about baseball. I saw him decide a man out on first base after the first baseman had acknowledged that the runner was not out. Such an umpire as that ought to be either fired or killed. Sullivan has a tact of living without working very hard, and he will probably figure in some other position in the base-ball world until he dies of old age."

Indeed, by late September, it was clear to even the thin-skinned Irishman that "baseball adjudicator" was out of line with his career path.

◆ 10 ◆

"Senator Sullivan"
Goes to Washington

*"Ted Sullivan is hustling for Washington. And there is a
rumor out that he is to manage that club next season. Ted
started the rumor."*
—*The Boston Globe,* September 29, 1887

By the end of August 1887, Ted Sullivan had found a truer calling—
as a scout for the terminally struggling Washington Senators. Scouting
proved to be the perfect gig for Sullivan, who loved finding and developing
young players. Within a month of signing on as a sleuth for Washington, he
searched out and signed W. E. Hoy, who many teams may have overlooked
because the young man they would call "Dummy" was deaf and dumb.
"Dummy" Hoy, of course, would prove to be one of the best all-around
players of his day. He was fast, attentive in the field, and laser-focused at
the plate.[1]

Sullivan fast became ingrained in the overall workings of the struggling Washington club. He promised the boys in the local newsrooms
that the Senators were going to "weed out all the old demoralizing element" and put together a strong team of good young material for the 1888
season.[2]

He spoke highly of the team's existing nucleus of catcher Cornelius
McGillicuddy, pitcher Hank O'Day, and that "big, fat, good-natured fellow" he had managed in Kansas City, batsman Billy O'Brien. He signed the
quirky but talented Irishman Pat Deasley and even went after his protégé,
Charlie Comiskey.

Robert Hewitt, the Washington club's baseball-loving but not-so-
business-savvy president, dispatched Sullivan to St. Louis on a bold and
secret mission to sign Comiskey, the fast-becoming-a-star first baseman,
away from Chris Van der Ahe's Browns. When a reporter in St. Louis
bearded Sullivan on the reason for his visit, saying "I know what you're here

Sullivan managed Washington's baseball Senators to a series of pre-season wins over amateur clubs throughout the south in the spring of 1888, before returning to Troy, New York, to tend his "training school" for minor leaguers. He was soon called back to the Capital City after the Senators started the season with an embarrassingly long losing streak.

for," Sullivan replied, "Now, for God's sake don't mention it. I always come over to see Charlie when he is here." Although reportedly offered a princely sum for Comiskey's release, the wise old beer and baseball magnate would not let his star go.[3]

In the meantime, Sullivan was actively putting together what might be considered baseball's first "farm team" up in Troy, New York. Hewitt let it be known he was interested in the Troy Club "as a training school or feeder for the Washingtons."[4]

By Thanksgiving, Ted Sullivan had not one, but three jobs: manager of the Troy "training school," franchise scout, and ad hoc manager of the coming-apart-at-the-seams-again Senators. The hopeful Washington press gobbled up Sully's optimism and wanted to believe his pledge to "stay away from the tail-enders and give the leaders a brush." They even soft-pedaled Sullivan's acquisition of some known "problem children," including "Sneak" Deasley, who had a reputation as a drunk and a head case, and "Old Reliable" Phil Baker, a popular journeyman ballplayer who had a seemingly insatiable taste for the fast life. "I know, I know," Sullivan would say, "To see him [Baker] juggling cigarettes and 'two-fers' in the vicinity of Ninth and

N streets, one would imagine him a fit subject for the retired list, but when he dons his uniform and gets upon the diamond, he has the life and activity of a young colt."[5]

In a few short years, the booze-chugging Baker would be destitute, and the fans would have to raise money to get him off the streets. As for Deasley, Sullivan expressed confidence that the sulky catcher would not go on a toot while in Washington, because his contract was only binding if he stayed sober.

Balancing the presence of those potential problem children was Sullivan's signing of switch-hitting outfielder Walt Wilmot, who would prove to be a fan favorite and a reliable big-leaguer for the next decade.

Sullivan promised team discipline and no slackers on his team in 1888. He said, "A man can't come the sore arm racket, either. If a man's arm can't serve him for two games a week, he is not a pitcher and we don't want him."[6]

Still, the Washington press was not expecting much, anticipating that the hapless, poor-drawing Senators would soon be dumped out of the National League. The good news was that in 1888, a backlogged Congress would likely be in session until mid-summer, providing plenty of be-suited tushes in the seats at the ballpark for half the season, anyway.

Ted "a Man of Grandiose Ideas"

> "He'd of made a suit of clothes for P.T. Barnum's famous elephant." —Connie Mack

"When Washington players reported at the Capitol in the month of March, 1888, we were introduced to a new manager, for during the winter, John Gaffney had resigned," recalled Cornelius McGillicuddy, the Hall of Fame player and manager better known as "Connie Mack."

> His successor was the irrepressible Ted Sullivan, one of the most refreshing characters baseball has ever known. He was a man of force, unyielding in his convictions, quick of tongue and with a flair for doing things differently from anybody else. He was a man of grandiose ideas.
>
> If he had been a tailor, he would have sought to make a suit of clothes for P.T. Barnum's famous elephant "Jumbo"; had he been a sailor he would have tried to discover the North Pole in a yawl; if he had been President of the United States he would have essayed to annex Canada.
>
> Always a nonconformist and ready to fence on any subject, nevertheless he was a likeable man, a missionary who did baseball a lot of good when it was in its swaddling clothes and besides, his knowledge of the game was profound. Everyone liked Ted Sullivan and his quaint ways.[7]

Getting in Shape
in the Gator State

As Mack said, "Ted was a man of grandiose ideas."[8]

Sullivan's grandiose idea of 1888 was for Washington to be the first professional team to go to Florida for training and exhibition games in the spring. A curious *New York Sun* noted, "Ted is very enthusiastic in speaking of the good to be derived from the prospective tour. He expects that it will prove particularly beneficial to several of the men who he has signed more from consideration of their ability to play ball than on account of their good habits."[9]

That sounded good....

Mack remembered meeting Ted Sullivan at the rail depot in Washington on the first day of

Cornelius McGillicuddy, a.k.a. Connie Mack, played for Sullivan at Washington in 1888. Himself a solid player, a stoic gentleman and teetotaler, Mack described his manager as "a missionary who did baseball a lot of good" (*Spink Sport Stories*, 1921).

March, just ahead of a great blizzard that socked D.C. in for weeks: "There were 14 members of the team," said Mack. "Ten were on the verge of being drunkards." To save money, he said, the fellows rode in coach class during the day, and at night slept two to a bunk in Pullman cars, before returning in the morning to the hot, smoky, scratchy coach cars they dubbed "Sullivan Sleepers."

On arrival in Jacksonville, Sullivan led his boys to a tract of woods outside of town, where a woman who owned two shacks put them up and provided three meals a day for a dollar per man per day.

Mack called the accommodations livable, but vile. "That lady never made much money on us," he wrote. "There was a fight every night and those boys broke a lot of her furniture."[10]

Albert Goodwill Spalding's about-to-be published 1889 *Guide to Base Ball* came out too late with this warning to young ballplayers: "The two great obstacles in the way of success to the majority of professional ball players are wine and women. The saloon and the brothel are the evils of the baseball world at the present day ... the evil of drunkenness is one which has grown among the fraternity until it has become an abuse that can no longer be tolerated. It will no longer pay to allow players of drinking habits in first-class teams."

It didn't take long for those 10 "drunkards on the verge" that Mack referenced to find a convenient source of booze among the locals in Florida and to proceed to "wake snakes."

"It was terrible—fights every night in front of those shacks," remembered Mack. "There was always at least one black eye in the crowd, and usually more." Yet Sullivan dispatched his usual happy press release to Washington sports writers: "The men arrived here in good shape and [have] surprised me by their excellent work."[11]

No Talk, All Action

Among the Washington rookies in "camp" was the deaf and mostly mute William Ellsworth "Dummy" Hoy. Sullivan had discovered the earnest and talented young fellow a couple of years before, when the then-boy had approached him in the Kirby House in Milwaukee with a note pad in his hand.

"He was not of the stereotypical description given by some managers, when they wish to describe the humble beginnings of a player," Sullivan wrote. "For this young man was neatly dressed, carrying a small satchel which contained, among other things, a pair of base ball shoes. As he approached me he gave no indication of his oratorical powers, but drew out a paper pad and wrote boldly that he was William E. Hoy from Findlay, Ohio, and said he came all the way from there to get me to give him a trial as a ball player.[12]

"He went through the form of practice [in Milwaukee] and I saw he was a ballplayer," recalled Sullivan. "I wrote on his pad, asking him what he wanted per month. He wrote: 'As a beginner, I will want $80 per month.' He was modest in all bearing. He was cheap at $100."[13]

That was the Ted Sullivan version of the story. Years later, in an issue of *The Deaf-Mutes Journal*, Hoy described the "discovery" differently.[14]

"Instead of him discovering me I really discovered him, as paradoxical as it may seem," the by-then star of the game wrote. Hoy agreed that he had approached Sullivan for a tryout and that the manager looked him over with "an itty concealed smile."

Using sign language, Hoy swore to the following:

> The idea of a mute playing professional ball evidently struck him as being rather unique. He asked me how I proposed to get into the decisions of the umpire, particularly on balls and strikes, and how was I to avoid being made a monkey of on the bases. The next day I was told to come out to the ball

grounds. The day happened to be a wet one, and nobody was at the grounds except the groundskeeper and Ted himself. He motioned me to put on my baseball togs and wade out to the field. For about half an hour he vainly tried to knock the ball over my head. Finally he motioned me to come in. He took the bat and scribbled in the wet sand: "How much?"

"Seventy-five," said I, making it out in a mud puddle with the heel of my shoe.

Hoy moved on from Milwaukee in 1887 to play for a team in Oshkosh, where his talents caught the attention of big league scouts.

Midnight Maneuvers

In the early winter of 1887, Ted Sullivan detrained at Findlay, Ohio, Hoy's hometown, followed close behind by New York Giants manager Jim Mutrie and a scout from Detroit, both looking to sign Hoy for their respective clubs.

On this story, told by Hoy when he was 81 and recorded in the *Louisville Courier-Journal* on December 20, 1942, he and Sullivan actually agreed.

All three talent hunters checked into the same local hotel, each conscious of the others' presence and intent, each planning to get up at dawn the next morning and beat their rivals to the Hoy farm, some 12 miles outside of town. But about 11 p.m. that night, Ted Sullivan sneaked out a back door, rented a hack at a nearby livery stable, and lit out after his quarry.

"It was a long, lonely ride that cold autumn night," wrote the *Courier Journal* scribe,

> With snow flurries threatening to develop into a heavy fall, but soon after midnight, Sullivan rapped at the door of the farm house, and after a seemingly interminable wait the door was opened by a young man, bearing a coal oil lamp and attired in a night gown. Then followed for half an hour an exchange of penciled notes—for Hoy, remember, was bereft of speech and hearing—and it was well on to two in the morning when Sullivan, with "Dummy" Hoy's contract with the Washington team snugly signed and tucked away in his pocket, began the return ride to Findlay, beguiling the way by whistling snatches of "Sallie, the Cuckoos Are Calling Now."[15]

Hoy—the *Evening Star* called him "Washington's sawed-off little center fielder"—proceeded to teach his new Washington teammates how to communicate with him, and he with them (lip-reading, sign language, grunts, and arm-waving).

Proctor Ted Sullivan kept an eye on his boys and scrutinized the contents of their travel bags as they hit New Orleans, Birmingham, and

Charleston for exhibition games, but did allow them to visit the horse tracks and bet a few nickels on the "brushtails."

Mack liked to tell how Sullivan kept the boys well fed in "untidy rooms" at "decrepit hotels" where ballplayers were not allowed to eat with the regular guests. Sullivan, he said, would take out a silver dollar and place it on the table with a conspiratorial wink to the waiters. The servers would, in turn, bring extra portions of food, but when it came time to leave, Sullivan would "slip the cartwheel" back into his pocket and make for the exit.

Telling the story in 1930, a few months after Ted Sullivan passed away, Mack lamented: "The old pioneer of baseball for many years always came to our hotel to chat with me, and did so just a few weeks before he passed away. I never failed to ask him if he still possessed his un-spendable silver dollar."[16]

The ever-clever Sullivan, in fact, put a bunch of shiny new silver dollars in the Senators' pocketbook by scheduling exhibition games in Southern towns along rail routes to and from the Capitol City.

Dancing on the Color Line

The previous year having witnessed more than a dozen talented Black players, like Fleet Walker, George Washington Stovey, Bob Higgins, and Sol White playing and succeeding in small leagues across the country, baseball's magnates that winter conspired to put a stop to it by instituting "the color line," essentially banning Black players from professional-level baseball.

As Ned Williamson, a white player who starred for many years with the Chicago White Stockings, candidly told *Sporting Life*: "The haughty Caucasians … were willing to permit Darkies to carry water to them or guard the bat bag, but it made them sore to have one of them in the lineup."[17]

In a March 1888 letter to the president of Ohio's Tri-State League, Fleet's brother, Weldy Walker, who had been playing in a segregated league in Pittsburgh, argued that the Tri-State league's recent repeal of a rule permitting colored men to sign with associated teams was "a disgrace to the present age," and that "there should be some broader cause—such as lack of ability, behavior and intelligence—for barring a player, rather than his color."[18]

Walker's logic was ignored, of course, and the inclusion of Blacks in the upper reaches of the national game continued to be limited to small Black boys, for, as Hall of Fame pitcher Christy Mathewson acknowledged, "a great piece of luck is to rub a colored kid's head."[19]

Superstitions like that were common in the early days of baseball.

When managing the Philadelphia Athletics in 1910, Connie Mack employed a hunchbacked bat boy, and the players would rub the boy's hump before going to bat.

"Dat Hot Club,"
Sporting Life,
December 30, 1893

There is nothing that catches a Southern darky's eyes as quickly as a flashy uniform. Ted Sullivan, with Celtic acumen, was not long in detecting this…. When the time came for spring practice he fitted the Senators out in a set of cheap, "loud" uniforms that could be heard in a bordering State, and started them through Dixie. The effect was magical. The colored people blocked the streets around the hotels where the Senators put up, and followed their carriages through the streets in droves, and packed the bleachers to see "dat hot club," as Ted's aggregation was termed. It was the first time in the redoubtable Sullivan's career as a manager that he made the gate receipts at the early practice games pay the current expenses of the club.

Picking Dixie's Pocket

But while Sullivan and the Senators were happily sweating—and making money—down in Florida, a secret meeting of the National League was

"Base Ball on Blackville Common," ca. 1889 (Library of Congress).

going on in Cleveland. Fretting that the emerging Players' League would cut into their attendance and revenues, the National League's team owners and league officials decided to cull (or "decapitate" as one newspaper put it) their Washington and Indianapolis members. Already suspecting that could happen, wily Sullivan had quietly applied for Washington to enter and play in the minor-level Atlantic League in 1889.

When the Senators returned from the Sunshine State, the *Evening Star* detected "gratifying improvements" and noted that the team's directors were taking on high expectations, predicting that Sullivan's new combination could finish as high as fourth place for a change.[20]

They Might Be Giants

Nevertheless, the boys looked sharp in pre-season exhibition games at home in D.C. They whipped up on Sullivan's minor league Troy team and made short work of Princeton's college boys before playing a three-game series with the famous Cuban Giants.

Beating and making fun of the famous Black barnstorming team from New Jersey was an annual tradition for the Senators. An enthusiastic *Evening Star* reported, "Fans loved the side-splitting hour or so of laughter at the odd antics of the Ethiopian athletes."[21]

As it happened, the 1888 series with the Cuban Giants included a match on Emancipation Day (April 18). "The notorious promoter," as *Sporting Life* had taken to calling Sullivan, went to town, touting the sure-to-be-hysterical contest with "Mr. Coons."[22]

Exploitation Day

"There are at least 100,000 colored people in Washington," Sullivan wrote. "I had to advertise the game, so I hit on the plan of putting two darkies in base-ball suits in the middle of the parade on two fantastic looking mules, with a banner on their shoulders, bearing the inscription, 'Come out to the Base-ball park today and see the Cuban Giants burn up the grass while practicing.'"[23]

According to Sullivan's telling, one of the mules walking behind a marching band balked, disrupting the parade, scattering bystanders, and infuriating the parade marshals. "The balky mule and the ludicrous sign was [sic] the center of all attention," boasted Sullivan, "and the great Cuban Giants game was advertised [successfully!] for the great Emancipation Day."

Washington sent the African American men, who were forced to pretend they were Cubans (even making up words that sounded like Spanish), home to New Jersey, humiliated, as always. NOT GIANTS, BUT DWARFS was the headline in the next day's *Post*, although the Black players were applauded for their "brilliant work in the field" and "clever base running."[24]

Come opening day, an ailing Robert Hewitt's son, Walter, was more or less in charge of the team's business affairs. "Grasshopper" Jim Whitney was designated player/manager, and Sullivan headed up to Troy to put the trainer team together. The mostly rudderless red, white and blue-suited Senators quickly slid into the losing column, scoring just nine runs in their first 10 games.

While Hank O'Day had a hard time fanning even himself, the former Boston ace, "Grasshopper" Whitney—so called for his long, stiff, skinny frame—held his own on the mound with 37 starts before a laser line drive caught him full in the chest, effectively ending his career. He would die a couple of years later, at the age of 33, as a result of the blow.

The play of Hewitt's mismatched nine got so bad, the *Washington Post* lamented: "A pitcher and catcher and Mr. Hoy now constitute Washington's base ball club. The other six men who accompany them are put on the field for the purpose of making errors."[25]

The speechless rookie continued to be the lone bright star in the Senators' lineup. By mid–June, the team's record was a dismal 10–29, and attendance at D.C.'s 6,000-seat Swampdoodle Park was often fewer than 500.

> "The outlook was flattering, but bad management, or, to put it more properly, no management at all, has brought about an unfavorable condition of things. President Hewitt is still a very sick man. Ted Sullivan is looking after the Troy club. Secretary Burkhart, Director Walter Hewitt and Jim Whitney alternate in running the machine. Confusion and disorder reign."
> —*Indianapolis Journal*, May 6, 1888

Ted's in Charge

The Senators continued to slide—at one point having to put a 40-year-old Civil War veteran in to pitch (and, yes, the opposing batters shot him full of holes). On June 12, it was reported that Ted Sullivan had been brought back from Troy as a sort of "consulting physician and the patient carefully goneover."[26]

"Ted Sullivan is now managing the Washington team," the *Cincinnati*

Enquirer reported on May 20. "The Keokuk Bible agent will get ball-playing out of that organization, if they are possessed of such an article."

The still-young manager reportedly hustled his Senators out of bed early and worked them hard at practice. It was reported that he even fined a majority of his players, telling them he would make them pay up if they didn't stop drinking beer and start playing better.

In Sullivan's first game at the helm, his Senators whipped Pittsburgh, 4–0.

As the season wore on, though, the Senators racked up more debits than credits, and during breaks in the schedule, Washington's ambitious manager would hop a train to anywhere in search of players to bolster his talented but struggling squad. Near the end of July, he was in New Orleans looking to snatch a couple of budding stars from the Southern League.

"Sleek and oily Ted Sullivan caught the boys napping in the negotiations for New Orleans players," noted the *Atlanta Constitution*, as said "oily" manager slipped out of the Big Easy with a couple of new prospects in tow.[27]

An Audience with the King

Still trying to hang with the National League competition, Sullivan's promising youngsters and hard-drinking journeymen were regularly bullied by baseball's established royalty, including the powerful Boston Beaneaters and their indomitable center fielder/catcher, Mike Kelly, whom the press called "The King" and "The ten thousand dollar beauty." Sullivan himself described Kelly as "a man whose head was a casket of baseball gems."[28]

"I was scared of him," Sullivan admitted. "I can tell you that candidly. He was as close to perfection in batting and base running as a human body can reach."[29]

Manager Sullivan's first face-to-face encounter with the great King that season came in a contest where Washington's own future Hall of Famer, Connie Mack, was catching and Hank O'Day, who would become one of the game's most respected umpires, was pitching. In the course of the contest, with Sullivan in the coach's box, Kelly drew a walk and advanced around the bases, but he got caught off third after a weak grounder was cut off by the Senators' shortstop.

Smiling all the way, the King strolled leisurely to home plate where Mack was waiting with the ball to tag him out. As Kelly sauntered up to Mack, he said, "Well, you sure got me that time, Connie." And at that, Kelly abruptly dropped to a squat and thrust his legs out in front up him, touching his heels to the plate. *Safe*.[30] "It was one of the neatest tricks imaginable," recalled Sullivan. "One of the greatest I have ever witnessed in my long years in the game. The King was some wonder."[31]

Of course, Sullivan was always one for the tricks, himself. In one game on a wet field at Boston, the two designated game balls became waterlogged. The Beaneaters' groundskeeper was instructed to chase, and "lose," any foul balls the home team hit, so that new—dry, better-to-hit—balls would have to be brought into play.

The trouble was that Sullivan had already anticipated Boston manager John Morrill's ploy, and, according to *The Sporting News*, "had borrowed all of their old practice balls, gone into the grand stand and, as fast as the balls disappeared, sent an old one back in its place."[32]

"The groundskeeper was livid," Sullivan remembered. "Vesuvius never threw up more lava and fire. He wanted to fight any one and all who threw the ball. While he was emitting fire I stole gently back to the bench." Sully's Senators won, 4–1.[33]

In early August, National League officials called another meeting to consider if and when to eliminate Washington and Indianapolis from the membership roster. Also on the agenda was a hearing on Sullivan's protest of a fine that was imposed on account of his uncalled-for pugilism during a game earlier in the season.

After a particularly embarrassing loss to Pittsburgh, the *Boston Globe* of August 20, 1889, noted that Sullivan's lame-duck Senators "actually drove people out of the park with their wretched exhibition."

By summer's end, the Senators and the equally hapless Indianapolis franchise were in a duel to the death for last place. Every additional loss represented one more step toward decapitation from the National League.

Not wanting to miss one of the last scheduled contests, Sullivan came up with an idea that would inspire future groundskeepers. Faced with cancellation of the game due to inclement weather, Sullivan reportedly spread canvas over the entire playing field and provided tents to be used by the players while not in the field. Unfortunately the game was called anyway, and Washington limped to the finish line with a 48–86 record, a mere 37 games behind the first-place New York Giants.[34]

Young Connie Mack was brilliant behind the plate, but he couldn't yet hit a wall.

Despite the team's lackluster record and his own inconsistent performance, Mack's talent did not go unnoticed. Opined *Sporting Life*, "Connie Mack, if thrown upon the market, would command more money than any of his Senatorial companions. He is unquestionably the best find Washington ever made, He is young, skillful and ambitious."[35]

Sullivan's 5'4" find, "The Dummy," was the team's best batsman and most popular player, hitting .274 and leading the league in stolen bases. Columnist W. W. Aulick joked that Hoy took out his frustrations by sneaking down to the Capitol Building at night and heaving a ball to the Treasury Department, the length of Pennsylvania Avenue, "and never hitting a soul."[36]

> *"Hoy, then, is one man who never sassed an umpire, never indulged in verbal taunts at members of rival teams and never hurled bitter remarks at the bleacherites of a foreign field. In a plain way of speaking Hoy was a deaf mute, and answered (in the sign language) to the name of Dummy."*
> —W.W. Aulick *Pittsburgh Press*, February 24, 1911

Blame for the team's woeful performance and finish was not all laid at Ted Sullivan's feet. Throughout the season, he had managed to juggle management of the Troy squad and oversight of the Senators.

The *New York Daily Clipper* concluded that "had Ted Sullivan been in charge of the Washington Club during the entire season, his team would assuredly not have come in last."[37]

The *Sporting News* acknowledged Sullivan's back-and-forth broomdance: "Once a week Sullivan would run over to Troy to see how the farm was getting along and to give some orders to his manager. So it may fairly be said that he was the first manager to run two clubs in one season—a major and a minor."[38]

◆ 11 ◆

Back to the "Auld" Country

After that rough summer of bouncing back and forth between Troy and D.C., Ted Sullivan found himself rootless again—not overly welcome back in Milwaukee, where the sporting wounds of 1886 were still festering, and uncertain of his professional and financial footing with the Senators. He told reporters that he would be delighted to stay with Washington, but that he would need a few more years and a better budget to build a contending outfit.

Around Thanksgiving, the itinerant manager announced that he would head for Europe in the spring as the agent of an English capitalist, and spend several months attempting to organize ball clubs in London and Dublin, before proceeding to Paris to take in the World Exposition.

In late 1888, the *St. Louis Post-Dispatch* reported his plan to arrange an "Irish Green Stockings" team to inaugurate the game in Ireland and said, "Manager Ted Sullivan expects to cross the ocean to eat his Christmas dinner with his relatives next year in Dublin."[1]

"Whether this is an April joke or not is not stated," noted a skeptical reporter back in Kansas City.[2]

A Christmas Tragedy

But that Christmas, Ted Sullivan made a sad and unfortunate decision to spend the holidays with friends back at his alma mater in St. Marys, Kansas, rather than travel to Ireland or return home to his family in Milwaukee, as he usually did. Early in the morning of December 26, his father, Timothy Sullivan, Sr., was asphyxiated by fumes from a faulty coal stove while sleeping at the home of his son, Detective Dennis Sullivan, in Milwaukee. Ted's and Dennis's brother, Eugene, who was sleeping in the same room, was found unconscious and died shortly thereafter.[3]

While the Sullivans were burying their dead in Milwaukee, the press in Chicago was predicting that Ted would not be back at the helm in Washington in 1889: "Manager Ted Sullivan, of the Senators, will not be with the Senators after April 1. Ted and the Senatorial crew are not in love with each other."[4]

After the funerals, Sullivan threw himself into planning his first trip overseas, now thinking he would organize a couple of teams, English and Irish, to play as a part of the Paris Exposition. He told the boys in the D.C. newsrooms that he had a gentleman in Washington who was interested in bringing teams of French, Irish, or English ballplayers to the U.S for a series of exhibition games in 1890.

As Sullivan was packing his grip for the trip, the boys who played for him in Troy were making noise about missing their last paychecks. By April Fools' Day, 1889—as Chicago's *Inter Ocean* had predicted—Sullivan was officially out as manager of the Washingtons and was hustling to get aboard a ship before the bill collectors could catch up with him. He told the papers he was going to Ireland for pleasure and historical sightseeing, but he would endeavor to establish a love of baseball while he was there.

Once safely on the Emerald Isle, Sullivan found a warm reception from his relatives and their neighbors.

> *"When I was in Ireland I made myself as much at home as possible by talking to every son of the auld sod that I came across. My name sounded well to them, and I guess I had made better progress than if I had given out cards reading 'Herr von Suddlebeck, champion pancake eater to the Emperor."*
>
> —Ted Sullivan[5]

Befuddled by Baseball

Ireland, "the home of heroes," Sullivan wrote, "always extends a hearty welcome to an American." As for baseball, the Irish were lukewarm, but they were curious.[6]

"The Irish people who love everything from America, told me they would be pleased to take part in the game and to see how it was played," said Sullivan. So, with a dozen Spalding league balls and a couple of bats in his grip, Yankee Sullivan promoted a game on the shore of Killarney's lower lake, an area popular with cricket-loving English tourists. The blighties expressed little interest in the "blooming American game."[7]

Ultimately, he was able to arrange a match between a band of locals and some begrudgingly willing English tourists. The game took place in a loosely cropped cow pasture with 15th century Ross Castle looming in the background. The first inning, with instructions, took half an hour. "The English parties got disgusted and said the blooming Yankee game was sillier than marbles, mumblepeg or quoits," went Sullivan's tale.[8]

Finally, a local Irishman—Michael Dempsey, "the crack hurler of Co. Kerry," according to Sullivan—proceeded to wield the "cudgel" and drove one of the Spaldings off the shin of the English pitcher. The game at that point fell apart, with the English pitcher grousing, "I wisht that blowsted, blooming Yankee and his blowsted, bleeding game was sunk in the middle of the blooming ocean before he [Ted] came over here."

Sullivan's subsequent sojourn to England, Land of the Anglos, did little to warm his Celtic heart toward the English people and their slow and formal game.

The Pittsburgh Daily Post reported that "While in London, he was beguiled into taking three days off from business and attending a cricket match. After it was all over Ted irritated his English friends a little by telling them that the American people could build a railroad and have through trains running while they were playing a game of cricket. They promptly hit back at our national game, referring to it as childish and wholly uninteresting."[9]

In June, Sullivan dropped a letter to the editor of *Sporting Life*, admitting there was not

J. J. CLARKE, Cleveland

In 1902, the Corsicana Oil Citys, featuring the home run hitting (he actually hit eight in one game) Native American catcher Jay Justin Clarke (callously dubbed "Nig" by newspaper sports writers, due his dark complexion), routinely drilled all comers in Ted's newly reformed Texas League. Clarke went on to play nine seasons in the American League. American Tobacco Co (souvenir card, Cleveland Naps, 1909–1911, Library of Congress).

a lot of interest in baseball in either Ireland or England, but that Paris might be ripe for a tour.[10]

Playing Ball with Buffalo Bill

In the spring and summer of 1889, William "Buffalo Bill" Cody and his entourage of painted Indians, trick-riding cowboys, sharpshooters, tent-builders, and ticket-takers drew a stampede of curious fans from all over Europe, Asia and Africa—everyone, it seemed, from viscounts, duchies, barons and earls, to peasants and peons wanted to experience America's legendary "Wild West."

Galloping into Cody's Paris encampment in the middle of May came one Timothy P. "Ted" Sullivan, smelling opportunity among the buffalo chips and wood smoke.

Having been relieved of his duties with the Senators of Washington in late March, Sullivan had been reading about the "fever" that had spread through France, indeed all of Europe, with the arrival of the famous frontiersman and his circus-like re-creation of America's "Wild West." Stetson hats had suddenly become the rage and, in Paris, virtually everything American was newly in vogue.

"In Paris, I think baseball would be a go," he told the papers, "and several parties are after me to bring two nines over here. They are encouraged, I suppose, by the great success of Buffalo Bill, who, by the way, is setting the Parisians wild."[11]

Ostensibly just on vacation to take in the historical sights and experience the Paris "Exposition Universelle" of 1889, Sullivan said he just so happened to have brought with him "a dozen official Spalding bullets and half a dozen bats to show the locals ... our national sport if the opportunity arose."[12]

A few months before Sullivan's arrival, the American sporting goods king, Albert Spalding, had siphoned barrels of good ink from the European press by staging an exhibition baseball game at the Parc Aérostatique, while Eiffel's towering achievement was being constructed in the background.

Sullivan wasn't in Paris but a week or two before he began sending his signature "letters" (forerunners of the modern press release) via cable to *The Sporting News* and other publications in the States. He was already conjuring a scheme to bring more baseball to Europe by hitching the sport's wagon, in the form of two traveling nines, to Buffalo Bill's European travel schedule.

On June 7, he sent a trans–Atlantic cable to contacts in New York saying Paris was interested in baseball, a group of wealthy ex-pats was behind the notion of creating a pair of exhibition teams, and he was hurrying back to the States to select the players.

Four days later, in a letter to *Sporting Life*, Sullivan conceded that trying to plant the seed of baseball in Europe was proving futile. Upon his return to the United States in July of 1889, the self-appointed ambassador of the National Game claimed he had obtained a commitment to place two baseball squads that would put on exhibitions and travel with Buffalo Bill's Wild West Show.[13]

As to whom that commitment was with is still unknown, as there is no record of any ball teams choosing sides in faux battles with Geronimo.

Back on Land with a New Plan

After watching Wild Bill sell gunslingers, wild Indians, and snake oil to the curious masses—at big profits—Sully set out to round up some moneymakers of his own. With renewed vigor, he took to the roads and rails again, scouring the U.S. for major league prospects, signing some good, legit prospects for Washington, Pittsburgh, and St. Louis along the way.

The *Omaha Daily Bee* reported that "Ted Sullivan [the *Bee* also called him 'The Illustrious Edward'] is making a handsome income dealing in the purchase and sale of ball players. He was in this city all last week endeavoring to secure at least an option on Crooks, Clarke, Nagle and Nichols. The Washington club wants Crooks, Brooklyn wants Nagle and Clarke, and Columbus and Cincinnati want Nichols."[14]

By September he was also hustling up and selling prospects to St. Louis and Pittsburgh—and, like Wild Bill in Paris, rustling up some good green. The *St. Paul Daily Globe* noted that "Ted Sullivan is a money maker ... and takes care of his earnings. He has not been jumping around the country for the sake of his health. He is worth $30,000."[15]

Meanwhile, reports were rampant that the scout/broker/manager/promoter was in line to take over management of the Washington club once more.

While Sullivan was raking in some nice fees from his baseball debutants, some of his lesser prospects had to borrow a buck to get to their minor club assignments. For example, when former big leaguer "Trick" McSorely and two semi-promising youngsters were signed to play in California, they didn't have, as one paper put it, "more money than a mule could carry, so they took a Sullivan Sleeper in an emigrant car and a big wash-basket full of edibles. They were forced to go on the cheap because the California people would not advance a cent."[16]

Besooted

"What a life!" Lefty O'Doul recalled of his days in the minors riding Sullivan Sleepers. "You'd get on a coal-burning train with the old wicker seats, carrying your own uniform and your bats and everything, and ride from Des Moines, Iowa, to Wichita, Kansas. All night and part of the next day. If you opened the window you'd be eating soot and cinders all night long. If you closed the window you'd roast to death. Get off in the morning either filthy or without a wink of sleep. Usually both."[17]

Still working out of D.C., scout Sullivan was commissioned to help his old boss, Walter Hewitt, secure players for the 1890 season. In late March, the *Pittsburgh Dispatch* reported that six "Senatorial Gladiators" (pre-signed players) showed up at the Washington team's clubhouse ready to don uniforms and start spring workouts, but neither Walter Hewitt nor Ted Sullivan was there to meet and greet them. Hewitt had gone to New York to attend an emergency meeting of the National League in an attempt to save his franchise from decapitation, as the league was getting deadly serious about dropping the blade.[18]

Sullivan's whereabouts were unknown, but the papers suspected he was "somewhere in the east" paving the way for Washington to enter the Atlantic Association, just in case the big league let slip the guillotine.

Sure enough, the National League chopped the Senators franchise just prior to the start of the 1890 season, and Washington was relegated to the minor Atlantic League. Upset with the National League's indentured servant reserve clause and penurious salary caps, the Brotherhood of Professional Base Ball Players was forming a circuit of its own that year, looting the established league's rosters and signing the best available minor league prospects. At the same time, the Hewitts—who, unbeknownst to their manager, were deeply entangled in legal and financial troubles—clutched tightly to their purse strings. Sullivan's budget to acquire ball players was so skimpy the *Post* joked that one of his prospects accepted as his advance a package of chewing gum and another signed for two cigarettes.[19]

Despite his standard promise of delivering a better brand of baseball, outside of a couple of proven veterans and a few promising rookies, Sullivan wasn't able put together much of a team, even at the minor league level. So the inventive promoter resorted to comedy and illusion to keep the fans entertained. And the cranks and scribes bought into it ... for a short while.

"Ted Sullivan is a coacher of the modern school, and his style is both unique and comical," Washington's *Sunday Herald & Weekly National Intelligencer* mused. "'Shaz-say' is his latest when he wants the ball bunted."[20]

Sullivan's Wild West Show

A correspondent for *Sporting Life* came out to see the odd-acting manager for himself.

> The quiet tip was given me to get behind Ted if I wanted to enjoy the game. Only the wire screen of the grandstand separated Ted and I. Forepaugh's Circus was tame in comparison with the time I had. Mr. Sullivan's dialect is unique, and the language in which he converses is a mixture of Cheyenne and Arapahoe, as near as I could catch it. Such expressions as "Shake a tree," "Sixty-six," "White Horse," "Tutti Frutti," and "Oshkosh" were understood by his braves, who nodded their heads in compliance with the instructions conveyed.... Ted is good natured and witty, which makes him very popular here.[21]

Ironically, Sullivan later called the myth that coaches used hundreds of secret signals to cue players "the bug-a-boo of baseball," something "commented on by a class of ignorant ball players for the edification of verdant and gullible reporters."[22]

Mixed Signals

The old fox admitted, though, that he was not above making up a few nonsensical signals to confuse the opposing players. "I made the gullible opposition believe that I had forty signs in a game of ball, and it was carried out to perfection by the wits that played for me, who joshed the other players that it was so."

Other players and managers picked up on Sullivan's tricks. When pitching for the Orphans and the Giants around that time, Dick Cogan suggested to his managers that they use Ted Sullivan's system of signals. "Ted had a great system," Cogan said. "He would sit on the bench and use verbal signs, howling across the field. The code ran something like this: 'High grass' meaning to hit it out; 'Low weeds,' bunt; 'tall timbers,' 'rag doll' and so on."[23]

Sullivan arranged for the Senators to practice on the campus of Georgetown University, where his team warmed up with pre-season games against the Lehigh and Williams college nines, and the old stand-by barnstormers, the Cuban Giants.

Early on in the regular season, Sullivan's nine managed to win a couple of games, triggering a rare fit of optimism in the newsroom of the *Washington Evening Star*:

> *Let loose the clarions of the sky,*
> *Let stars to planets call*

The joyous news that Washington
Did win two games of ball.
And then we may to some extent
Our sorrows less recall,
That Washington in other years
Lost every game of ball.[24]

But long strings of losses followed, and Sullivan's entertaining diversions soon wore thin with Washington's frustrated baseball fans. The lines at the Senators' ticket windows got shorter and shorter.

Following a late-inning loss to the New Jersey Gladiators, Sullivan, in what the *Washington Post* called an "Explosion of Managerial Wrath," went after the umpire, calling him "a robber" and several other endearing titles. He reportedly raised his arm to strike the umpire but was brought down by the captain of the Jersey team. The Washington fans were not impressed. "A manager who cannot control himself is not the man to be placed in charge of a team," the newspaper huffed. "He went so far that he even shouted at players while in the field and running bases."[25]

Senator for a Day

In order to bolster fan interest and income, Sullivan defied convention and the law, opting to schedule some games on Sunday, as ticket sales were nearly always good on God's working day and the people's day off. The long arm of the law in D.C. immediately issued an edict saying, in no uncertain terms, that any contest attempted on a Sunday would be stopped if every man had to be carried off the field on a stretcher.

"This is not a Sunday town and there is no sympathy for a club that will play on Sunday," opined a righteous *Washington Evening Star*. So Sullivan opted to test the holy waters with a game across the Potomac near Alexandria, Virginia. As he anticipated, there came a visit from the local sheriff, who proclaimed that the game was "in violation of the law and desecrating the Sabbath, and must be stopped."[26]

"He wanted to arrest everyone connected with the game, from the manager down," Sullivan recalled. Wearing regular business attire, as was the norm for managers of the day, Sullivan flatly denied that he was the manager named Sullivan, but rather "Senator Timothy Sullivan of New York."[27]

In the classic style of a Southern politician, "Senator Sullivan" offered to introduce the sheriff to some of his lawmaking colleagues who were, at that very moment, caucusing in the stadium office over a bottle of Old Bourbon from Old Kentucky. In the office were baseball men posing as members of the House and Senate from Virginia, Alabama, and Kentucky. They commenced to regale the young sheriff with long, funny stories over swigs of the nectar, while the baseball Sullivan quietly slipped back out to the field and finished managing the game.

The hustling manager pushed his team hard, scheduling extra games and exhibitions in order to shore up shaky relations with the bank.

"No base-ball manager in the country chases the nimble dollar longer and harder than Ted Sullivan," said the *Cincinnati Enquirer*. "Ted plays as many games as it is possible to work in during a season. Discomforts for his men or chances of injuries, have no influence with him. He will date his team for an exhibition game in the morning, and play a championship game in the afternoon if he has to take a gravel train or a hand car to make the 'jump' between towns."[28]

Chief Mourner

By June, Sullivan's promotional smokescreens could no longer hide the lack of heat in the Senators' bats. The *Sunday Herald and Weekly National Intelligencer* no longer beat around the bush, saying, "This is horrible and the team, with Ted Sullivan as chief mourner, should be sent home in ice-boxes."[29]

To make matters more dire, the Atlantic League was looking to slap him with a fine and possible expulsion from the league for playing a Sunday game with an "outlaw" team from Gloucester called the "Hardly Ables."

Judging from other news reports, it appears that Sullivan stepped away from the team sometime in June, only to return at the tail end of July—by which time the team had been deemed dead and insolvent and the Atlantic Association had pulled the franchise from Hewitt. The Association then turned the franchise back over to Sullivan, who said he would use his contacts to hustle up financial backing and form a stock company.

Will Work for Food

Sullivan went ahead and rolled the remnants of the team onto the field for a few more games, including one of the first ever played under the lights in D.C. Having not touched a paycheck in a while, some players sold tickets and worked concessions, while others passed the hat in hopes of putting some lunch money in their pockets.

The *Post* encouraged local lovers of the game to turn out and give the boys a lift, while the *Evening Star* rued the hit-and-miss play of Sullivan's Senators, writing in late July:

> The five hundred people who went out to Capitol park yesterday saw more than twenty-five cents' worth of base ball; they had at least half a dollar's worth in a game that was begun, and, after progressing for three innings, ended in a row that finally culminated in a forfeit to the Baltimore Club.... Manager Ted Sullivan had an excellent opportunity in the squabble that terminated in the forfeit of the first game to show how completely he could lose his wits as a base ball manager."[30]

A few days later, the same paper tried to put a good spin on the situation, saying:

> It now looks as though the Washington club had been benefited by the collapse of the Hewitt reign. Manager Ted Sullivan on Saturday secured the expulsion of the old club and the admission of a new one in his own name.... Thus has Manager Ted emerged from the obscurity of managerdom and sits athwart the presidential chair, assuming the dignity of a magnate. But that is not the only change. There are others promised by the hustling Ted, whose feet and hands have been heretofore tied by the penury of the club. He has secured the backing of two or three Washingtonians who have some spare cash to sink in base ball.[31]

Ted Sullivan's new-found financial backers quickly backed off, unhappy with the team's state of affairs. On August 5, prior to a game with what was left of the nine from Newark, his poverty-stricken players traded their places on the field for porch chairs in front of the Imperial Hotel, where they chewed tobacco, told jokes, and said goodbye before packing their grips to go home.

The few die-hard fans who showed up for a game to be played under the lights with Newark found the gates to the park wide open, the clubhouse shuttered, and the ticket window, through which so few quarters had been pushed through lately, closed up tight.

On August 10, manager Sullivan conceded defeat, saying, "I can get plenty of backing for next year but the capitalists I have met are timid about putting money in for what must be for a time a losing venture."[32]

The *Sunday Herald and Weekly National Intelligencer* blamed the poor showing and untimely death of Sullivan's team not on him, but on the embarrassing stigma that came with having only minor league ball in the nation's most important city:

> The demise of the club is conclusive proof that the people of this city do not want to be members of a minor association. Their lack of patronage of the cheap-admission games is abundant proof of this. To drop out of the National League, where the pick of the base-ball talent was to be found, to take a place in a very much reduced minor association, did not exactly catch the ideas of the enthusiasts. Washington wants first-class ball.[33]

Sullivan quickly proclaimed that he was through with baseball and was going to Atlantic City to take a rest, but he must have gotten lost on the way to the resort because on August 11, he was in Pittsburgh pitching the last-place Alleghenys (they would finish the season with just 23 wins against 113 losses) on a young pitcher he had found. The lad, Bill Phillips, threw the next day against Cap Anson's Chicago Orphans and gave Pittsburgh their first win in forever and a day. Crowed the next morning's headline in the *Pittsburgh Dispatch*: "The Chicagos Could Do Nothing with Sullivan's Wonder" and speculated that Sullivan would be Pittsburgh's next manager.[34]

Kicks a New Idea Around

He wasn't in Atlantic City long enough to have a brat on the boardwalk before he announced he was expanding his interests beyond baseball, and that he had a new scheme: "To win British gold" by taking a crack team of American football (soccer) players to England to beat the Brits at their own game.

The Washington Post, like dozens more American newspapers took the bait:

> Ex-Manager Sullivan's plan is to collect a team of the best football talent in this country, take it over the briny and play a series of games with the English cracks, and come back here in time to go into baseball next season with a pocket full of British money. Not that Ted is a-wearied of baseball, but the season for baseball is about over, and Ted isn't the one to do nothing for half a year, if an honest penny is to be turned in the athletic sport line.[35]

Up in Connecticut, it was reported that "Foot-ball is now Sullivan's new hobby. He doesn't know much about the game, but he sees money in the scheme he has evolved from his fertile brain."[36]

After a months-long tour and educational sojourn through England, Ireland and Wales, scheming Sully questioned the wisdom of taking a bunch of novice American "foot-ballers" into the bellies of the sport's beasts. Instead, he would bring an English rugby team over to the states to play Yale at the Polo Grounds, then Princeton, Harvard, Johns Hopkins, and Columbia. Then on to Canada. He told potential backers it would be great entertainment and a sure-fire moneymaker.

Finding a jobless Sullivan hanging around in the press box at Washington after his return from Blighty in 1891, a *Sporting Life* reporter listened to the traveler's tales and wrote:

> Ted Sullivan—there is but one Ted, and he just returned from a trip to Europe. Ted never looked better. He is of that queer shade that is just betwixt and

between the hue of a white man and a Negro that comes from a trip on the water, and Ted says that he would not take fifty dollars for his tan. He has brought back with him plenty of funny stories and lots of cockney talk about the ways and means of the game that is very odd. Ted always was droll, even in his serious moments, but he is very funny in his periods of relaxation.[37]

Without sufficient backing, the scheme to win British Gold didn't pan out, so the celebrated seer of baseball's future turned his fertile brain to planning baseball tours of Cuba and Australia.

Before the year was over, he was searching out and trying to snatch players for the sputtering American Association, which, as it turned out, would be forced to merge with the National League the following year. But that October, Sullivan was in Cincinnati to sign the handsome, ambidextrous, Irish-born pitcher and outfielder, Tony "The Count" Mullane.

"Ted had Tony corralled in the rear of a Vine Street beer joint for over two hours Saturday night," confided a snoop for the *Cincinnati Enquirer.* "He is here on behalf of President Von der Ahe. The St. Louis chief wants Tony, and he wants him like a tenderfoot wants a gun in a border unpleasantness."[38]

The *New York Sun* indicated that Ted Sullivan's trademark charm wasn't working, that Mullane sensed the "chloroform in his nectar."[39]

◆ 12 ◆

Things Go South

Chattanooga and "The Dry Grins," 1892

During the 1892 rebirth of the Southern League (remember Memphis?), Chattanooga Chatts fans got the full Ted Sullivan treatment—a winning team, a losing team, a whiff of scandal, umpire abuse, and special attention to the manager's finances.

As usual, Sullivan's announced involvement in the rebirth of Southern baseball was lauded by fawning sportswriters as evidence of the league's legitimacy and viability. In fact, he attended the February organizational meeting on behalf of the A. G. Spalding sporting goods company, and when the meeting was completed, the Spalding ball was adopted and Sullivan was sent to investigate the prospects of enlisting franchises from four other cities.[1] Newspapers reported that, by the close of the month, the little hustler was out "working his jaws" and predicting success.[2]

Not surprisingly, Sir Ted Himself was one of those enterprising managers attracted by Southern baseball. When the season opened in April, Sullivan's Chattanooga Chatts were leading pennant contenders in a field that included the Atlanta Firecrackers, Birmingham Grays, Macon Central City, Memphis Giants, Mobile Blackbirds, Montgomery Lambs, and New Orleans Pelicans.

The Chatts ran out to a fast start and led the standings through June before falling flat in July. Sullivan blamed his team's swoon on rigged umpiring,[3] but still drew flattering press coverage. The fact that he coached from the baseline while wearing a business suit was noted in newspapers across the country,[4] and his status as a baseball evangelist, master strategist, and accomplished scout was routinely splashed across newspaper sports sections. Sullivan was a Southern League star.

> *"Teddy, however, is one of the best, most genial, warm-hearted Irishmen in the world, and everyone who knows*

him likes him. Then Teddy loves every one—even the
umpire who robs him."
—Atlanta Constitution, May 15, 1892

The chief of the Chatts was at the peak of his powers in July, when his team clinched the league's first-half crown with a win over Birmingham.

Typical of the time, the Southern League divided each year's campaign into two seasons, with the winners of the first and second halves facing off in a championship series. Chattanooga edged Montgomery for the first season title with a 52–28 record, good for a .650 winning percentage, securing them a berth in the title series against the second-season champs.[5] The Chatts went on to perform as if they had nothing to play for, but manager Sullivan's run of positive press continued through August.[6]

His decision to wager $900 on a prizefight ($500 on John J. Sullivan, $400 on James J. Corbett) was reported as straight news,[7] and he was lauded for having his franchise about $5,000 in the black by early August. His local support crested at the same time, according to a column by Ren Mulford, Jr. "The next time Ted Sullivan crosses the Atlantic to free Ireland he will wear diamonds," Mulford wrote. "His Chattanooga admirers put a big sparkler in his shirt front this week. Ted is the biggest man in the Southern League these days."[8]

A month later, Mulford reported that Hustling Ted's roving, team-moving eye had settled on Nashville.[9] And the news just kept getting worse for Sullivan.

By mid–September, the Chatts were buried in last place with a 9–22 second-half record, and manager Sullivan had seen enough. During a five-error outing in Atlanta, he walked out of the ball park in disgust before his team had completed their 5–2 loss.[10] During the following weeks, he ramped up his scheme to move to another Southern market for the 1893 season.

Southern baseball observers knew Sullivan was looking for a post-season exit, and Chattanooga fans were eager to hold the door. The Chatts drew about 50 fans on their good nights during the final weeks of the season, and Sullivan himself was persona non grata in town. If you could find him. According to one press account: "All Chattanooga is howling for the jolly Irishman's scalp, and for the first time in his life Teddy has the dry grins. Sullivan and the people who once smiled upon him now barely speak as they pass by."[11]

Still, Chattanooga had won the first leg of the 1892 season, and now the matter remained of a nine-game final series against second-half champs Birmingham. Unsurprisingly, the denouement of the 1892 Southern League season smacked of scandal.

The series ended in a suspicious 4–4 draw, and Game Nine was not played. Sullivan, naturally, claimed the season crown, explaining that the Birmingham players opted not to play the final game because they were no longer under contract.[12] That explanation was widely dismissed, and the league awarded the title to Birmingham based on overall winning percentage.[13] The story that stuck in baseball circles, however, was what sportswriters called "the bogus saw-off" of the fixed series, which was later confirmed by the complicit umpire.[14]

By then, the media's newly-christened "little magpie" had held his Chattanooga franchise hostage, only releasing it after he was awarded the Nashville club. Sullivan reportedly pocketed a stack of cash, bailed on the debt he incurred when the local grounds were built, and pointed his walking shoes toward Nashville.

Judging from the newspaper scribes' post-season chatter, he wasn't missed.

Another "Sullivan Sneak"

As the echoes of Chattanooga's jeers faded, newspapers across Dixie reported that now Ted Sullivan was headed toward Tuscaloosa, where he was engaged to work as a baseball coach at the University of Alabama.[15] He had the Nashville franchise in his pocket and predicted that he would make his new location "the banner city of the circuit" in 1893.

Cranks across the region were enthusiastic about the upcoming Southern League season. On balance, the 1892 renewal was considered a success, with all eight teams playing at least 120 games and the league hosting a championship series, such as it was. The 1893 season promised to be different, however, with an ambitious 12-team circuit in place.[16] But at a time when leagues regularly folded prematurely, those ambitions proved to be a triumph of hope over experience.

Ted Sullivan had built a reputation during his days in Dubuque as an eagle-eyed scout who could find players who were young, fast and talented. But in pretty short order, Nashville's baseball fans came to suspect that Sullivan's talent evaluation was based more on his pocketbook than pennants.

His Nashville Tigers opened their season on the road April 10 against the Memphis Fever Germs, and the Nashville nine quickly stumbled out of the gate. And they kept stumbling. Just a week into the season, the Tigers were humiliated in an eight-error loss, and the tone of their season was set. Hustling Ted Sullivan's aggregation was dismissed as a doormat.

"A big crowd was out to-day to see Ted Sullivan's team try to play base ball."
—*Daily Commercial Herald* (Vicksburg), April 21, 1893

Before May was out, Southern newspapers were shelling Sullivan for the poor showing of his team. Clucked the *Nashville American*: "After a while they will find out that the Majah's [nice-guy Sullivan's] hide is impervious to newspaper shafts as a canvas-back is to water. Ted's been there too often."[17]

The beatings kept coming, and by June 15, now-christened "Bluffing Ted Sullivan" was riding herd on the tenth-place team in the 12-team league, sporting a 19–28 record and a .404 winning percentage. A month later, the Nashville talk was all about Sullivan cashing in and moving on.

The Southern League magnates met July 15 in Chattanooga, and reports from that meeting were headlined by the news that Sullivan had bolted from the circuit. He politely informed his colleagues via telegram that he had completed the sale of the Nashville Tigers franchise to a group of local businessmen who planned to choose a new manager and finish out the 1893 season.[18] His departure led to a blizzard of comments, mostly criticizing Sullivan for greed and venality in his dealings with the league and the Nashville fans.

"Skipped"

The local newspaper was unsparing when noting that Ted's Tigers had fallen into the league cellar (*Nashville Banner* May 30, 1893).

Within days after his departure, stories flew that Sullivan had been shopping his best players on his way out, including an offer to sell his three best starters to Charlie Comiskey for $1,000.[19] He was rumored to have pocketed cash from player sales, $2,500 in road receipts, and $5,000 from the sale of the franchise. His former supporters said he "deserted" his team, and a dispute arose regarding whether Sullivan abandoned his players in Montgomery[20] or instead thanked them for their service and paid them what they were owed.[21] Regardless, he was condemned as a money-grabbing carpetbagger by the press, fans and former colleagues. "Ted's made about $5,000 with the Nashville team, and where is Ted?" asked *The Sporting News* before answering its own question: "Skipped."[22]

Sporting Life was less kind: "It is to be hoped that Ted Sullivan has quit the South forever. The little magpie has been a mischief maker ever since he has been in the South and has spent the season bluffing instead of trying to get together a winning nine to represent the Tennessee capital."[23]

The Nashville Tigers finished the first half of the season in last place with a 20–44 record. The owners of the Birmingham and Charleston clubs followed Sullivan's lead and surrendered their franchises to the league. A brief second, same-year season was commenced, but the Southern League ultimately collapsed on August 12.

By the end of October, rumors had it that the enigmatic manager was to take over the Atlanta franchise … and Ted Sullivan was in Richmond, Virginia, as an ambassador for the Spalding sporting goods emporium, looking to start a Virginia State League.[24]

Atlanta, 1894

Just Like Nashville, Only Quicker

Unlike earlier stops, town-hopping Ted Sullivan brought a trunkful of reputational baggage with him when he made his managerial move to Atlanta prior to the 1894 Southern League season.

To be sure, he drew some of the typically laudatory preseason coverage, with one sportswriter predicting that he would eschew accomplished but pricey veterans in favor of ambitious young hustlers who would bring winning baseball to Atlanta.[25]

> *"Manager Sullivan is popular in the southern cities for the fact that he makes his men play from the start to the finish, and fights gamely until the last man is out in the ninth. It has been said of Sullivan that he would rather lose the United States treasury than a game of baseball."*
> —*The Atlanta Constitution*, January 21, 1894

But this time, the locals seemed to view Hustling Ted's arrival with more than a little skepticism.

Sullivan shrugged off the suspicions and misgivings with humble bombast, prefacing his pre-season evaluation of his team with, "I never liked to be considered a blower, but…." He went on to predict a successful season for his Atlanta squad, which he noted was peppered with plenty of young ("like a lot of three-year-old colts"), unknown (and cheap) players. All players, he hastened to add, were unknown at one point in their careers.[26] That caveat did little to silence his detractors.

Early in the season, Sullivan took a few knocks in the sports pages over his penurious reputation. One joking allegation had him outfitting his Atlanta team in whitewashed uniforms from the previous Nashville season, while another crack had him saving travel costs by replacing Sullivan Sleeper cars with "bicycle rail cars."[27]

One element of Sullivan's Southern reputation held up during the 1894 season—his young, cheap unknowns were never going to be pennant contenders. Among the cheap unknowns on Sully's roster was the tiniest man (5'2" and just 95 pounds) in professional baseball, who was described as "throwing twisters that give the wind a tussle in reaching the plate."[28]

The Atlantas had a losing record by mid–May, and the manager's seat was getting hot. Waxed a scribe from the *Atlanta Constitution*, "Ted Sullivan's" (the scribe teasingly called him "The Frenchman") "stars are not shining with that luminous brilliancy that Atlanta fans would fain gaze upon and be dazzled by."[29]

After their New Orleans boys roughed up his Atlantas, 13–3, the *Times-Picayune* predicted, "Tales of sorrow will be told by Teddy Sullivan, principal of the Atlanta Baseball Kindergarten, for years to come. Poor, weeping Ted was hoodooed, and often lost the combination to his secret-coaching methods."[30]

Sullivan made vague public comments about bolstering his roster, and at the end of May he offered to buy the Mobile team for $1,500 and bring those players to Atlanta.

Typical Sullivan: if he couldn't bring a town a winning team, he could at least put a little color into the game. Often it was the color green. He had a big Irishman by the name of Burk playing third base for him, and the story went that Burk had a runner out by a mile, but umpire McCloughlin called the guy safe. Seems Burk just shrugged and rolled the ball back to the pitcher—which sent Sullivan into conniptions.[31] "Don't you ever tell me again that you are Irish and stand there and take a deal like that without kicking," Sullivan shouted. "There ain't a drop of Irish blood in your veins. It takes a Norwegian to keep quiet under such circumstances as that!"[32]

Nevertheless, the Atlanta franchise, along with about half of the league, was on the verge of collapse. Things were so bad that a by-now gimpy Sullivan was playing right field for his team during the final weeks of June. Still, the hustling manager bristled with faux outrage at reports that his team had disbanded. In a very Sullivanesque telegram on June 24, he complained to the league president that Charleston had disbanded owing him money, and that he wanted to collect.

"The Charleston club quietly and sneakily disbanded, and then wanted to make it appear, for some reason, that it was Atlanta that had disbanded," he claimed. "It is what I call a mean, malicious piece of business.... I have come here to fill my honorable engagements, and if they all live up to contracts as well as Teddy Sullivan the league would be all right."[33]

The Southern League held a special meeting two days later, and Sullivan's team was out. The league tried to play a second season with four hangers-on, but that effort failed, too, and the 1894 Southern League was disbanded for good on July 8.

At the time of their departure, his Atlanta team was in seventh place of the eight-team league, ending with a 21–37 record and a .327 winning percentage. The famous Ted Sullivan's apparent disinterest in fielding a competitive team generated deep hostility among baseball fans. "He is a rank quitter. He has ruined his team," fumed the *Constitution*. "In other words, he has simply been true to his past record."[34]

Naturally, Sullivan didn't stick around. A couple of weeks later, he sprouted up in the Garden State trying to sell the Southern-news-insulated locals on a proposed New Jersey League.[35]

> *"Ted Sullivan, the baseball organizer, will devote his attention to the North next year, as his Southern League experience has not been a pleasant one."*
> —*New York Tribune*, September 15, 1894

◆ 13 ◆

A Tale of Two Sullivans

"Bejabbers, begorra, 'tis a circus for sure,
'Round my house on a summer's night,
When the lads in the neighborhood do meet
And put on the gloves for a fight."
—*Boston Globe*, October 2, 1887

Although the baseball Sullivan certainly had his own clever ways of slipping away from antagonists who wanted to beat the daylights out of him (e.g., umpires, investors, small-town chambers of commerce presidents), he didn't have the powerful fists or the manly size and physique of his hero and fellow Irishman, the great John L. Sullivan.

But Ted Sullivan grew up loving boxing almost as much as baseball. "I never saw a prize ring battle before in my life, although the literature of former great encounters, in England and America was consumed by me, when a boy," he wrote.[1]

Even before he exploited the soft heart and popularity of the great John L. Sullivan on that baseball field in St. Louis back in 1883, Ted Sullivan idolized the Irish warrior and followed him from fight to fight. Before spring ball commenced in Wisconsin in early 1882, he joined the mass of hero-worshipping Hibernians drawn to Mississippi City, Louisiana, to see for themselves the Boston Strong Boy (just 24 years old at the time) chew up and spit out the 31-year-old reigning American champ and fellow Celt, Paddy Ryan.

"The novelty and excitement to see the two great warriors of the roped arena stripped to their waists, fighting for first honors of the world's supremacy in a grand assault of arms thrilled me with joy," the scrawnier Sullivan wrote.[2]

Much to the joy of John L.'s faithful gamblers, like Ted, the illegal (but official) fight, held out of view in a grove of trees on the grounds of a hotel in Mississippi City, didn't last long. Paddy Ryan went down like a sack of spuds after nine rounds and 11 minutes. Ryan is reported to have said afterward: "When Sullivan hit me, I thought a telephone pole had shoved against me endways."

Ted Sullivan said of Tipperary-born Ryan: "Although outfought and outclassed ... he never once in that nine rounds dropped tail and ran. He could not. He was of the same race, Irish, as the man who was delivering the blows."[3]

The baseball Sullivan walked away with some of that gambling money, and the fighter Sullivan carried the $2,500 winner-take-all purse back to Boston. "There was but one John L. Sullivan," Ted later wrote. "He whipped men drunk, and he whipped men sober, he whipped them shaved and unshaved." Indeed, Big John L. was, as Ted gushed admiringly, "a giant amongst pigmies." At least until fast living robbed him of his dignity, health and career.[4]

> "Ted Sullivan has circulated the story in Texas that he is a brother of John L., but he doesn't offer to prove it."
> —*Kansas City Daily Journal*, March 23, 1895

Faithful "Fan" ... to a Point

For the next decade, Ted Sullivan and his long-time buddy and fellow Hibernian boxing fanatic, "Dirty" Jack Doyle, the New York Giants' first baseman, traveled to many of John L.'s fights and bet on the champ, nothing but confident that the rugged Irishman—famous for saying "I can lick any sonofabitch in the house"—would knock out yet another tomato can and put more bucks in their pockets.

Until September 7, 1892, that is, when an aging Strong Boy (by then a graying, overweight, hard-drinking, out-of-shape 34-year-old man) ran up against Gentleman Jim Corbett. Busy managing the Chattanooga club that fall, Ted had sent $500 to be placed on big John L. Sullivan to win ... and, just in case, another $400 to be placed on Corbett.

Ted recalled that his idol was looking old now, "with gray hairs and patched up stomach, with belts and plasters around it to give some semblance of his former self ... the steam in the ship of vitality exhausted long ago."[5]

Sure enough, the Great John L. went down like a boat anchor in the 21st round.

A few years later, in 1897, the *Kansas City Journal* noted that "Ted almost went broke when Corbett whipped Sullivan, but he [later] got part of his losings back on the Corbett-Mitchell fight and now he wants to get even on his life by betting on Corbett at any price."[6]

Not Ted's Brightest Idea

If it was a sport, Ted Sullivan naturally wanted a piece of it, whether "it" was baseball, soccer, rugby, Gaelic football, or boxing. In 1895, baseball's best-known promoter bobbed a management agreement in front of a promising young Black fighter from Texas named Scott Collins, who carried into the ring the fearsome moniker "Bright Eyes."

It was reported in December of that year that "Ted Sullivan is down East filling the ears of reporters with wonderful stories of the prodigious valor and exploits of 'Bright Eyes,' a new pugilist he has recently discovered." Sullivan claimed his discovery had never lost a fight.[7]

Fortunately for Sullivan, Collins never signed on the dotted line, as the prodigy's next fight was against future welterweight champ "Barbados Joe" Wolcott. "Bright Eyes" lost that match before the singing birds could even get tuned up. And as a matter of record, Sullivan's guy never won a bout in his entire (four-fight) career.

Rumble at the Opera

Ted Sullivan loved anything that sold tickets. The man with baseball's shortest attention span once filled an early spring evening by going to an opera house. In March of 1901, he promoted and refereed what was called "a scientific exhibition of the manly art" at the Opera House in Athens, Georgia, including a bout between "a well-known local boxer and one of the best light weights in the country."[8]

Ted Saw "Soccer" in America's Future

Coming off the worst months of a financial panic that saw banks teeter and unemployment rise to double digits, America's major league baseball owners in 1894 were grasping at straws to bolster revenues. Looking across the pond to Europe, they could see that the game of soccer was packing stadiums with fanatical, money-waving fans and, with cities along the eastern seaboard teaming with first- and second-generation immigrants from Western and Central Europe, the idea of putting soccer teams on America's baseball fields in the winter months was born. Sullivan, of course, was picked as the midwife to raise it up.

Clear-headed Ned Hanlon, owner of the Baltimore Orioles, figured he would get the jump on his fellow baseball owners (Brooklyn, Philadelphia, and New York) who had joined him in forming a new American Soccer

League.[9] Recalled Sullivan: "Ned looked at me and smilingly said 'Ted, I know you will find a ballplayer if he was in the bowels of the Rocky Mountains. I would like to spring a surprise on our opponents.'"[10]

In the fall of 1894, while the attention of America's baseball men and their fans was focused on the pennant races and the World Series, Sullivan quietly slipped aboard a ship headed for the British Isles. His mission: to surreptitiously find, recruit, and bring back a crack team of soccer players for Hanlon's entry into America's new professional soccer league.

Sullivan's first stop was Manchester, where he watched a championship match between the Manchesters and the Blackburn Rovers. The match was exciting, he reported to Hanlon, "but the fun that [Charles] Dickens has often written about is in the bleachers."

Determining that many of the best players in the established European game came from Scotland but played for British clubs, Sullivan prowled a pub popular with the Brave Hearts and lured a handful of crack Scottish and English players into his and Hanlon's scheme with steady rounds of "uisce-beatha [whiskey]."

"I treated them to six or seven bottles of stout bought at the 'En and Chicken," wrote Sullivan, "and they were hypnotized by my proposition at once ... they thought the Yank was a great man."[11]

Posing as a wealthy Glaswegian (even mastering the guttural dialect of Scotland's gritty industrial city), Sullivan secured the players' temporary releases from their English clubs by saying he was simply taking them all to Scotland for a vacation and a few home exhibition matches.

By Thanksgiving, Sullivan's ringers from the UK were thrashing America's home-grown "football" (soccer) teams in a series of lopsided matches. "They were supposed to be nothing but scrubs left over from the pickings of Hanlon's rivals," Sullivan boasted, "but Holy Heavens! It was nothing to those English experts to dribble the ball through the legs of the Washington players."[12]

It was reported "Foxy" Ned Hanlon was "so well pleased that he gave Sullivan a check big enough to make the money-loving Irishman's eyes sparkle."[13]

A government inquiry into the legal status of Sullivan's imported aggregation was begun. But it didn't matter. The games proved so one-sided that, according to Al Spink, "the whole scheme to establish soccer as the winter game in the major league baseball parks of American was abandoned."[14]

Ted Sullivan blamed the soccer tour's failure to catch America's fans on fire on the baseball magnates, saying they didn't "boom" it properly. He maintained that the sport had unlimited potential and that bringing it back for another go would "render a service to the sport-loving people of America and give work to hundreds of lively youths. Mark me, people will take to it."[15]

◆ 14 ◆

At Home on the Range

"Ted Sullivan, now in the south, is the king of the hustlers, and could write a big book about his long experience, from the national league to sizing up the rising talent in England."
—*Boston Globe,* March 25, 1895

After learning just enough about soccer to hustle it for a season, Ted Sullivan traded his English bowler for a wide-brimmed derby and ventured into the land of longhorns to round up a new baseball league.

It is difficult today to consider America's minor league system without the Texas League. But when Sir Ted arrived in the Lone Star state in late November 1894, America's game there was on the rocks. An initial version of the league had shut down the previous year after a chaotic and money-losing four-year run. During the three seasons he came to spend in sunny Texas, the pale Irishman oversaw record-setting success and pitiful teams, charmed his friends, enraged his enemies, abandoned cities, and became known as a founding father of the Texas League.[1]

When he first got there, though, his reputation was in tatters across the Southern map. He had been roundly criticized for his oversight of the 1894 Atlanta club, which had limped to a 21–37 record before it disbanded on June 25. The full Southern League crashed on July 8, and Sullivan's antics were widely blamed for the league's failure.[2]

But the enigmatic manager's sketchy record didn't matter to the Texas baseball enthusiasts who embraced his effort to resuscitate the Texas League in the waning months of 1894. One Lone Star reporter, apparently unfamiliar with the formula that calculates the distance between two points, claimed that Sullivan was so enthused about Texas baseball, he had broken all records for traveling by making the trip from Liverpool to Dallas in eight days. In the era of 19th century steamship and western rail travel, that was some tall (and surely mythical) hustling.[3]

Following the initial organizational meeting, there was some early chatter that Sullivan had done an end run around the locals and finagled the Houston franchise for himself. By the time league officials gathered in March to discuss a schedule, a rival ownership group from Houston was making a play for that franchise, and league president J. C. McNealus was pressuring Sullivan to take over the Dallas operation. Sullivan responded with umbrage that he could not bring himself to desert Houston. He then quickly handed over his claim to Houston and moved on to Dallas.[4]

Sullivan's decision to move his team to Dallas was seen as an unforgivable betrayal by Houston fans. Indeed, that bitterness was still on display in a 1914 column in the *Houston Post*:

> The criticism of this action was bitter indeed. Sullivan had guaranteed to put Houston in the field with a winning club. He had every encouragement. And on the eve of the league race he left the Bayou City without a team and literally in the ditch.[5]

Eventually, a schedule was completed, and baseball buffs began to look forward to their new Texas-Southern League's 1895 season. As previous league organizers had learned the hard way, franchise viability depended largely on good scheduling.

The biggest hurdle that Texas baseball organizers faced was simple geography. The league's massive footprint made scheduling costly and difficult. The availability and cost of rail travel—the "jump" between league cities—was always a chief consideration for franchises. And when it came to rail travel, what worked for Connecticut or Iowa baseball leagues wouldn't necessarily work in sprawling Texas.

For the 1895 season, the league's eight teams were scheduled to travel a combined 34,218 miles on road trips. Individual franchise travel schedules ranged from Sherman's low of 2,803 miles to Shreveport's 5,249 miles, and nearly every team had at least one road trip in excess of 400 miles.[6] Even traveling on the cheap with players sweating and trying to catch a wink in hot and dusty Sullivan Sleepers, rail costs remained among a franchise's leading expense.

Finally, the time came to start playing some games, and the great promoter was quick to talk up his Dallas Steers. In fact, three years after the end of the season, Ted Sullivan could still uncork his legendary bombast and blarney when discussing his 1895 Steers.

"Bracketlegs Charley"

Bad Breath and a Mean Disposition

Sometime that spring, Sullivan reportedly rustled up his Steers and drove them into Texas's Indian Nation for a series of exhibition games with a team of select Native Americans. According to Sullivan's telling, the umpire for the first game was called "Bracketlegs Charlie," a man so tall (6'6") that most of the spectators eyed the action through his bowed legs. According to Sullivan, Bracketlegs carried two revolvers and a jug, and made calls blatantly partial to the home team.

> He robbed us of the game, and I thought at the time that he would be just the proper caper to crush the "Muggsy" McGraws and Jack Doyles. If he couldn't do it with his guns he could do it with his breath. If I didn't have a warm regard for the insurance company that has been carrying me for years, I would have filed an objection to some of his decisions. I made one kick, however, and that was when my left fielder chased a high fly and took a header in the river that fringed the field. I asked "Bracketlegs Charley" for the privilege of a pair of life preservers for my outfielders. He looked at me and then at his guns, and I retreated to the bench.[7]

• • •

Reporters noted that Sullivan was particularly eager to play well in Atlanta, given the previous summer's criticism of his lousy team and the blame he shouldered for the Southern League's collapse after he folded his franchise.[8] For his part, "the irrepressible" Sullivan was unfazed by the grudge match atmosphere. "I'll make monkeys of the Atlantas," he said. "My team is one of the best minor league aggregations the South has ever seen, and I'll make it warm for any of 'em."[9]

Despite his cocky claim, Sullivan had to watch the Atlantas lay a 14–3 shellacking on his Dallas nine in front of a big, howling home crowd. He kicked and wailed about umpire Jim Lynch, and following the game he derided the Atlanta team and predicted that they would finish in the Southern League cellar. A reporter, perhaps in an act of charity, found one complimentary note from the Steers' performance—their red socks, gray pants, and blue shirts made for an attractive uniform.[10]

Not all of the team's 1895 exhibitions were as well-documented as the scrap in Atlanta, but more than 10 years later, one of Sullivan's Steers was still talking about the abrupt end of another exhibition game.

False Alarms

Today only ghosts play ball among the ruins of the dried-up railroad town once known as Peru, Texas. But back when Peru's grass was still green, Ted Sullivan took his Steers there to be fed and watered, and to play an exhibition with the local nine—comprised mainly of the town's firemen.

"They played pretty good ball," Cleveland mailman Jimmy Gilman, who played for Sullivan in those days, remembered.

> But we took it easy and let them have their own way for a while. Well, when the sixth inning began, the score was 4 to 3 in favor of the firemen and the crowd was frantic with joy. We went to bat and began to get busy. We had driven 12 men across the plate and had the bases full, with nobody out, when I noticed one of the Peru's substitute players leaving the grounds at a signal from his captain.
>
> About three minutes later, after a home run hit by one of our men, the bells began ringing as if all of Texas was ablaze. You should have seen that team scatter. Over the fence went the outfielders and over the turnstiles went the battery and infielders. The game ended then and there, the score reverting to the fifth inning with Peru one run ahead.
>
> The fire? Oh, there wasn't any fire. The ringing of the bell was just the Peru method of winning a game."[11]

Where's the Money?

With the exhibitions behind them, the Dallas Steers started the season at a furious pace, rolling out to a 21–5 record and sitting comfortably in first place on May 19. Oscar Colquitt, the young governor of Texas and a big baseball fan, declared Ted Sullivan was now more popular in Texas than he was. Although, after sizing up rotund Teddy, the governor quipped, "I'd make a better baseball player than you if I had a chance to train."[12]

But despite the on-field success and the governor's accolade, not all was well in the manager's world. In late May and early June, an open letter Sullivan penned to the *Dallas News* was the talk of the Texas-Southern League. In his letter, he bemoaned his team's lack of support at the turnstiles, despite a strong first-place showing that included a record 23-game winning streak. As the franchise's sole owner, he explained, he relied entirely on his team's cut of the gate to make payroll and meet other expenses, but with weekday games drawing fewer than 200 fans, and weekend contests fewer than 1,000, the Steers were in rough financial shape. According to Sullivan, a group of Dallas citizens had guaranteed him $300 to move to that city, but the cash was never forthcoming. In his letter, he contended that a wealthy Denison man had offered him $500 cash plus $50 per game if Sullivan would move his team to Denison, and that a Norfolk club had offered him $500 cash for three of his players. Sullivan suggested that Dallas fans might want to deliver $500 to him soon so that he would not be forced to sell those players.

"I am no 'jollier' nor a dead beat, but I speak to the point like any straight man," Sullivan explained in his financial plea.[13]

Not long after his open letter, the minor league magnate challenged the winners of either the Western League or the Eastern League to play his Texas Steers for "the minor league championship of the United States." He proposed a seven-game series in October at the Texas State Fair, which would be highlighted by a Corbett-Fitzsimmons heavyweight title fight. It was predicted that the prizefight would draw a massive crowd atop the 10,000 to 15,000 daily visitors to the Fair. The winner of the minor league series would walk away with a $1,000 purse and half of the gate receipts. While the proposed fight and baseball series generated plenty of chatter throughout the summer, of course, neither of the events took place.[14]

Maybe the Greatest Game Never

A story that Ted Sullivan told and retold over the years was of a game that may or may not have actually taken place, but became legend nonetheless. When *The Sporting News* reported it years later, the headline read:

SHOT THE BALL
Greatest Game of Ball Ever Played in Texas
Had a Most Sensational Ending

Newspapers across the nation reported that more than a thousand cowboys escorted Sullivan and his Steers onto a ball field in Waxahachie, and that the cheering of the crowd of 30,000 "was like the roaring of Comanches."

According to Ever-Truthful Ted's account, the event was an exhibition grudge match between his Steers and a nine from Abilene, and he and the Abilene manager concocted a ruse aimed at keeping the rowdy Steers players from starting fights and abusing the umpire

> When we got to the Abilene grounds we saw no fence, but all at once the manager drew a revolver and fired into the air three times. The retort was dying away when we saw a man galloping like the wind toward us. He halted near us, took off his hat in real cavalier style, and the manager, going through the same formality, said: "Colonel Sullivan and Capt. O'Connor [team captain Mike O'Connor], allow me to introduce you to Cheyenne Pete, the Mayor of Bleeding Gulch." Pete bowed and said … "I wish to politely inform you that I guard a square mile and among the many sights is a well-stocked cemetery of my own."

Crowds of cowboys began to pour into the grounds. After returning from a short ride, Pete discharged his revolver again and said to the Abilene manager: "Colonel Crawford, you will pardon this intrusion, but I have just killed eight men, who were trying to steal into the grounds, and I want to ask you what I shall do with their bodies?"

"Let the bodies remain where they are," answered Crawford, "as there will be others killed in different parts of the field, and we will want to bury them all at once."

According to Sullivan's razor-sharp recall, he and O'Connor were introduced to "Sure-Shot Bill," who was to umpire the game. They were warned by the Texas ump that there would be no questioning his calls. But the first time an Abilene runner was called safe at first, O'Connor ran toward the ump, ready to jaw his complaint.

Sure-Shot Bill (in another of Ted's tellings, the umpire was the Navasota Tarantula, Ned Garvin) stood firm and said: "'Capt. O'Connor, I wish to pay my compliments to you and the Steers,' at the same time picking up a pebble, throwing it in the air, and, like a flash, drawing his revolver and shooting it to pieces: 'but if memory serves me right, Captain, I think I said that the runner was safe.'"

As Sullivan recollected, all was quiet until the ninth inning, when his Steers were up two runs and Abilene's best hitter was at bat with two men on. The Abilene batsman proceeded to hit a long, high fly ball to center, when, according to Sullivan, "A tall horseman suddenly rode from the crowd, crying 'Boys of the panhandle to the rescue!' Five thousand revolvers were emptied at the descending ball and nothing came to earth but an old piece of yarn."[15]

Ted's "Grapevine Curve"

The Steers ran roughshod over their league rivals, making manager Sullivan so cocky that he put himself in to pitch the second game of a doubleheader against Shreveport. By now well into his mid–40s, Hustling Ted tossed looping bouquets. On June 21, the newsboys at the *Shreveport Times* called his tosses "grapevine curves," which arrived so slow they gave the befuddled Grays' batsmen "the sore eyes."

The *Times* observed, "Mr. Sullivan wore a happy smile the entire evening, even though he lost the games. He used 'Santa Anna,' 'Missip' and the balance of his 'hoodo' bag, but lost after all. He 'stood in' with the large audience from the start and was winning the admiration of the rootertorial representatives when the last man in the ninth yelled enough and the blackboard showed 8 to 3 in favor of the Grays."

Steers Stomp on League Rivals

Dallas ended up winning the league's first half-season title with a 43–14 record on June 22. They were also in first place with a 28–7 mark on August 7, when the second half-season was upended by the collapse of the Shreveport, Austin, Houston, and San Antonio clubs. From that point on, the Steers faltered just enough to allow Fort Worth to overtake them and win the second season crown.

The championship series of the 1895 Texas-Southern League was set to start on September 7. The 15-game series was designed to provide up to seven home games each for the Dallas Steers and the Fort Worth Panthers, with the 15th game, if necessary, to be played at a mutually selected site.[16] The series stumbled out of the gate, however, when Fort Worth manager Billy Ward wired Sullivan that the rain was coming down heavy in Fort Worth, and the Panthers would not be heading to Dallas. According to a published report, "Sullivan read the dispatch, uttered several un–Sunday remarks," then went to the telegraph office and dictated his poetic reply:

> *Be still, Billy Ward, and cease repining;*
> *Over in Dallas the sun's still shining;*
> *Thy fate is the common fate of all—*
> *Come over here and we'll play ball*
> —Ted Sullivan[17]

The first game of the series was awarded by forfeit to Dallas, but eventually Billy Ward and his Panthers got on the trail with Sullivan's Steers and won the championship series, seven games to six. But by just about any estimation, the 1895 season was a success for Ted Sullivan. He guided his team through an entire season, worked through financial struggles, and oversaw a strong, record-setting club.[18]

In early August, he was credited with salvaging the league after the disbanding of four franchises, and one columnist opined: "Ted is no chewing gum manager, and what he don't know about the game isn't worth knowing."[19] But Ted Sullivan being Ted Sullivan, there would be no victory lap or warm feelings for him at the end of the successful revival of Texas baseball.

And the Horse You Rode In On

In the opening days of 1896, news broke that Ted Sullivan's Texas Steers had found a greener pasture in New Haven, Connecticut, as members of the Atlantic Association. The news took people in Texas by surprise.

Not all Texans were sad to see Ted Sullivan go, particularly Houston fans.

Prior to his move to Dallas, he had assembled a strong team, but with only a month before opening day, new Houston owner W. F. "Billy" Hepworth was forced to assemble a roster of local amateurs and a couple of semi-pro players. Hepworth lost money throughout the season and ultimately ran 29 players through his payroll. The fact that Sullivan's Steers were wildly successful while the miserable Houston Mudcats were unable to complete the 1895 season fueled Houston fans' disdain for the bombastic hustler. Nearly 20 years later, a Houston sports columnist described the 1895 revival of the Texas League as the "incursion that has always deluded Sullivan into christening himself 'The Father of the Texas League.'"[20]

One of his contemporaries, Sam Taub of the Houston franchise, put his feelings toward Sullivan more succinctly. Upon hearing that Sullivan had declined ownership of the San Antonio franchise for 1896, Taub said he "wouldn't eat taffy off the same stick with Ted."[21]

"Teddy Sullivan always gave me the marble heart, and right glad I am that he has decided to stay away from Texas," said a happy Taub.[22]

◆ 15 ◆

Ted Herds His Steers
North to New Haven

Come fall of 1895, news reports had the old sport managing a prize fighter in Texas, considering a job in Virginia, and taking his Steers up the trail to fresh grass in New England.

His young boxing hopeful, "Bright Eyes" Collins, was turned into mincemeat after only a couple of fights, and a job managing the Norfolk Clams didn't pan out.

There was speculation in the sporting press that Sullivan would yet return to Texas in 1896 and take over the San Antonio franchise. In the meantime, Hustling Ted was "handling the fortunes of a theatrical troupe" in partnership with "Colonel" Ned Green, the rich and free-spending manager of the Texas Midland Railroad and son of New York's famous "Witch of Wall Street," Hetty Green, a miserly multi-millionairess known for dressing like a beggar woman.[1]

At Christmas it was announced that Ted Sullivan had been awarded the Atlantic League franchise in New Haven, Connecticut, and would compete with nines from Newark (Colts), Paterson (Silk Weavers), New York (Metropolitans), Wilmington (Peaches), Hartford (Bluebirds), and Philadelphia (Athletics). His New Haven team would include many of the talented Steers players who had just torn up the Texas League.

Although an admirer of Sullivan's promotional skills, the *Boston Globe's* syndicated columnist, Tim Murnane, didn't give the new Atlantic League much chance of succeeding. "Too much Ted Sullivan for real business," he wrote.[2]

Need More Green

Sir Ted immediately endeared himself to the baseball fans of immigrant-heavy New Haven by promising that most of his players would be Irish.

There's only one German on the team. Read my list of players—O'Connor, O'Hagan, Driscoll, Boyle, Killacky. Reads like the register of a Donegal ship, eh?[3]

The Irish and the Yankees are the best ball players. I am not stuck on Dutch ball players; artists are very scarce among this class of players. Figuratively speaking, they always ride with their backs to the engine and never see anything until they have passed it.[4]

In fact, good-natured grudge matches between amateur Irish and German ball teams were a popular attraction in cities along the East Coast on St. Patrick's Day.

As was his wont and style, Ted Sullivan added a dash of hyperbolic intrigue to his herd by claiming that one of his new pitchers was an American Indian named Wolf-Eating-Bear, the first (not true) Indian ever to play professional baseball, and that he had another pitcher who was a genuine, 6'5" Texas sheriff with 125 notches on his gun, marking the number of desperadoes he had killed in the line of duty.

"The latter, he (Sullivan) says, has killed 265,000,000 in a legitimate sort of fashion, but he doesn't consider him very ferocious," said the presumably tounge-in-cheek *Richmond Dispatch* of April 4, 1896.

The *Wilmington Evening Journal* dubbed the new New Haven team "Sullivan's Baseball Freaks" and called Sullivan "the funniest humorist and most entertaining romancer in the base ball business."[5]

The scribes back in Texas didn't think Sullivan funny at all. In hearing that the itinerant Sullivan had sold the San Antonio franchise to Jim Nolan of Galveston and moved his Steers to New Haven, *Sporting Life* noted, "the people of San Antonio ... don't know what to think of his actions. The papers are printing all kinds of yarns about what he intends doing here, there and everywhere. Ted is a great fellow to get the fans worked up."[6]

In fact, the promoter king wasted no time in cranking up his pre-season press machine. The *New York Sun* reported, "Ted Sullivan, the Hibernian troubadour, comedian, and baseball exploiter," had already signed "a couple of crackerjack players for $30 advance money" and had discovered a phenomenal pitcher from Minnesota who had spent the winter putting holes in barn doors for practice.[7]

To warm up his "freaks," Sullivan wanted to take on the college boys from nearby Yale, but when the school declined, he turned to his favorite foil, the Cuban Giants. Next in line was a nine from Norfolk, Virginia, where Steers catcher Hodge chased after Norfolk's pitcher, got him against the grandstand, and "'gored' him."[8]

Throughout the exhibition season, Sullivan's outsized claim of having a six-shooting Texas lawman on his team drew big numbers of infatuated fans to the ballpark. By opening day, Sullivan's pug nose had grown to a length longer than Pinocchio's.

Ted's Notorious Texan

In a letter to *Sporting Life*, the manager claimed his hard-throwing Texas sheriff, "Bullet-Proof Ned will be the greatest sensation in the box that was ever known to baseball, and it may border on dime novel story when I say Wolf Eating Bear is a legend among his tribe with a record of 60 scalps."[9]

Sullivan's comical exaggerations of Ned Garvin's prowess with a pistol and Wolf Eating Bear's

WAS FOURTEEN TO TWO

Bullet Proof Ned and Wolf Eating Bear Easy Marks for the Truckers Yesterday.

FAST FIELDING, RUNNING AND HITTING.

Eddie Leach and Patrick Rollins in the Points for the Home Team, and With the Good Work of the Other Members "Ted's" Herd Was Nicely Rounded Up for Slaughter.

There was a very good crowd at League Park yesterday afternoon to witness the second game of the series between "Ted" Sullivan's New Haven Club and the Truckers, and those present saw a very good game of ball, not simply because the home team won, but just simply because it was a very fair game—a game which was interesting from all standpoints. Clever base running, good team work, excellent hitting and fairly clever fielding was the rule, and what more a "crank" may wish to see is something beyond the comprehension of the writer, and suffice it to say that if the Truckers will…

Upon moving his talented Steers to New Haven, Connecticut, Sullivan titillated fans and increased attendance at games by making up colorful names for and fearsome stories about his players, including Bullet Proof Ned (Ned Garvin) and Wolf Eating Bear (Gus Mackey) (*Norfolk Virginian*, March 31, 1896).

GARVIN, P, Brooklyn

The "Navasota (Texas) Tarantula," Ned Garvin (Chicago Orphans souvenir card, 1900).

accuracy with a carving knife were total fiction, of course, but "Bullet-Proof" Ned's penchant for mayhem was quite real. After playing for Sullivan in New Haven, Garvin—whose Irish surname translates in the Gaelic to "rough or cruel fate"—went on to a career in the big leagues marked by equal parts brilliant pitching and inexplicable violence.

Sober, Garvin was said to be gentle as could be, but after ingesting a few highballs, he would turn into a raging demon. A notorious drinker with a hair-trigger temper, "The Demon Texan," as he was also called, once beat and shot a saloonkeeper and a policeman in Chicago, stomped a shoeshine boy in Milwaukee, crushed a beer glass in the face of a teammate in Brooklyn, pounded a meek insurance salesman in New Jersey, and used an elderly team secretary as a punching bag.

Still, those flashes of genius on the mound kept Garvin in the game until 1904, when Brooklyn Superbas manager Ned Hanlon gave Garvin his unconditional release after the beating of the club secretary, which occurred during a beer-bottle-throwing melee on a train headed for St. Louis.

Back in Connecticut, Sullivan's Yankee-ized Steers played well in exhibition games, including a lopsided 15–2 win over manager Sullivan's favorite foil, the Cuban Giants. New Haven's *Morning Journal and Courier* reported on the Steers' offensive stampede with enthusiasm: "The Steers plowed deep into the ground, tossing the giants from horn to horn, stamping, bellowing and tearing up the earth with the inanimate bodies of the former Giants, and when last seen of the colored brigade they were looking like pigmies instead of Giants after their encounter with the terrible Steers."[10]

But the paper had to admit: "This colored club plays no poor game … which was demonstrated by their clever work in the number of fine plays they made … and the team that will beat them will have to play ball from start to finish."

New Haven baseball fans turned out in force for a warm-up match with Sullivan's old team, the Washington Senators. Knowing him as they did, the boys in the *Morning Times* of D.C. newsroom poked a little fun at the loquacious manager in their pre-game coverage. "For a curtain raiser," they wrote, "Ted may be induced to make a few remarks from home plate on the tariff, the silver question, women's rights, and the general cussedness of umpires."[11]

The *Times* dutifully reported "the twirling marvels with the Fenimore Cooper sobriquets" would be backed up by Bill Joyce and Jack Crooks, a "full blooded 'soo' from the Kerry Patch reservation," and that fans would be guaranteed "a war dance with pyrotechnic trimmings."[12]

Sullivan announced that his Texas Demon lawman, who he claimed was also an accomplished trapper and poet, would pitch the game, and that the umpire would wear a full coat of armor and keep tab on strikes by firing a six-shooter every time notorious Ned cut the plate.

Feeling himself bullet-proof and chivalrous that season, the 5'7" Sullivan took up for an insulted waitress ... and made darn sure his pals in the press knew all about it.

TED SULLIVAN A SLUGGER
He Punched Two Salesmen for Insulting a Waitress
Boston Daily Globe
May 1, 1896

Manager "Ted" Sullivan of the New Haven baseball team laid out two New York commercial travelers, one of whom insulted a waitress in the Westmoreland Hotel yesterday morning. Two drummers were seated at the table with "Ted." One of the drummers called a waitress, and when she came he seized and kissed her. The girl resented the insult and then rushed from the room crying.... The baseball manager reached over and slapped the drummer in the face. The two knights of the road then came at "Ted." The insulter made a pass at him, which was easily dodged. He countered and caught the drummer on the mouth landing him in the arms of his companion. The latter came at Ted, but his rush was checked and his desire for fight quenched by a right-hander square on the nose. The first drummer renewed the attack with a fork, which was an unfortunate move for him. Sullivan met his armed antagonist with a terrific blow on the stomach, staggering him, and sent in another on the jaw, which knocked him completely out. The drummers called on no merchants yesterday, but nursed their wounded bodies and feelings in seclusion.

Chances are good to excellent that chivalrous Ted Sullivan ghost-wrote that story to make things easier for an overworked reporter pal. His noblesse had dissipated, however, in time for the next ballgame, at Norfolk, where he was ejected for using language offensive to ladies, the umpire, and most everyone else within earshot. Said a *Sporting Life* correspondent who was covering the game: "I regret very much to take up so much of 'Life's' valuable space in rehearsing this matter, but unless I did the outside world would think this town unfit for civilized people. Sullivan said he would never come here again, and I hope he never will, unless he acts in a more gentlemanly manner than he did this trip."[13]

Ted's Close Call

By the middle of May, New Haven fans were ready to run the manager out of town. He narrowly escaped the vengeance of his patrons following a game where the opposing team didn't show up and he refused to give refunds to the hometown ticket-buyers, offering rain checks instead.

That offer apparently didn't sit well with the fans, who wanted their 50 cents back. They went after the manager as he stepped off an electric car and set to pummeling him before he was rescued by police and escorted back to his hotel. The city attorney later determined that Sullivan's offer to provide rain checks was sufficient and that the fans needed to leave him alone.

By early June, there were rumors that Sullivan was scouting players for other teams. A sarcastic scribbler for the *San Antonio Sunday Light* conjectured that the little Irishman was enlisting recruits for an attack on England and might be forming a brigade "in case of war and at the same time have a chance to set old Ireland free, which has been Ted's ambition all his born days."[14]

By the end of July, after more losses (38) than loyal fans in the stands, New Haven was no longer part of the Atlantic League, and Ted Sullivan was once again circumnavigating the minor league map. The truth is, his Steers had been corralled by some pretty fair competition, as a number of young ballplayers in that year's Atlantic League would prove to be stars in the bigs, including a young shortstop for the Paterson Silk Weavers named Johannes Peter Wagner, who went by "Honus."

In late September, the *Macon Telegraph* reported, "Ted Sullivan, the erratic, fat, wide awake baseball man" would be taking charge of the team in Savannah the following season.[15]

Come October, frequent traveler Sullivan was in charge of a deck chair on a passenger ship headed to England, with an eye to organizing a post-season exhibition tour for Hanlon's World Champion Orioles.

By the first of November, he was back in Baltimore, the bearer of bad news: He didn't see much hope for baseball in England due to the cold and clammy weather and a general disinterest in the sport. Togged out in a Savile Row suit and an English overcoat, the avowed Irishman admitted he was not a fan of the denizens of Blighty.

"The English can't help it," he told the *Baltimore Sun*, "but they are cold-blooded in their manners. After leaving the congeniality of America, I always feel when I enter England as if I had stepped into an iceberg."[16]

Caught boarding a train for a Yale-Princeton football game in November of 1896, Sullivan told a scribbler for the *Washington Evening Times* that he'd rather be "condemned to live on the Eastern Shore and eat acorns for the rest of his natural life than to have to reside in 'deah Lundon.'"[17]

Come Christmas, after a little duck hunting in New England, Sullivan was off to Wisconsin to spend holidays with relatives.

Without a team to start, hype, manage, or abandon in 1897, the freshly rested baseball phantasm haunted ballparks and newsrooms from New Jersey to Nevada. In March, he appeared next to a reporter's desk at the *Baltimore Sun*.

Mexican Pipe Dream
Baltimore Sun
March 7, 1897

The witty, widely known Ted Sullivan, who has managed base ball teams from the Rio Grande to the Bay of Fundy, rolled into town yesterday and spent the afternoon at the Baltimore base ball office, on South Street. Mr. Sullivan came from Washington, and since he was in Baltimore last he has been swinging round the circle out west, spending a good deal of time in Wisconsin.

When asked if he would go back to the Texas league this year, he said that the San Antonio franchise had been offered him, but he hardly thought he would take it. He was asked what he intended doing the coming season and he replied with a characteristic gesture, embracing the whole country, that there were so many great opportunities he did not know which to accept. He declared that he would certainly see the Corbett-Fitzsimmons fight on St. Patrick's Day, and that he intended betting on "Pompadour Jim." Mr. Sullivan has a big project on hand, which he discussed with McGraw and Doyle, of taking the "Four Time Champions," as he expressed it, and another all-league team on a tour after the season of '97, taking in cities from Baltimore to San Francisco and returning via the City of Mexico, where the teams would play a week or more. "We shall have President Diaz at the games, of course, to give his sanction to the national game," said Mr. Sullivan.

In late August, Sullivan was in New York, arranging details of what the *Times of Washington* called another "gigantic scheme which his fertile brain has evolved."[18]

"It is not an opium dream," stated a confident *Cincinnati Enquirer*. "When Ted and his merry troupe of ball players invade the land of cactus, opals and bullfights, it will be an event of national importance."[19]

Before the "gigantic scheme" could be hatched, Sullivan fell off the wagon—literally. In November, an uncle was taking him to the railroad depot from a farm outside Milwaukee, when the horse pulling their buggy got spooked and tipped the contrivance over, injuring Sullivan's leg. The tour was postponed, indefinitely, so that the manager could take time to recover ... and go hunting for ducks.[20]

◆ 16 ◆

Dubuque, Part II

"After several years of 'knockabout' sports, he has returned to be our Moses."—*Dubuque Times,* February 24, 1898

Recovered from being banged up by the runaway carriage, Sullivan eased his way back into the business in early 1898 by agreeing to train and coach the ball team at Washington and Lee University, at least for a month or two—until spring training began for the pros.[1]

It appeared that the majors were not standing in line to hire him for that season, but he was still a hero to at least a few folks back in Iowa, where his fame in the game first took flight. In fact, a serious and most enthusiastic effort was made by the people of Dubuque to bring the miracle worker of 1878 and 1879 back to "The Key City" on the Mississippi.

"Dubuque has been frantically endeavoring to get Ted Sullivan to manage its team but the wily Ted cannot be located and Dubuque's hopes are going glimmering," noted the *Burlington (IA) Gazette* in late February of 1898.[2]

Dubuque's town fathers and their more upstanding citizens were disgusted with and embarrassed by the teams they had been fielding. It seems the previous managers and players had endeavored to put the local brewery out of business.[3] The town folks insisted it was "high time that the toughs should be eliminated from the game … their rowdy actions and obscene talk worked a material falling off of attendance. Some of the visiting players used language in the presence of ladies, for which they should have been brought before a magistrate. With Mr. Sullivan at the helm, it is assured there will be no more of it."[4]

In his back and forth negotiations with Dubuque's town fathers, Sullivan publicly expressed a sentimental connection to people of the old Mississippi River town. It was a tough decision, he said, as he would rather fail a million times elsewhere than one time in Dubuque.

Tired of fielding mediocre ball teams made up of "rowdy inebriates" who tried to drink the town dry, Dubuque in 1898 was ready for some disciplined management. The call went out to serious and sober Ted. Mulvihill's Tavern, ca. 1905 (author's collection).

"Ted is impulsive and big-hearted," wrote a thankful fan. "But what Irishman isn't?"[5]

When Sullivan did at last accept the town's offer, the news sent fans and the Chamber of Commerce into paroxysms of joy. A poem was written of prodigal Ted Sullivan's arrival in the company of a town booster named Joe.

SULLIVAN'S RIDE

Up from the east in the cold winter night,
Bringing to Josie's heart delight,
The train it rolled in with a rumble and roar,
Telling the bridge had been crossed o'er,
And Teddy was in old Dubuque once more.

By the flash of Joe's eyes and his gay, happy way,
He seemed to the fans there assembled to say,
I have brought you Sullivan all the way
From Washington City to save the day![6]

Dubuque's baseball-starved fans had visions of dominance dancing in their heads once again. The local paper was in Sullivan's lap, gushing that he was the dean of baseball men and a virtual native son—having dug pumpkins and picked oats in Hawkeyedom—who would surely field a top-notch nine of young, ambitious, and well-disciplined players.

Ted Sullivan had become something of a living legend since leaving Iowa behind more than a decade and a half earlier. As a special correspondent for *The Sporting News* put it: "Ted Sullivan's popularity does not come of base ball alone. It is strong personality and intellectual attainment that have made him famous throughout the United States."[7]

The people of Dubuque, especially, saw Sullivan through kaleidoscopic lenses—as not just a famous baseball genius, but as a writer, actor, comic, and sophisticated world traveler.

The local papers and *The Sporting News'* account said the Dubuquers were looking forward to thespian Ted presenting and starring in a sketch of his own composition entitled "Baron Goldstein, the Old Clothes Dealer," featuring conversations between a Jewish pawnbroker and an Irish shopkeeper. The opening act was to be "a cakewalk by local colored people."[8]

Bachelor-Manager-Thespian Sullivan even caught the eye of the fairer sex. One of the town's best-known ladies (the gossips wouldn't name names) was reportedly "dead gone" on him. In turn, the manager ordered "neat and nobby" new uniforms and promised Dubuque fans his squad would present "the prettiest appearance of any team in the association."

On deck for a spring exhibition game were the Unions, a popular "colored" team out of Chicago.

Ted Sullivan's Dubuque Tigers opened the season on Easter and lost a series of mediocre ball games, but by mid–May they were looking better. In reporting a win over the St. Joe (Missouri) Saints, the *Dubuque Herald*—still in Sullivan's thrall—said, "Ted Sullivan donned a uniform and coached. His tactics are good, and his work yesterday showed that he is cunning and well posted on the strategy board, using a good many signs instead of noises to rattle the pitcher. Ted's team is doing good work now, and with good weather and liberal patronage he will make a record that will surprise the most extreme enthusiasts."[9]

Stabbed in the Head

But the weather continued to be lousy, and Sullivan's luck turned even lousier, starting at midnight on May 28, in his office in Dubuque's Merchant Hotel, where he was stabbed in the side of the head by a local bicycle race promoter after an argument over the promoter's pilfering of Sullivan's ballpark's seat cushions.

"The baseball manager said he was stabbed, without warning, while sitting in a chair, unable to defend himself," reported the *Herald*. "Officer Riley responded to the bloody scene and escorted the cyclist to the hoose-gow. Why such an uncalled for assault as this should be made on a man as good-natured as Ted Sullivan is a mystery. He is known here among all of our citizens as a pleasant easy going man, who never had an altercation with anyone."[10]

Six stitches and Sullivan's good nature couldn't stop the whims of Mother Nature, either. Persistent cold and rainy days put a damper on attendance in Dubuque and throughout the Western Association. By the first of June, all the teams in the association were losing money. At an emergency meeting in Cedar Rapids, officials talked of disbanding in mid-season to stop the bleeding.

In fact, the Western Association did fall apart mid-season, and sentimental Ted Sullivan scooted out of town a few quick steps ahead of the team's creditors, leaving the townspeople and his players lost and confused, with the keys to an empty ballpark.

The local papers were sympathetic to Sullivan's plight—at least initially. "Sullivan has suddenly dropped into oblivion," the *Dubuque Daily Times* said on June 11. "We are thankful to Ted for giving us a good team. Thanks are due him for that much, at least."

The boys at the *Herald* agreed that the manager had kept his promise to furnish the town with sober, clean ball players. "The team is a good one," they wrote, "and should the season be played through, his team stands an excellent chance of winning. But Mr. Sullivan has sunk a large sum of money, and does not propose to continue in this way."[11]

But after stewing on the matter for a couple of weeks, the *Times* fumed: "If the members of the Dubuque club could put their hands on Ted Sullivan they would lead him to believe that they were tigers in earnest. They are very angry over the outrageous manner in which he has treated them. He lied to them almost all the time, and never paid a full month's salary. He is the most gigantic fraud in the baseball line that Dubuque has ever known."[12]

Baseball's phantasm was next spotted by the *Cincinnati Enquirer*, sitting in the bleachers in Chicago "among the old-timers who crawled out of their holes to see the Reds' series."[13]

Off to Conquer Cuba

The smoke from the Spanish-American War had barely cleared before it was announced in September of 1898 that Never-Sit-Still-Sullivan was now at work on a plan to invade Cuba and preach his baseball gospel to the game-starved natives there. "If Cuba is to be Americanized, one of the first things it needs is baseball," he told reporters. His plan was to take a team of National League players to the near-isle that winter and arrange exhibition games for the entertainment (and coin) of the 50,000 American troops stationed there. He claimed to have the blessing of General Fitzhugh Lee, the head of American military operations in Havana, a baseball fan he had met when managing the ball team in Richmond. With all those troops, reasoned Sullivan, "there should be plenty of protection for the umpire, and patrons for the gate."[14]

Baltimore's John J. McGraw agreed. "Muggsy," said the *Lincoln State Journal*, "[is] the latest one to have the Cuba bee buzzing in his sky-piece."[15] McGraw recalled being with an American team barnstorming through Cuba in the early 1890s, and his team losing every game but one. He thought Sullivan's idea was a good one, saying, "There is no doubt the Cubans enjoy the game and are hungry for it. I have seen crowds of 12,000 and more at a Sunday game in Havana."[16]

Added Sullivan: "The Cuban people love sport, and baseball, wherever it has been introduced and understood, is one of their favorite pastimes, and I honestly believe it will finally supersede that antique, barbarous and alleged sport, bull fighting."[17]

Back in Iowa, the men in the Chamber of Commerce and the keepers of the spittoons in the *Dubuque Daily Herald* newsroom were still smarting from Sullivan's hasty midsummer exit from their town. Following rumors of Charles Comiskey's involvement in "the Cuban scheme," the Dubuque sheet spit this editorial comment: "If Comiskey can fix it so Ted will catch the yellow fever and thus relieve the world of his offensive and crooked personality, Dubuquers will be satisfied."[18]

And the paper didn't let up. A few weeks later, it expressed pity for Cuban baseball fans who might cross paths with Sullivan and noted, "the fans of Dubuque wish him success. NOT."[19]

But little Ted Sullivan kept working his scheme, leasing the Almandores Park stadium in Havana and planning a parade in the Cuban capitol. He boasted that Major General Lee was going to toss the ball to the umpire to start the first game, that there would be more generals in attendance than seen in any one city since the Civil War, and that every American in town would be on hand for the occasion.

In January of 1899, a syndicated article reported that "The irrepressible Ted Sullivan, of baseball fame, known to the ball cranks in every state, has been here [Cuba] arranging to develop the national sport of America. Ted is the magnate of Havana." The games, it was reported, were scheduled to begin in two weeks.[20]

By February, though, Sullivan was back in the States, saying he had really been in Cuba scouting potential sites for winter and spring training facilities for unnamed American teams, but that he hadn't given up on his pet scheme to take some American professionals to Havana for a series of games against "native Cubans." He said the Cubans, having learned baseball from the American soldiers occupying the island since the Spanish American War, were getting pretty good at the game. "They have arms like iron, great speed and succeed in walloping every team American soldiers produce," he said. The native food, on the other hand, "would resist an attack of the Rough Riders."[21]

It would be another 12 years before America's baseball magnates truly discovered the wealth of talent on that little island barely 100 miles off the coast of Florida. Armando Marsans, signed by the Cincinnati Reds in 1911, became the first Cuban star of America's big leagues, to be followed, as we know, by a whole lot more.

Encounters with "The Demon Base Ball Gun"

Ted's tale describing the original pitching gun being unpredictable and dangerous made its way around the baseball world in 1904 (*Chicago Times-Herald*, 1897).

By the 1890s, baseball's "twirlers" were delivering a crazy new mix of pitches to ever-wilier hitters wielding wider bats. In addition to the old illegal standbys, like spitters and cutters, the men on the mound were bringing knuckleballs, curve balls, forkballs, changeups, and livelier fastballs. The exertion it required and the toll it took on a thrower's arm limited how many innings a pitcher could go, requiring managers to add more fresh arms to their rosters. Batters needed more practice to prepare themselves without wearing out their own pitchers. So along came the pitching machine.[22]

As early as 1897, Charles "Bull" Hinton, a

math professor at Princeton, was experimenting with a gunpowder-powered baseball pitching machine that could fling horsehides at variable speeds and even simulate a curve. The contraption, which he called "a base ball gun," was ingenious, but it could be noisy and frighteningly erratic.

Prior to the start of spring training in 1904, "The Old Fox," Clark Griffith, then manager of the New York Highlanders, learned that several colleges were planning on using pitching machines for the first time.

> That makes me smile, for the very mention of a pitching machine calls to mind the story Ted Sullivan tells of the one tried out at Yale[actually Princeton]. This machine, after sending in one ball straight—it was loaded with something like 144 charges—skewed around on its pedestal and began sending its freight at the professor who invented it and who happened to be standing by first base. The professor made tracks for the fence, but, running in a straight line had to take several thumps before reaching a place of safety."[23]

Griffith said he himself would have nothing to do with a "pitching gun."

> A fellow who had invented one brought it around to show me and set it up in a vacant lot. I put on a glove and started to catch a few just to see how the thing worked. The first ball came out four times faster than Rusie [Amos Rusie, "The Hoosier Thunderbolt" of the New York Giants] ever threw one in his palmy days. Nobody could have stopped the ball, let alone catch it. Right through my hands it ripped and "zing"against my chest. I dropped, the breath knocked clean out of me and as I was sitting up, "whoosh!" comes another, just grazing my hair. That was enough; I flopped down flat and rolled out of range. Never again for me.[24]

"Same Old Trick"

Southern Postscript, 1899

*"Ted Sullivan as the Montgomery people know is an Irish-
man, pure and simple, a Celt of purest ray, a Hibernian of
Hibernians. Ted gave great assistance to St. Patrick when
that good saint skiddooed his celebrated bunch of trained
snakes from the uttermost confines of the Emerald Isle. Ted
also discovered, invented and revised the stone of Blarney. Part of that stone—a big part and a greatly improved
one—he brought to Montgomery."*
—Montgomery Advertiser, March 1, 1906

After a five-year hiatus, Ted Sullivan returned to the Southern League
for the 1899 season. He might have hoped for a more successful curtain call.

It started the way it nearly always started: Famed baseball impresario
Ted Sullivan was coming to town, and league pennants were sure to follow.

From the middle of January through late February, partisans in Alabama and Texas launched competing campaigns to charm Sullivan to managerial openings in Montgomery and Houston. Sullivan excited the local
cranks in late January during a visit to Montgomery,[1] but a couple of weeks
later, reports surfaced that Sullivan had informed the president of the Texas
League that he would accept the Houston franchise and was on his way to
take over a roster of players.[2] Nevertheless, local columnists in Montgomery remained optimistic that Sullivan would return to the Southern League
and bring a championship to Alabama's capital city.

When Sullivan teamed up with John J. McCloskey and chose Montgomery, the *Montgomery Advertiser* hallelujahed, "If Montgomery don't
have the fastest ball team this summer that ever cavorted around a diamond all the signs of the zodiac are sadly at fault."[3]

Eight hundred and ninety-one-point-four miles to the north, in Iowa,
a cynical scribe, under the headline "SAME OLD TRICK," wrote, "Ted

"TWO STRIKES AND THE BASES FULL"

Illustration by Charles Dana Gibson, 1904.

Sullivan is still in the 'conning' business … he has caused himself to be lionized by the fans [in Montgomery] who sang his praises in the highest key."[4]

Sullivan's early "conning" indeed mesmerized local baseball fans. Looking back a few years later, the *Advertiser* would say, "To say he took the Capital City of Alabama by storm is putting it mildly. It was a whirlwind. After a few minutes talk with Ted the Montgomery fans were convinced that the game of baseball was in its incipiency and would remain in swaddling clothes until the Montgomery aggregation should startle the world with its flashes of brilliancy and teach the American people the art of baseball."[5]

Sullivan's blarney quickly proved hollow, and on April 24, more than 100 Texas baseball fans met at the city hall in Dallas to discuss his scheme to bring his only recently acquired Montgomery Senators team to that Texas community. Days later, a package of incentives was approved, and the franchise was on the move. On his way out of Alabama, Foxy Ted broke his silence—"so far he has made the Sphynx go to night school and learn her biz all over again"[6]—and managed to vilify himself even further by telling Montgomery fans the team's move was their fault. He justified his decision by complaining that only 11 season tickets had been sold in Montgomery and that attendance at games never covered expenses.[7]

Déjà vu—Sullivan was accused of fielding a cheap, lousy team unworthy of the fans' support.

"Then came the 'team,'" the *Advertiser's* retrospective went on to say,

And such a collection of dubs and frapped has-beens has never been gotten together before. The predominant feature of the aggregation was Charlie-horse in a most acute and advanced stage. The bunch looked like a hospital list and it was actually painful to see one of them getting on and off the street car. Such a thing as base running was of course a dead letter. One or two of them could hit the ball occasionally when there was no chance of getting out of the way, while as for throwing—say, that was the limit. A bunch of old maids playing ping-pong could have beaten them by several city blocks. Ted should have been arrested for obtaining money under false pretenses.[8]

Despite his wretched roster, Sullivan made no apologies for his priorities.

Organized baseball was "a commercial enterprise exclusively"[9] that should be played in the best-paying cities, Sullivan explained. And Dallas fit that bill, agreeing to purchase 1,000 grandstand tickets and handing over $500 to Sullivan as part of the relocation agreement. In a nice bit of blarney, Sullivan dismissed the notion that any monetary inducements were behind the move, saying that all he sought was "the friendship and patronage" of Dallas fans.[10]

But his old friends back in Alabama were still smarting from Sullivan-style benefaction.

He had reportedly stiffed the Western Railroad on the debt he owed for the ballpark grounds he had leased in Montgomery, and a local brewer was out several hundred dollars for donated stadium upgrades. Meanwhile, some angry fans had contacted attorneys to seek civil action against Sullivan.

The *Advertiser* jumped in on the controversy, saying, "It is hard to understand how a man with the reputation of Ted Sullivan bears in the baseball world can demolish that reputation in this way. The purchasers of season tickers here say that they will attach the gate receipts of all games that Sullivan's team takes part in until they get their money back."[11]

As the Dallas Steers—uncompetitive and already deep in the cellar of the four-team league—took the field for a May 22 game at Mobile, the police cuffed Ted Sullivan, placed him under arrest, and pitched him into a nearby jail cell. Entrepreneur Sullivan was charged with taking money under false pretenses from the Montgomery resident to whom Sullivan had sold the liquor concession for the entire 1899 season at Senators' home games.[12]

The president of the Mobile team posted Sullivan's bond, and upon his release, Sullivan pronounced his intention to head directly to Montgomery and clear up his legal issues. He then hopped on an afternoon train and got himself out of Alabama as quickly as he could. His incarceration and flight out of state spared him from having to watch his Dallas team's 18–7 loss, highlighted by their seven errors, in an exhibition described as "a disgrace to the national game."[13]

Less than a week later, Sir Ted Sullivan cashed out for the final time in the Southern League, selling his Dallas franchise to a local buyer and telling reporters, "I am through with the minor league game, and I am going on to New York to see the Jeffries-Fitzsimmons fight."[14]

On June 9, he was at Coney Island as a correspondent for *The Sporting News*, covering the historic, bloody mismatch between heavyweight boxers Bob Fitzsimmons (167 lbs.) and James Jefferies (206 lbs.). But then it was back to the bushes. In September, it was widely reported "the baseball promoter and agent of everybody" was quietly working (unsuccessfully, as it turned out) on behalf of Ned Hanlon to sign Baltimore's star third baseman, John McGraw, for the Reds for $10,000.[15]

And all the while the cagey impresario was working with Charles Comiskey and Al Spink on a scheme to create a brand new major league.

The next spring, as the nation's talk turned back to the national game, irrepressible Ted Sullivan, in cahoots with his old boss, W.H. Lucas, was sliding in and out of Minnesota and Wisconsin, making noise about starting a northwest minor baseball league. Then he was in Washington and Idaho, painting pictures of a new Utah-Montana League.

The *Spokane Daily Chronicle* was soon complaining that "Hustling" Ted Sullivan had hustled away from that city, leaving it in baseball limbo, saying, "he vanished in a hurry, and it is even hinted that he left behind him some souvenirs in the form of unreceipted bills."[16]

Baseball fans in Salt Lake weren't starting a Ted Sullivan fan club, either. "Sullivan sat around and twiddled his thumbs and expected the necessary money and the men and everything he wanted to come rolling along his way," grumped the *Salt Lake Herald*. "Since that time he has been enjoying himself saying there is positively no interest here, and that it is the deadest ball town that he ever struck."[17]

◆ 18 ◆

A Midwife
of the American League

"One day when time hung heavily on his hands, he looked at the clock and said, by George, he hadn't organized a league in five minutes. So, to make up for the lapse, he went out and gathered together some folks of his own good sort, and they set the American League in motion, and when Ted had done that he had done something, which nobody can deny."
—*Bluefield (WV) Daily Telegraph,* June 11, 1911

Accounts involving baseball's "queer genius" vary widely, of course, but it is generally assumed that Sir Ted Sullivan was, at the very least, a fly on the wall at the Republican House in Milwaukee when lawyer Henry Killilea drew up incorporation papers for a new American League.

Former sportswriter Byron Bancroft "Ban" Johnson and Charlie Comiskey had purchased teams in the minor Western League in the early 1890s and, by giving fans a decent (no obscenities or ungentlemanly behavior allowed) brand of baseball, had met with much success at the ticket gates. In 1899, the two emerging moguls turned their eyes to a bigger prize.

According to Al Spink, founder of *The Sporting News*, sometime in the summer of 1898, he and Sullivan discussed the poor practices and parsimonious ways of the established National League, planting a seed that would eventually sprout the enduring institution we call the American League. After making a list of cities they thought could support a new professional circuit, Sullivan and Spink invited a group that included Charlie Comiskey and Tom Loftus to meet in Chicago, in secret, at an "obscure hotel" in order "to avoid notoriety and the criticism of an unfriendly press."[1]

Spink claimed, "It was the first meeting ever held for the purpose of placing the American League in the field and as a result of the work of Mr. Sullivan and myself there was a fair attendance [which] gave us great hope for the future." Spink said he read letters from John McGraw of Baltimore and William Barney of Brooklyn, each promising to help place teams in those cities, should a new league be formed. And, again according to Spink, as a result of that meeting, Comiskey first mulled the idea of forming and placing a team in South Chicago—which he would indeed do two years later.[2]

Sullivan was apparently assigned the unsavory job of negotiating a pre-war treaty with the existing league's power brokers. Not to worry, he assured his fellow insurgents, "the brains of baseball are outside the bulwarks of the National League."[3]

Secret Conference

Chicago's *Inter Ocean* newspaper reported on July 1, 1899, that big (300 pounds) Ban Johnson, president of the Western League, had returned from an eastern trip and met Comiskey of St. Paul, Loftus of Columbus, and Killilea of Milwaukee by appointment at the Great Northern Hotel at another "secret conference."

The paper acknowledged that "The National League is in a bad way. The Western League is prosperous. The promoters have plenty of financial backing and a number of clever managers. As a result new and startling developments may be looked for any day."

By mid–July 1899, reporters were chasing Sullivan—who likely made himself easy to catch by showing up in their offices and taking a chair by the window fan—asking him about rumors of a new baseball association being organized for the purpose of opposing the National League. "There is only one Ted Sullivan, and if there are any new leagues in sight he is liable to get mixed up in them in some shape or other," was the conclusion of the *Watertown (NY) News*.[4]

The *Boston Globe* confirmed that Sullivan was "personally interested" and heavily involved in organizing the new league and that Cap Anson and Tom Loftus were expected to lead a new Chicago club. But the paper was skeptical, saying the would-be league was having a hard time getting to first base and declaring, "Ted Sullivan and Chris Von der Ahe must keep moving or the fans will think the whole thing is a fake sprung by Ban Johnson."[5]

Sullivan responded, "The new league is a certain go. Everyone in Chicago is talking about it."[6]

Although claiming he had nothing to do with the inner workings of the new league, Sullivan was clearly working public relations for Comiskey and Johnson.

As the 1899 season came to an end, papers around the country noted that "Sullivan has been acting for the new league magnates in the capacity of general missionary to see what direction the wind is blowing and incidentally to prepare the way for the organization."[7]

Posing as an unattached, casual observer with inside knowledge, Sullivan made sure he paid courtesy calls to newsrooms in cities being eyed by backers of the new league, including St. Louis.

THE NEW ASSOCIATION
Ted Sullivan Says There is Plenty of Room for It
St. Louis Post-Dispatch
August 4, 1899

Every day the new American Association is making new friends. Ted Sullivan, the little Irishman who put the champion St. Louis Browns together, is one of the latest to endorse the new movement. Sullivan has been in St. Louis and Chicago recently, where he has heard the players say a lot about the new league.

"The boys who are now on the pay rolls of the big league teams," said Sullivan, "all appear to think I have something to do with this proposed organization, and they have been rubbing up against me, looking for a chance to play in the new league. I really know nothing about it, other than what I have read, and it may be a phantom and it may be a reality."

The Evil Magnates

Ever-thinking, Ted Sullivan fed the press's growing contempt for the National League's smug, controlling, and parsimonious moguls. "These men who seem to have an idea that a Divine Providence ordained them as guardians of the national game, are on the wrong track," he was often quoted as saying. "This syndicate business in baseball might go in the land of the Czar, but not in this free country. The major league magnates can take a few lessons by watching the workings of this league."[8]

Knowing that Sir Ted had a penchant for blowing smoke, some thought he was acting as a double agent. On August 5, the *Indianapolis News* said: "Ted Sullivan, the baseball impresario, was in the city yesterday, as he said, in the interest of the proposed new league. But those who know the wily Ted think he is acting as the agent of some National League club, and is here looking over material in the Indianapolis and Grand Rapids teams."

Whereas Sullivan wasn't acting as a double agent—*yet*—it's likely he was looking to get in on the action by counseling and partnering with would-be investors in cities like St. Louis, Cincinnati, Detroit, and Washington who might support a franchise in a new American League.

"I also have a quiet tip," he told the *Pittsburgh Press* on Aug. 11, "that

William C. Whitney, Rockefeller, Carnegie, Havemeyer and one or two others are behind the scheme."

In mid–August of 1899, syndicated news articles reported more and more rumors of a new, potential major league forming. "An informant" and "most authentic source" had verified that the first official meeting of this new organization was to take place September in Chicago. That informant was, very likely, you-know-who.[9]

Cock-a-doddle-do!

On Saturday, September 16, the organizers reported present—Cap Anson (Chicago), Tom Loftus, Connie Mack, George Schaefer and Chris Von de Ahe (St. Louis), Al Spink (*The Sporting News*), Frank Hough (*Philadelphia Enquirer*), M. B. Scanlon (Washington), Frank Buckley (New York), C. S. Havenor and H. D. Quinn (Milwaukee)—sat down in a private chamber at the Hotel Norwood in Chicago for a Last Supper of sorts. A cock must have been crowing nearby.

Ban Johnson was telling reporters he would not meet with promoters of the by now not-so-secret American League. And "Honest John" Comiskey's son denied having anything to do with the new league, either.

If the two of them were not at a meeting of the American League promoters on that following Sunday, September 17, one Ted Sullivan certainly was there, at least long enough to be counted present. A reporter who was present wondered why "Ted Sullivan spent 15 or more minutes in the counsel chambers, which was fragrant with the fumes of good tobacco and eloquent with the chatter of 'wise men,' but then suddenly disappeared."[10]

The baseball press was of two minds whether the new league would succeed. In a report that ran September 18, the *Chicago Tribune* said, "The new league, which is to put clubs in the field, break the power of the trust, and break the national agreement, was fairly launched, and all that it needs now is money." Two paragraphs later, it opined, "it looks like the new league will 'die abornin.'"

Various predictions that the new league would surely be a winner drew only laughs from the cigar-smoking magnates of the National League. James J. Corbett, the famed pugilist turned sportswriter, wrote in his syndicated column, "Corbett's Corner," that the audacity of the announced new league was "greeted by ridicule and sneers from practically all of the baseball experts of that time, who figured that the American, if it ever did actually open gates, wouldn't last two full seasons."[11]

"Local baseball people don't take the formation of the new baseball league seriously," yawned the *Brooklyn Daily Eagle*.[12] The unfazed manager of the Brooklyn Superbas, Ned Hanlon, gave the new league no chance, saying, "They have as much show as I have of jumping over the Eagle Building."[13]

A month later, in October, the Western League leaders—Comiskey, Connie Mack, James Manning, Ban Johnson, and Tom Loftus among them—came together again at the Great Northern Hotel in Chicago and changed the name of their organization to the American Baseball League. Comiskey formally announced his intention to locate a rival team in Chicago, while his trusty backstop worked the press: "Ted Sullivan figures that Chicago, with its 2,000,000 people, can support two baseball teams. She now supports ten theatres," reasoned one Ohio editor.[14]

With attendance down and their attendant stacks of gold diminished after the 1899 season, the NL's cigar smokers finally stubbed out their stogies and took notice.

Where's Sullivan?

An irritable James Hart, president of the NL's Chicago Orphans franchise, refused even to talk to reporters about the new league, prompting the *Chicago Tribune* to gibe: "He will retire to his den and hibernate, and from his windows watch the sea waves and scan the Michigan City shores with a telescope to see if Ted Sullivan is hunting players in that direction."[15]

Public support for Ban Johnson and his brand of cleaner, more pocket-friendly baseball grew as plans began to emerge for the upstart American League to enter play in 1900. "To have a war on the question of territory would be deplorable," Sullivan was quoted as saying, "yet it would hurt the National League ten times more than the American. This Monroe Doctrine in base ball should not be operated against the citizens of this country, but it seems that only the strong can stand this luxury, but as expansion is the craze the American League should be one exception."[16]

On March 5, 1900, the Milwaukee lawyer, Henry Killilea, drew up articles of incorporation for the "American League Base Ball Club of Chicago." That same day, papers reported that "Ted Sullivan will likely look after the Chicago team in the American League."[17]

The war was officially on.

And the timing was perfect. Hurting financially, the old league was getting ready to reduce its number of cities and teams from 12 to eight, leaving a good number of decent and great players looking for better-paying jobs.

A not-so-easy-to-find plaque on the site of the old Republican House Hotel in Milwaukee commemorates the founding of the American League:

Birthplace of the American League

The Republican House was the birthplace of baseball's American League. On the night of March 5, 1900, Milwaukee attorney Henry Killilea, his brother Matt, Connie Mack, Byron (Ban) Johnson, and Charles Comiskey gathered in room 185. In defiance of the existing national league, Comiskey's Chicago White Stockings (later Sox) were incorporated, and the league's eight team alignment was completed. After the 1900 season, the league reorganized, placed teams in Baltimore, Boston, Philadelphia, and Washington, D.C., and achieved major league status.

With the help of their fast-footed, flannel-mouthed scout, Johnson and Comiskey were able to scoop up dozens of reputable players for the new league, which, as part of a reluctantly offered concession with the senior organization, had agreed to enter play in 1900 at the minor level.

Although they went through the 1900 season categorized as "minor" players, the new league's recruits played some pretty competitive ball, the teams being the Chicago White Stockings, with Comiskey in the manager's box; the Milwaukee Brewers, under the management of Connie Mack; the Indianapolis Hoosiers; the Detroit Tigers; the Kansas City Blues; the Minneapolis Millers; the Cleveland Lake Shores; and the Buffalo Bisons, managed by Walt Wilmot. Comiskey's newly sewn White Stockings took the minor crown in ought-ought. Feeling guilty for leaving St. Paul high and baseball dry, the emerging magnate Comiskey dispatched his handyman Sullivan to organize a new minor league to accommodate the fans there.

Once the new league's season was under way, Ted Sullivan was on his way to Colorado. The papers reported in early April that Sullivan's "shrewd Irish phiz" had been spotted in Denver and that "he has a bug in his hat which is urging him to put a professional team in Colorado Springs ... and is using his oleaginous tongue in an effort to interest some of the Springs capitalists in his scheme."[18]

Before the ink was dry on that story, baseball's nomad had slipped into St. Joseph, Missouri, and quietly snatched up catcher Johnny Kling for his client-of-the-moment, the Chicago Orphans/Cubs of the National League. Kling, of course, would go on to earn a reputation as one of the greatest catchers ever to wear a mask.

In August, the ecumenical mercenary was spotted attempting to "weave a baseball romance" around James D. Burns and George Stallings, the new owners of the American League Tigers.[19] As one report had it: "Ted Sullivan dropped by Charlie Bennett's cigar store in Detroit and after buying a nickel's worth of stogies the two veterans decided to put a National League Club in that pretty town for 1901."[20]

Experienced sports writers like those at the *Detroit Free Press* smelled smoke: "Ted Sullivan, good fellow that he is, and well-known to all baseball men in the country, is used as a tool. Ted was represented as coming here in the interest of the major organization for the express purpose of offering Burns and Stallings a franchise in the National League, [when] the fact of the matter is that his solo mission was to look up promising young players" for the upstart new league.[21]

"The National League magnates were crawling through transoms, hiding behind garbage barrels and holding gum-shoe sessions at Cleveland and other [baseball] cemeteries," the *Buffalo Times* observed, "to prevent other philanthropists from engaging in a sport simply to amuse the public."[22]

After a series of contentious meetings with team owners in Chicago, an impatient and frustrated Sullivan declared: "These gatherings of magnates are so full of warm vapor, I thought I was in a Turkish bath. But I swam to land and now want to say that they are all good fellows and that they have forgotten but one thing—how to please the crowds which pay the half dollars at the gate."[23]

Acknowledging that most sporting writers on the National League circuit didn't believe Ban Johnson and company would go so far as to inflate the status of the American League in 1901, one scribe warned, "They may be forced to change their tune very shortly."[24]

In January 1901 the white flag went back into Ban Johnson's pocket, and the American League officially declared itself a major, ready to challenge the old monopoly for the benefit of players and fans.

IS IT A STAMPEDE? was the headline in the March 2, 1901, edition of the *Philadelphia Enquirer*, which reported that the "lusty young" American League—with no salary caps—was snatching marquee players like Cy Young, Willie Keeler, Joe "Iron Man" McGinnity, and Clark Griffith away from the NL. In short order, more than 100 known National League players had "kangarooed" to Johnson's new circuit.

The Panic of '01

Ban Johnson's policy of not divulging the names of the players he had signed had the effect of creating panic among, as one paper called them, "the very tiresome magnates of the older organization."[25]

"The magnates of the old league blundered badly," the *Cincinnati Enquirer* of May 19, 1901, concurred. "They regarded the declaration of independence by the American League as a bluff and counted on Ban Johnson and his associates suing for forgiveness and returning to the national agreement fold."

Like politicians facing a tough re-election campaign, the old guard of the NL hired a new consultant, one with inside knowledge of the other side: Timothy Paul, a.k.a. "Hustling Ted" Sullivan. The silver-tongued scout the *Washington Post* called "the best Irishman of all" was employed by the senior league to help snatch players back.[26]

"I am for the National League myself," Sullivan admitted, "and have sided with the big show. But I must admit that the American League has made the National look like 30 cents."[27]

Ironically, Ban Johnson sweet-talked John J. McGraw into becoming manager and part-owner of his "new" Baltimore Orioles franchise, and made McGraw (of all people) chairman of the new league's rules committee, charging him with making the game cleaner, faster, fairer, and more family-friendly.

One of the most significant rule changes made by McGraw and his committee was one that Ted Sullivan had advocated for years: Allowing a designated hitter to bat for the pitcher because, as, Sullivan always said, "twirlers are a lot of whippoorwill swingers."

The *Buffalo Courier* proclaimed, "Ted Sullivan is a queer genius."[28]

"Nobody wants to see the pitcher at bat," explained Sullivan. "They go to the plate, make a bluff at the ball, and sit down. Nobody expects a pitcher to do anything, and it is seldom that one of them gives a surprise party."[29]

As for cleaning up the boozing by players and fans, McGraw, of the vile temper and preacher-melting vocabulary, joked to a reporter that he was thinking about starting a theatrical company and engaging Carrie Nation as the leading lady in a tour of the classic temperance play, "Ten Nights in a Bar-Room."[30]

Sporting writers and fans alike embraced the new league from the get-go. At Baltimore's first AL contest of 1901, posters and banners hanging from the girders read: FAREWELL, NATIONAL LEAGUE SYNDICATE BASE-BALL AND MERCENARY METHODS *and* WELCOME, AMERICAN LEAGUE, HONEST BALL, AND SPORTSMANLIKE METHODS.

Along with the Baltimore franchise (Orioles), the new "big league" fielded teams in Boston (Americans), Cleveland (Blues), Washington (Senators), Detroit (Tigers), Philadelphia (Athletics), Milwaukee (Brewers), and Chicago. Among the fans in the stands was Ted Sullivan, the newly minted "general agent of the National League," eating peanuts and waving invisible contracts at the new league's best players.

"He [Te]) is wearing no masks, no green whiskers, no gum shoes," the *Washington Post* acknowledged on August 18, after Sullivan was spotted at the park in D.C., "and he is not carrying a dark lantern. He makes a clean breast of his mission here."[31]

"I have been employed by the National League to visit the American League and minor leagues of the country to watch the work of ball players,"

Sullivan conceded. "Now, just because I am in this business it must not be inferred that every time I drink a bottle of pop with a player I am buzzing a $10,000 offer for next season in his ear ... and trying to get a stranglehold on him for the National League."[32]

Having nearly scraped clean the NL's rosters of star players, and promising and (for the most part) delivering civilized, highly competitive baseball, the AL outdrew its older rival in each of the three cities in which both leagues fielded a team in 1901. The new league was clearly not going to do "the Old Ted Sullivan" any time soon.

"The American League's history shows that, at least, in baseball, brains can beat money," boasted everybody's friend and pinch-picket, Ted Sullivan. "There was some fellowship and reciprocity of feeling in the whole combination. It is demonstrated that the American League got their present standing by energy, pluck and perseverance."[33]

As soon as the first real competitive two-league baseball season was over, Sullivan was in Chicago with his still-friend Charlie Comiskey at an inaugural meeting of the Association Foot Ball League, with a scheme to start another professional soccer circuit. Sullivan claimed a franchise in Milwaukee and Comiskey one in Chicago. That second attempt at soccer also missed its goal, ran out of money, and did "the old Ted Sullivan" about halfway through the season, taking chunks of Sullivan's and Comiskey's wallets with it.

Where exactly the celebrated hustler hustled to next was unknown. A blurb in the eastern sports columns read: "Ban Johnson and Charles Comiskey have gone to Indian territory, ostensibly to hunt bear and deer. Privately we learn they are leading an expedition in search of Ted Sullivan."[34]

"Ball Spielen!"

From somewhere in the hinterlands in January of 1902, have-typewriter-will-travel sent his newspaper pals across the country the outline of his latest vision: to form a couple of all-star teams, one German, one Irish, to play for the championship of the world. "The teams I selected would draw a large crowd," Sullivan promised, "as the games would undoubtedly be exciting and a novelty. There would be no hippodromes, either, as that class of men would be too patriotic and dignified to be parties to such a scheme."[35]

"Someday," he added, "other ethnic groups in America might be invited to play in similar competition," including "that sport-loving people, the Hebrews, who are today the staunchest supporters of the national game," the Italians, "who have already shown their castor in the prize ring," and even "the colored race, which has been represented by excellent men, namely Walker, Stovey and Grant."[36]

He thought the Poles would be there—once they got over their disappointment with Charlie Comiskey.

"To their horror and chagrin," laughed Sullivan, "I told them Charlie's father was one of those educated and refined Irishmen from County Cavan. Poor fellows, they left with a heavy heart to think their idol belonged to the Irish race."[37]

◆ 19 ◆

The Prodigal
Hustler Returns

In his time, it was said that whenever Ted Sullivan needed money, he found his way to Texas.[1] In fact, the Irish rover was no stranger there. Whether scouting players, evaluating markets, establishing franchises, organizing leagues, or setting up spring training sites, Ted Sullivan knew his way around the Lone Star State. And if his activities ended up padding his pocketbook, well, Foxy Ted was never opposed to turning a dollar.

The first version of the Texas League was organized in 1888, and for the next 14 years it was defined by instability. Some years there were organized leagues; other seasons were dark. Teams folded, teams moved, cities proved supportive, and cities were deemed unviable. Sullivan himself had enjoyed on-field success with his 1895 Dallas nine before his return in 1902.

It was that return that led to Sullivan being called the father of the Texas League. He identified the cities, assembled the necessary financial support, worked with railroads, built a schedule, and generally did everything needed to launch a league. As it turned out, his 1902 efforts ultimately weren't measured by profits or final standings, but rather by what came in their wake. With the exception of a three-year hiatus during World War II, the Texas League hasn't missed a season since being resurrected by Ted Sullivan in 1902.

On the field, the story of the 1902 season was the Corsicana Oil City team's domination of the Texas League. But the team that posted a 27-game winning streak and won both halves of the split season wasn't even on the pre-season list of franchises.

Sullivan arrived in Texas in the autumn of 1901 and quickly set about organizing a league. Ten cities were represented at the preliminary meeting, and Sullivan was appointed as "a committee of one" and charged with visiting cities and evaluating their viability. Experience taught him to emphasize a compact league with favorable transportation rates, and the final

149

choice of cities—Corsicana, Dallas, Fort Worth, Paris, Sherman-Denison and Waco—fit that bill. The longest jump in the schedule would be just the 101 miles between Dallas and Paris.[2] Corsicana was a late addition to the league, and when Sullivan reportedly asked, "Where the devil is Corsicana?"[3] he had no idea how emphatic the answer would be.

J. Doak Roberts' Corsicana club rocketed out of the gate and went on to put together one of baseball's legendary seasons. The team won the first-half title with an eye-popping 58–9 (.866) record, a stretch that included a 27-game winning streak from June 8 through July 5. The streak was highlighted by a cartoonish 51–3 burial of the Texarkana Casketmakers. Because Sunday baseball was outlawed in Corsicana, the game was played at the compact Ennis grounds, and the hits just kept on coming.[4] Of the 53 hits the Oil Citys pounded out, 21 were home runs. Catcher Jay Justin Clarke went 8-for-8 at the plate, each of those hits a homer. Within a month of that game, the Texarkana and Waco clubs disbanded, and league officials started the second season on July 9.

Corsicana continued to run roughshod over the Texas League, winning the second leg with a 30–14 record, negating the need for a playoff series. Apart from the domination by the Oil Citys (they particularly feasted on the Paris Homeseekers, beating them 24 times in 27 games), the 1902 Texas League had its share of typical minor league hiccups and oddities.

Franchise stability was a factor early in the season with the Sherman-Denison Students moving to Texarkana on May 8 following a miserable 1–10 start marked by meager fan support. Charles Eisenfelder, the undercapitalized owner of the Paris Eisenfelder's Homeseekers franchise, hit upon a novel answer to staunch his failing franchise's red ink. When league officials rejected his plan to relocate to Houston, Eisenfelder decided he was done playing home games in front of small crowds of Parisians. Instead of paying out $50 guarantees to visiting clubs, Eisenfelder took his team on the road for the second half, pocketing that precious $50 guarantee for 41 of their final 56 games.[5] Despite a bit of shuffling, the 1902 Texas League season was a success, with four franchises finishing a full season. Even though Sullivan's Fort Worth Panthers finished below .500, there was no question that Sullivan and his league would be back in 1903.

> *"Ted is the supreme mogul of this baseball order."*
> —Grantland Rice, *Atlanta Journal* sporting editor[6]

At a meeting held in late September, the decision was made to add four franchises to the four that had completed the 1902 season. To that end, Sullivan headed south to investigate the prospects in Houston, Galveston,

Beaumont, Waco, Austin, and San Antonio.[7] Sullivan quickly gave the nod to Houston and San Antonio, and just as quickly he was awarded the Houston franchise, with his former Fort Worth franchise offered to local citizens.[8] October and November were marked by rounds of gamesmanship between franchise owners, wannabe owners, and local interest groups. Houston was deemed "a good ball town" by most parties and was the object of much of the jockeying. News that Sullivan had been awarded the Houston club was met with hostility in that city, where he remained unpopular since his attempted franchise grab in 1895. Concurrently, the owner of the Southern League's Shreveport franchise coveted the valuable Houston market with an eye toward incorporating it into the South, perhaps with the addition of the Galveston and Beaumont franchises. Eisenfelder's plan to swap Paris for Houston was rebuffed by his peers, while a local group of Houstonians made a play for the home market.

But when Beaumont and Galveston proved unable and uninterested, the cost of the jump to only two Southern cities sealed the fates of Houston and San Antonio. Those four cities would compete in a separate South Texas League in 1903.[9] Despite earlier ambitions of an eight-team Texas League for 1903, a four-team circuit was close to complete in January. In what was believed to be a final organizational meeting during the first week of January, franchises in Corsicana, Dallas, Fort Worth, and Waco appeared to be locked in. Would-be owners from Paris, Texas, and Shawnee and Oklahoma City, Oklahoma, were anxious to join the league, but were turned away. In the final week of January, however, Sullivan indicated that his arrangements with Waco had turned sour, and he said he was likely to take his team to Paris. Sportswriters were bullish on the prospects for Texas baseball, with the sole exception being the viability of Sullivan's Paris franchise.

The sportswriters were both wrong and right. In terms of on-field success, the Paris Parasites were a juggernaut. At the box office, however, revenues never met expenses.

It wasn't as if Sullivan didn't offer up an entertaining and competitive team. The team led the standings by four games on May 1, and the Paris Parasites took the first season title with a 32–20 record, eight games ahead of second-place Dallas. They also made news in national publications with a nine-homer outburst in a win over Corsicana.[10] Along the way, Sullivan maintained his reputation as a manager of kickers and complainers who focused more on his bank balance than league standings.

As the chirpy Irish manager began to wear out his welcome in Paris, his relationship with local writers became so frayed that he was still being bashed by the local newspaper 48 years after leaving town. In a 1951 column, the *Paris News* editor, A.W. Neville, recalled his days as a beat writer covering the Parasites, and still harbored a disdain for "Irishman Ted Sullivan, already old and cranky, who acted as if he was doing Paris a favor by managing a club here."[11] Sullivan's days of doing favors for anyone in Paris came to an end in June. Sullivan and Doak Roberts, the Corsicana manager, arranged to play their June 12–14 series in Waco, and the considerable fan support—coupled with significant transportation savings—convinced Sullivan and other league officials to relocate the Paris team at the conclusion of the first season.[12] The move to Waco may have brought Hustling Ted more fan support and greater gate receipts, but the team plummeted in the standings, going from first to worst in the second season. The newly christened Waco Tigers finished 1903's second leg with a 20–36 record, trailing the winning Dallas team by 16 games. Their first-season title put them in the championship series against Dallas, and the Giants took the pennant fairly easily.[13]

After completing a second consecutive full season, Texas League fans and officials were optimistic about the 1904 season. Ted Sullivan presided over a January 17 organizational meeting in Dallas, where franchise owners considered membership applications from Paris, Sherman, Ardmore, and South McAlester.[14] By then, however, Sullivan had sold his best and marketable players to teams in other leagues. He took that cash, packed up, and headed out, leaving behind him the foundation of what would become a solid and storied minor league.

Borderline Drunk

By the conclusion of the 1904 season, old Ted Sullivan was a worldly figure who had created several teams and leagues, had played with and managed future Hall of Famers, had written for numerous publications, and had traveled broadly across Europe.

But according to published accounts—including an item in the April 23, 1905, edition of the *Salt Lake Tribune*—for at least one afternoon, he was no match for a nasty combination of mescal, hubris, and a rigged street game.

Sullivan had visited El Paso with an eye toward creating a Texas League franchise in that town. He abandoned his effort when the T&P Railroad refused to cut him a deal on transit to away games. Before he left town, however, a group of locals asked if he was interested in joining them for a Sunday afternoon trip across the border for a bullfight. Sullivan jumped at the offer.

Following "a couple of tastes of the famous third rail El Paso brand," the group stumbled onto a streetcar and crossed the river into Mexico. They arrived at the bullring early, and the normally puritanical Sullivan passed up a variety of gambling options in favor of another crack at the local liquor. Then, as his (bad/dumb) Irish luck would have it, he spied a gaming temptation he couldn't pass up.

For 25 cents, a player would throw a baseball at a contraption that was marked by holes, trapdoors, nails, and other impediments. In the unlikely event that the baseball fell to the bottom of the device, the game paid 5-to-1. Sullivan put down his quarter, threw a baseball into the sketchy device, and came away a winner. But he was no match for the lure of easy money and the game's sly operator.

"Now, the promoters of this hoary swindle might as well have made it 50-to-1," the account goes. "The game was old when Noah was in the National League and a man as wise as Ted Sullivan should have known it. But the third-rate mescal was getting in its work, and his view of life was rosy enough to warrant any 5-to-1 shot. Besides, anything with a baseball in it looked good to him."

When Sullivan was asked about a wagering limit, he was told, "The blue sky was the only barrier." So he threw down $25, which he promptly lost with his second toss. When an observer and suspected compatriot put down $10 and received $50 after the ball reached bottom, Sullivan's hazy judgment gave way to his greed and pride. Sullivan wagered his entire roll, threw the ball into the device and watched his $50 disappear. After quickly realizing he had been conned, Sullivan reportedly "then went away into a corner and turned himself inside out."

Without the $1 admission fee for the bullfight, or even money to ride the streetcar back to El Paso, Sullivan was then seen weaving his way on foot back across the bridge to the United States. According to the *Tribune's* account, he fled El Paso at his first opportunity:

> The next morning Mr. Sullivan was astir at 4 in the morning, catching the first train out of El Paso. He has never been there since, and if you ask him about Mexican games of chance he will go to the floor with you. But he will not deny that this story is the truth.[15]

"To this day," wrote the *San Francisco Examiner* columnist "Van," "the mention of bull fighting will start another kind of fight with Ted Sullivan."[16]

◆ 20 ◆

"The Original
Gumshoe Man"

Beating the Bushes for Prospects

"In a few games I can tell if a player has the fiber in him or not. Your Uncle Ted can pretty nearly tell a player in the dark. I've taken many a rough diamond to the lapidaries."
—Ted Sullivan[1]

Travelers riding trains pretty much anywhere in America between 1890 and 1926 were likely to spy a portly little man in a dapper derby, sitting alone, perusing *Sporting Life* or *The Sporting News*, on his way to who-knows-where.

In describing Ted Sullivan's travel habits, *Sporting Life* said: "Like the Kilkenny feline, old Ted has more than a single life and he has bobbed up as serenely as any jack-in-the-box ever shot forth when the cover was raised."[2]

Sullivan was a ubiquitous rider of the rails, traveling to small towns, burgs and backwaters across America looking for—and often finding—ball-playing diamonds in the rough. In the early days, he pretty much had the scouting game to himself. His office was a railroad smoking car, where he spent endless hours scanning letters from prospects and game reports from local newspapers, and penning press releases, opinion pieces, books, and plays.

A typical opening paragraph in a baseball town newspaper went something like this one that ran in *the Cincinnati Enquirer* in the fall of 1891: "The first to appear on the scene was Ted Sullivan, the dark-lantern, gum-shoe hustler from the western banks of the Mississippi."[3]

Unmarried and generally unattached, for the better part of 50 years Sullivan made his real home on the road. The former player, scout, and league-starter turned sportswriter Tim Murnane once asked in his popular column: "Who in the south or far west has not heard of this baseball

154

Bohemian? For Mr. Sullivan, like his favorite poet 'would rather live in Bohemia than any other land.'"[4]

The heralded player-hunter, or "pinch picket," as some called him, slipped into towns anonymously, looking like a hardware drummer or farmer come to market. "'T. Sullivan, Cincinnati, Ohio,' scrawled across the register of the Charles Hotel, to the ordinary individual who scans the pages means nothing," observed a reporter for the *St. Joseph (MO) Gazette* in the late summer of 1905.

> When Ted Sullivan calls for his key at the desk and a bellhop directs him to his apartment, the average commercial man would wager ten to one that this T. Sullivan owned a half section and yesterday marketed two cars of tops on the St. Joseph Exchange.
>
> Of rather heavy build, his rosy features and sharp, penetrating eyes command immediately the attention of those with whom he comes in contact. A light brown, medium weight suit is usually worn by Mr. Sullivan. A plain brown straw hat covers the florid, jovial features of this artist of baseball. That close scrutiny, backed by years of experience, gives to Ted Sullivan the power to instantly determine the value of a piece of base ball machinery.[5]

Sullivan himself said, "Personal observation is the only proper test of a player's worth" because "baseball is a queer game. The freaks of fortune are sometimes so queer that one year the jackdaws may look speedier than the homing pigeons in the dope, but they don't last."[6]

> *"Ted Sullivan is the greatest spotter of coming players in the country.... He is a regular Christopher Columbus when it comes to discovering new things in the baseball world."*
> —*Des Moines Register,* July 2, 1905

Beginning with his talented young Rabbits in Dubuque in 1878, always-on-the-move Ted Sullivan was recognized as an accomplished spotter of youthful potential. Recognizing that "a good scout is a pearl beyond price," *The Sporting News* said, "his abilities as a baseball hustler and judge of a player's merits are well known throughout the country" and that he had "signed more good men ... than any other man we know of, and in choosing players he very seldom makes a mistake."[7]

Sporting Life credited the million-mile rail passenger with putting into successful operation baseball's first scouting system and discovering many of the game's greatest stars. In 1907, the *Washington Post* anointed him "the Sherlock Holmes of the diamond."[8]

Under the headline "Quest for Gold Detracts from the Interest in Athletic Events," the *Chicago Daily Tribune* "Special Correspondent" Ted Sullivan, who was sniffing out prospects along the Pacific coast in 1901, expressed concern that many of America's aspiring athletes were trading their bats for shovels and picks and following get-rich-quick rumors to the wilds of the Alaska territory.[9]

> *"Let it be understood right here, that Mr. Sullivan is a Big League scout, one of those gentlemen whose presence at a ball game immediately sends the players into an agony of suspense as to whether he will notice their work. By one word he can send them to the Major Leagues, the aim of every ball player with ambition."*
> —*The Edmonton (Canada) Journal,* August 3, 1911

Making Kids Nervous

When Ted Sullivan was spotted in the bleachers at Topeka, Toledo or Timbuktu, young players grew nervous and excited. Opportunity had come to call in the form of the best-known talent scout in baseball.

"Now, what do you think Ted Sullivan, one of the God-fathers of baseball, is scouting around Muskogee for?" asked the *Muskogee (OK) Times Democrat* upon the legendary scout appearing in the stands in October of 1911. "Ted, or Sir T.P. Sullivan, as some thousands of persons know him, has been here for some days. He didn't come to see the fair."[10]

Anticipating a visit from the noted scout, the *Pittsburgh Press* said, "Scouts of balldom are ever on the lookout for talent. Ted Sullivan hasn't been heard from recently, but he will turn up before long with a car load of youngsters."[11]

The pioneering scout was not all that easy to impress. He relied on hot tips, news reports, and the smoke of rumors to find his future stars, but was always skeptical.

Sullivan was known to put the sign of "DEAD RABBIT" on many ambitious youngsters who looked good in their home cities but would never make good in the major leagues. He would pull aside players discombobulated by stage fright and say: "My brother, hike back home. You will never be a ball player. You might be a success as a tombstone in a graveyard, but you'll never do on the diamond."[12]

Sullivan liked to say the clearest test of a major league prospect was "headwork," and he recalled working with ballplayers "so obtuse were their brains that you could not take a Winchester rifle and shoot an up-to-date, bright baseball idea through their heads."[13]

Many modern (early 1900s) players, he said, "have good whips, and are fast on the bases, but as a rule have ivory heads." He once joked that smart managers should tie strings to the legs of their ivory-headed fielders and tug left or right to tell them which way the batter was likely to hit.[14]

His advice to young players thinking of making baseball their profession was: "Cast aside any false idea of the game, take up the idea when entering professional baseball, as when you first entered school, to know you have a pile to learn."[15]

Upon shipping his chosen ones up to "The Show" (another term he is often credited with coining), the patriarch of the game would leave them with the following bit of advice: "Good hours and sobriety will enable you to remain long in your profession and enhance your reputation among major league managers."[16]

A syndicated article picked up by dozens of papers across the country in the winter of 1913, declared: "Ted has picked up ball players from almost every state in the union. He has found them in Oshkosh and he has weaned them away from the grandeur of Medicine Hat, Neb. Where ever the game is known in this country, Ted has been looking around for talent in the rough. Baseball men generally will give the distinction of being the first scout to Ted Sullivan."[17]

The Washington Post jokingly blamed him for plunging New England "into deepest mourning by declaring there are no good players there."[18]

Lazy and overworked sports writers loved to see Sullivan coming through the newsroom door. They knew he'd have some good stories to tell, which would help fill up the pages of their broadsheets come deadline time. But a few sports sleuths refused to swallow the wily scout's blarney. "Ted Sullivan, the baseball impresario … has been selling gold bricks to unsuspecting managers," spat the *Cincinnati Commercial-Tribune*.[19]

The *Des Moines Register* acknowledged him as "the greatest of all scouts," but called him "a total farce in all other departments of baseball."[20]

On Village Heroes

"In every village or city in the country," Sullivan wrote,

You will hear the fans say: "I know of a great player of so-so city, but you can't get him. His folks will not allow him to play professional baseball," or "he is rich, he don't have to." (The fact is) He don't have to, because he knows down in his heart that he has not the speed or nerve to take the chance. If he thought he had the ability to earn $300 on the ball-field, with the luxuries of fine hotels and sights of the best parts of the United States, he would butt his head through a brick wall to get there and leave his $25 a month job.[21]

I know what it is like to be taking those open lot stars from the ranks of amateur clubs of large cities, who are touted by the newspapers to be "so and so."

So they are "so and so" once a week in a Sunday game at home, but when they enter the real profession in a minor league, no matter how small, and campaign from city to city for the championship of that league, the first shout from the bleachers will send a cold sweat through this hero of the open lot at home or college campus, that will put him in such a trance that he can't tell first from third.[22]

One of the old scout's favorite and most oft-told yarns was about a young prospect from Vermont named Gillfeather; not a bad ballplayer, but a serious prima donna who, deep down, knew he wouldn't cut it in the big leagues. The New England boy claimed he could not be talked into going to Texas to play ball because he knew the Lone Star state to be a crude and untamed place, full of rough, vile-talking cowboys and ballplayers.[23]

"Why, Texas, is all right in every way, Mr. Gillfeather," Sullivan said he told the boy,

And I am sure you will not be contaminated in your affiliation with professional baseball players…. Mr. Gillfeather, this is my proposition to you: If you want to pitch for me in the Texas league, you will work only a day a week, which will be on Ladies' Day. A valet will be furnished to you, free of charge, and will be with you throughout the entire season. He will carry your bat to and from home plate, and if the ball is too heavy for you to hold before you deliver it to the batsman, he will hold it for you. This attendant will fan you between innings and serve you cream and strawberries.

"And would you believe it?" Sullivan would laugh, "The boy still didn't sign."

Not Impressed with College Boys

"Of the many college men that have entered the professional ranks," Sullivan wrote, "very few have made a success of it. It may be startling and astounding when the essayist of this article states to the baseball world that he had under his management one time men who could only make their mark to sign a contract, yet who could teach the highest classical scholars of Yale, Harvard and Princeton the chess of the game."[24]

Sullivan maintained that college baseball men were some of the worst problems managers had to deal with, and that "the men who do the best headwork for us in the game of today are the ones who graduated from the vacant lot leagues."[25]

Watching a ballgame once from the bleachers at Harvard, Sullivan sat next to the university's president. Recalled Sullivan: "I mentioned to him that we needed brains in the game today, and he told me he thought the college men could furnish that. I told him 'no,' that we could not get it from the colleges. Then I mentioned one ballplayer who had to make a cross as a signature but he was getting $4,000 a year—as much as a U.S. Senator—because he had it in his head to play the game."[26]

How to Find a Phenom

Sullivan was a master at planting rumors to raise his stock with the press and with major league managers looking to purchase fresh talent. As far back as 1886, he was floating hints of great discoveries he had made way back in the bushes, well off the beaten scout trail.

In 1896, the Irish seanachaí (storyteller) floated one of his greatest masterpieces to the media in the form of a letter to a friend, in which he confided to said-friend that he had discovered a pitching phenom in the far-and-gone woods of Minnesota.

Somehow, of course, the letter was "leaked" to the press.[27]

Dear Smythe,

There is one man who arrived here today, from Wild Bear, Minnesota, and styles himself the Minnesota Terror. He will prove a wonder indeed as a pitcher,

Sullivan didn't spend much time rooting among the ivy for prospects. He called academia "the nursery of egotistical snobbery," and was of the mind that prep and college boys were too full of theory to understand "the hidden science of the human nature of the game." Photograph 1901 Cathedral Commercial School, Kansas City (author's collection).

if the shattering of three inch planks and the breaking of door knobs means any-
thing. For the past ten days I have been deluged with letters from this individual,
and among the many feats of speed, he claimed to possess, are such as knocking
branches off a tree and the felling of an ox at the distance of 40 feet. From these
Munchausen stories I believed he was a genuine crank but to my astonishment
he came all the way to Milwaukee, introduced himself and asked if I would not
go to some gymnasium or building where he could show to my entire satisfaction
that he could duplicate what he had been talking about. Three friends and myself
went to the gymnasium with him. I gave him three League balls to select one
from. We then measured fifty feet. We put up a two inch board. He shattered it as
if it was a piece of paper rent by the wind, at the same time cutting the ball. We
were indeed astonished. I said to him: "My friend, such speed I never before wit-
nessed. If your accuracy equals your speed, you are indeed a wonder." He replied:
"There's where I am at home, and I have not spent all winter pitching through a
hoop for nothing." We next marked a cipher on the wall about ten inches square,
and to our astonishment, he hit the bull's-eye four out of five times, and made
the League ball as oval as an egg. This was done against a brick wall. He spied a
tin cup on the floor. He says put that up on a stick fifty feet away. He hit that cup
where it will never again reshape. I said to him: "You are a regular Bogardus, but
there is one if not two things against you. I can never get a catcher to hold you
and if you ever should hit a man, his ball days would be over forever." At the lat-
ter assertion he became very indignant. He said, "I can put a ball nine times out
of ten over the centre of the plate and if a player gets hit it is because he wants to."
I engaged him and will give him work as soon as the national agreement papers
are signed.

T. P. (Ted) Sullivan

SULLIVAN CLAIMS TO HAVE
A "PHENOMENAL" PITCHER FROM MINNESOTA
Spent the Winter Breaking Barn Doors for Practice
Milwaukee Sentinel
March 27, 1896

"The baseball fraternity are eagerly awaiting for funny Ted Sullivan to announce the name of the 'phenomenon' that breaks two inch planks at fifty feet," wrote a tongue-in-cheek scribbler back in St. Louis,[28] while the *Omaha Bee* cagily noted that Sullivan, "a sharp, shrewd man and one of the best known base-ball men in America" was a bit like George Washington, "for once in a while—alack—he is known to tell a story."[29]

Tossing out phenom stories was part of the veteran scout's MO. He didn't like his bosses or his prey to know where he was or where he was going at any given time. "The perennial manager, who has developed more baseball players than any one man living, has a grievance," reported the *Chicago Tribune*. "Ted maintains that the magnates watch his movements too closely. He says: 'If I was in the middle of Alaska and should bow to a man, Van der Beck [the Detroit Tigers' nefarious magnate] would claim him, and if I shook hands with him he would sign him.'"[30]

The former ballplayer Tim Murnane, when serving as Baseball Editor for the *Boston Globe*, wrote, "I want to take my hat off and say that Ted Sullivan was the equal of them all, and when it came to using judgment in selecting new players, he had the modern bench managers skinned to death. Ted Sullivan on the players' bench was just as valuable as Mike Kelly on the field."[31]

Illustration "Chips from the Diamond," by E.W. Kemble, 1909.

Diamond Was This Girl's Best Friend

> *"A schoolhouse without a baseball diamond within hailing distance would be a complete and colossal failure. Girls are no longer content with skipping the rope."*
> —*Parsons (KS) Weekly Eclipse*, April 8, 1914

A regular and eager participant in the feasts and "fanning bees" (baseball gossip sessions) held at Comiskey's getaway lodge in the North Woods of Wisconsin, Sullivan generally out-whopped the managers, ballplayers, umps, and sports writers who each fall gathered there to tell lies over aged libations and fresh-cooked venison. In one such session in 1907, Sullivan claimed to have discovered the first female major leaguer while umpiring a girls' game at a Wisconsin resort. "Talk about ballplayers," went his story over dinner, "why that girl had Johnny Evers and old baldy Isbell [White Sox first baseman Frank] skinned a block. The way she did grab off liners and tag out the runners with one hand made me think of the old association days, when we had real ball players in this country. And hit! If she didn't smash out a home run and two three baggers in four times up I'll bet on the Cubs to beat the White Sox this fall in the world's series."[32]

Sullivan swore to it, of course, but said he just couldn't bring himself to sign her, because that would be betting against his pal and host, Charlie Comiskey.

Chicago-area sports writers among the guests fanning at Comiskey's lodge in the chilly North Woods found Sullivan a regular source of warm air and amusement. After one such session, the *Chicago Tribune* snarked: "Ted Sullivan, who is running a sort of Lick observatory for the discovery of nebulous baseball stars up in the wilds of Wisconsin, ran down from Milwaukee one day last week to get into touch with civilization again, and, incidentally, to tell President Hart and Comiskey of the two local baseball industries what a mine he had located up there for managers in need of infant prodigies."[33]

> *"Ted Sullivan, who has been out scouting for Comiskey, has bagged an Indian pitcher named Jack Warhoop, who was found running at large at Freeport, Ill. Warhoop is said to be so tame he will eat out of your hand. Comiskey doesn't need him particularly, but he must keep Ted busy until the bird season opens."*
> —*The Chicago Tribune*, July 31, 1907

When Sullivan came across a young prospect from Illinois named "Warhop," he added an extra "o" to the boy's name and proclaimed his find a genuine Native American. Of course, young Jack was no more Indian than Christopher Columbus, but thanks to Sullivan, he quickly got some looks from big league clubs and went on to spend eight seasons knocking off pale-faced batters for the New York Highlanders and Yankees.

Partial to O's and Mac's

Ever faithful to the Auld Sod, Sullivan was likely only half-joking when he said—and he said it often—that baseball needed more Irish players: "Irish make the best ball players, not one that comes from Ireland but one whose veins are filled with the blood of the Celt."[34]

Naturally, his fellow Hibernians tended to agree with him. "The last time Ted was up to see me," the Irish-born former manager Mike "Cap" Scanlon told the *Washington Post* in 1906, "he said he thought a few more O's and Mac's mixed in on the Nationals would help the team a whole lot. He's got a barrel of horse sense."[35]

The Go-to Guy

Although Ted Sullivan never had just one job, after his book, *Humorous Stories of the Ball Field,* was published in 1903, and he had taken a few stabs at writing sketches for vaudeville, he devoted a majority of his time to scouting for his friend, White Sox owner Charlie Comiskey, and for a host of minor and major league clubs, including the Cubs, the Reds, the Orioles and the Senators. For at least one year, he was the official talent sleuth for the National League.

"The league in its time has bought a good many gold bricks," Sullivan said of the NL. "It's not safe to take a man to the major leagues on the showing of the scorecards for the season. They are too often doctored. Some manager in a minor league has a man for whom he expects a good price; he will see that the score shows that man plays a brilliant game, when in fact he may be only a second rate plug."[36]

> *"Colonel "Ted Sullivan," who holds a roaming commission in the Army of the Mags, has bobbed up at Milwaukee."*
> —*The Cincinnati Enquirer,* December 6, 1903

In 1906, the *Washington Post* labeled Sullivan "one of the keenest baseball scouts … famous the country over." Ironically, that same year, he was fired by Cincinnati for muffing a few recruitments and for saying publicly that Reds star Cy Seymour, the previous year's NL batting champ, had "asphalt for brains," causing the Reds to trade him and then regret it.

Sneaking Behind Enemy Lines

The following winter, however, Sullivan was dispatched to track down and bring back first baseman Bob Unglaub, who had defected to the Williamsport Millionaires of the outlaw Tri-State League. He boasted:

SNAPPED ON THE DALLAS DIAMOND.

TED SULLIVAN. ·	HARRY STEINFELDT.
The Famous Minor League Manager Was Caught By the Camera While Talking With "Steiny" Over the Red Prospects.

The *Cincinnati Enquirer* of March 28, 1904, confirmed that scout Sullivan was "carrying the bait box" for the Reds.

Any scout during these times who dared enter this forbidden territory to claim and coax back Organized Ball property took his life in his hands. And when it was known that he [the scout]) was inside the fences of the enemy, telegraph managers and operators and telephone girls formed themselves into an alliance to inform the outlaw managers of the substance of any message sent out by the scout of Organized Ball.[37]

To dodge and circumvent this network of espionage by the outlaws, a plan was arranged … the name of each player was agreed in our code of correspondence by wire or long distance telephone. The star first baseman we were after was to be named "preferred stock" and the lesser prospects were to be named "common stock."

Sullivan was so professionally ambidextrous that he actually took a bit of umbrage at being called a mere "scout," thinking of himself as more of a "sleuth" and a "senior advisor" to team owners.

"I am not a scout, as so many papers have it," he grumbled to the *St. Louis Post* in 1911. "I get around the country a whole lot and naturally see a lot of minor league baseball. I have had a whole lot of experience with base-ball players and I know a good player when I see him. It's only natural that I would tip off my friends to promising youngsters."[38]

The celebrated Irish-born sportswriter, John B. Sheridan, concurred. In his popular column in *The Sporting News* in 1919, he wrote: "As a matter of fact, Ted Sullivan is so much more than a scout that I cannot class him as one. Ted is part of baseball itself. I regard him as one of the great makers of baseball, as the great philosopher of baseball, rather than a mere scout."[39]

Ted Sullivan's clients didn't always listen to him, though. When Cincinnati rejected a couple of Sullivan's prime choices in 1906, Reds skipper Ned Hanlon took a beating in the press. One report, under the headline "IS HANLON JEALOUS?" said:

> Ned Hanlon has made several very serious mistakes in releasing ballplay-ers whom Ted Sullivan, the agent of the club, had secured in various parts of the country. It is very peculiar that he should give up so many stars whom Sullivan has unearthed.... It was not a case of Sullivan going out and picking up stars from the minor leagues, but of selecting stars from the ranks of the almost unheard of clubs in small leagues. It is up to Ned Hanlon now to acknowledge that old Ted delivered the goods and he gave them away.[40]

> *"Ted Sullivan's name has burned up a good many wires since he first entered the baseball business, and it means something to have his John Henry at the commencement of hostilities. Ted says he is done with baseball, but he don't look it. We'll wager a telephone pole against a tooth-pick (this is an old one, but it's a bet we've never lost) that Ted discovers somebody else before the coming season is out. As long as we are celebrating Columbus Day, why not institute a Sullivan Day for the baseball clan. As an explorer, Ted has them all jumping sideways."*
> —*Davenport (IA) Daily Times*, January 12, 1909

Sullivan believed a good scout was a winning team's most valuable asset. "What value is a scout to a baseball club?" he asked. "Immense," he answered himself. "A mediocre manager can make a success of a team of high class players, while a good manager will fall apart with a team of medi-ocre ball players. So it's up to the man who gets the players for the team."[41]

Since Sullivan changed employers frequently and often sleuthed for teams in either league at the same time, it was never clear just what he was up to. He was generally sitting in a railroad smoking car between there and everywhere, or in a hotel lobby or small Anywheretown newsroom, regaling captive audiences with tales of yore.

As the *Dubuque Daily Times* put it: "Whenever the magic hand of good fellowship lifted the veil that hides the past, genial Ted Sullivan told stories."[42]

The crosstown sheet, the *Dubuque Telegraph-Herald*, took a shine to the middle-aged troubadour as well, noting that Ted Sullivan was "one of those irresistibly funny fellows who is always saying the most fetching things without any apparent effort. He is constantly bubbling over with mirth, and his fun is simply infectious. He has earned the reputation of being one of the funniest men in baseball."[43]

Bag the Scouts?

"What is to happen to the mysterious scout?" was the lead in a November 29, 1909, story in the *Chicago Evening American*. According to the paper, some clubs were considering doing away with their scouts altogether, claiming they were costing their teams too much money.

The byline over the story read "Bill Bailey," a pen name for a young Bill Veeck, the same Bill Veeck who became president of the Chicago Cubs and spawned the Ted Sullivan–like promoter, Bill Veeck, Jr., who brought radical entertainment (e.g., a 3'7" batter; players in Bermuda shorts) and innovation (he integrated the American League) to the game. "When the baseball scout came a new leaf was turned in baseball, and an expensive one" Bailey/Veeck wrote.

> Any time a team escapes with a scout bill of less than $3,000 said team is getting off cheap. Many a baseball club has paid $10,000 for a year of scouting. The Cincinnati Reds claim that it's all a waste of time. On the other hand, you couldn't convince Charles A. Comiskey of that.
>
> Ted Sullivan is one of those old time scouts. He gumshoes into town. Ask him what his business is and he's as likely to tell you that he is a book agent as he is that he is a retired millionaire. Maybe he won't tell you either story.

Whereas Sullivan might not have been a millionaire, ten grand a year, adjusted for inflation, would add up to about $275,000 in 2019. And Sullivan rarely had just one client.

The old "player hunter," as some writers called him, believed that good scouts were undervalued and deserved a lot more recognition, respect and money.[44]

> A good scout can save his employer a lot of money by stalling him away from players who are highly touted by others but have no chance to prosper in the

majors. It [the making of a good baseball team] is just like putting up a building. The hod-carrier does the hard work. He works eight or 10 long hours a day packing up brick, but it's the architect to whom ethereal credit for the handsome building is due. You don't send a bricklayer out to select a diamond.[45]

Despite Sullivan's slick loquacity and vaunted reputation as one of the game's foremost gumshoes, longtime followers of the human enigma had their doubts about his cabled reports from the bushes. *Sporting Life* reasoned that Sullivan "always runs the chance of developing one or two fairly good players from the lot, and then by a system of judicious talk and advertising succeeds in attracting the attention of the big league managers to his great find or 'phenom.' These managers are always on the lookout for strengthening material, and for that reason are easy victims."[46]

"The oldest man in baseball," as more than one sports hack called him, was still sending players for tryouts as late as 1925. And his familiar moon face under a derby hat could be spotted in the stands at a Senators or White Sox game until he could no longer climb the stairs.

Sadly, by then most of those many young men whom Sullivan discovered and who had gone on to careers in professional baseball had forgotten their old mentor.

◆ 21 ◆

Sullivan's Off-Base Humor

"Ted is universally recognized as 'the whitest man in base-ball."—Winnipeg Tribune, May 27, 1911

Ted Sullivan liked to use the word *"amadan"*—Irish for fool or stupid.

He thought African Americans were cute, like children, but inherently *"amadan."* Whereas he was among the first to see big potential in athletes from Japan, Cuba, and South America, he didn't think America's "darkies," as he called them, were smart enough or disciplined enough to play professional baseball. But they made for mean sport in the books and plays he wrote, and in after-dinner dialogues he delivered at smokers and banquets.

Sullivan's first attempt to share his self-described warm and sympathetic observations of Blacks came during a winter spent back home in Milwaukee, after being nearly chased out of Memphis in 1885, when he wrote a play called *Ball of the Darkville Rifles.*

In 1896, Sullivan mailed out "syndicated letters" carrying short stories he had written. The *Atlanta Constitution* and other papers in need of filler picked up and ran a two-part "darky" story titled *The Yaller Chicken Club,* the plot having to do with a "colored ball club" in Georgia that was having a hard time coming up with a catchy name for itself.[1]

Reviews of the story ranged from "clever" to "side-splitting."

Virtually unemployed in the summer of 1899, Sullivan told anybody who would listen that he was out of the game for the rest of his life but had compiled enough stories to write a book about baseball.

But first, as announced by the *Wilmington Sun* on Dec. 20, 1898, there was "Ted Sullivan's Southern Refined Colored Minstrels and Louisiana Cakewalkers."

Between baseball seasons in 1899 and 1900 "the irrepressible Ted Sullivan," as he was often referred to, put together a troupe of Black performers and took them on a barnstorming tour of the Pacific Northwest. Sullivan

168

boasted, "I will have nothing but negroes in my troupe, who give real representation of negro life in the south."[2]

The farcical and demeaning presentation was described by the *Ogden (UT) Standard* as "an entire negro show off the beaten paths of theatricals and minstrelsy," featuring ragtime piano playing, a "buck and wing" dancing contest, and "the most amusing feature," a battle royal sparring contest between four Black men in barrels, wearing oversized boxing gloves. To keep things

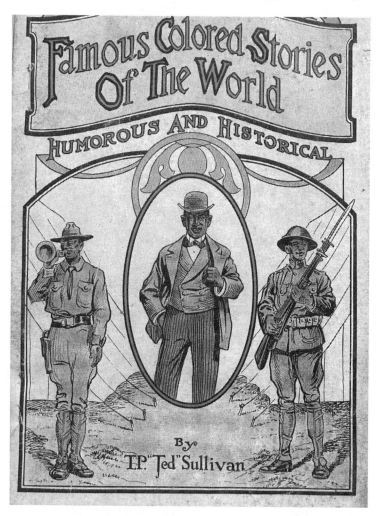

Sullivan looked down on Blacks as intellectually and athletically inferior and relished telling stories and writing plays in what he called "the Negro dialect." But in 1915, he published this book, dedicated "to the brave colored American soldiers who fought and died on foreign soil for liberty and world's democracy."

ecumenical, the promoter tossed in a gladiator contest between two actors from the local Chinese theater.[3] The *Standard* reported, "The gate receipts were good, and Ted Sullivan, the manager, was correspondingly happy."

In 1903, he proudly (as he did everything) rented an office in downtown Chicago and hung out his shingle as a writer and dramatist. Among the talents and services listed at the top of his letterhead was "Publisher of Plantation Negro Stories."[4]

Not giving up his day job of scouting for and brokering talent, Sullivan also had another letterhead printed up proclaiming him "The Chief Builder of Baseball." To put Ted Sullivan's writing in context, it was right around this time that Thomas Dixon was writing his best-selling book *The Clansman: An Historical Romance of the Ku Klux Klan*—the tome that gave birth to the film *The Birth of a Nation* which conveniently justified white America's disdain for, and persecution of, Black Americans, who were portrayed as ignorant, out-of-control looters and rapists.

In 1904, it was reported that Ted Sullivan had retired to Texas for the winter and was writing a new play called *The Mississippi Cotton Pickers* that would debut in St. Louis the following summer. Nineteen months later, he was in Chicago preparing to give the world a new book of Negro yarns. In 1906, in between scouting missions, he was busy promoting a book called *"Plantation and Up-To-Date Humorous and Negro Stories."* Reviews—very likely penned by Sullivan himself—appeared in an odd variety of publications across the country, including this one in the June 1906 edition of *Vegetarian Magazine*:

Book Review
Vegetarian Magazine,
June 1906

This book is vibrating with first-told Negro humor and, as set forth by the author, with his own native and sharp wit, scintillated with an antidote for the blues, in any clime and under any sky. Mr. Sullivan has spent many years among the denizens of the South, with a desire to turn into account their quaint characteristics, and has made a close study of the dialect, songs and individual traits of the southern Negro.

Familiar with the plantation scenes in "Dixie Land," "Way Down in Alabam,'" and also among the éclat of Washington, during the social season, then back amongst the everyday life of the cotton field toilers again, as well as with the aristocracy, the author has woven into his book much instructive and interesting history, all characteristic of American life with the picturesque slave days gleaming through it all. To interpret these quaint Negroes with the folk lore and superstitious ways, their childish beliefs and mirthful personalities, require more than a student of human nature. It requires a man with a warm, sympathetic heart, keen, penetrating mind and a responsive sense of humor which only one of Mr. Sullivan's make up would do.

The prolific profiteer followed *Plantation* with a widely publicized but seldom seen Civil War drama titled *Ole Virginny*, and touted a forthcoming work, to be titled simply *"Coon Stories."*[5]

An admiring Tim Murnane of the *Boston Globe* wrote: "I would not be surprised to see Mr. Sullivan among the successful playwrights of the year. Ted Sullivan stands alone as the great independent character in base ball, thoroughly posted and a man who has carried the sport into the darkest corners of the country. The brunt of it is that Ted Sullivan can draw a check for $80,000 and get the cash. I guess Ted is easy money."[6]

Prior to baseball's celebrated World Tour in 1913–1914, with only part-time work in organized baseball (scouting players, conjuring missions to South America, and managing the Clinton [Iowa] Teddies in 1910), Ted Sullivan supplemented his time and income by taking his monologue of "short dialect stories" on the road, speaking at fanning bees, baseball banquets, and Knights of Columbus smokers. He delighted and amused audiences with his impersonations.

His pal Al Spink bragged that Sullivan could mimic a German Jew to a T and that no one was better at satirizing the drawl-talk of a weary Texas farmer. Spink's *Sporting News* added: "He is such a fine mimic, and master of dialect that he can pass muster anywhere as a British bagman, as a French courier, a Scotch piper, a veteran Canuck, or a down-east Yankee. He has played all these parts in his day."[7]

How Many?

It had to be a typo ... or Ted Sullivan's nose had grown long enough to reach across the Mississippi River. Whatever the case, the *Dubuque Times Journal* said in July of 1923 that "the leading old timer in baseball ... has written several books, one of which, *Folklore: Negro Stories of the South*, has had a sale of 3,000,000 copies since its publication seven years ago."[8]

Ted's 25-Cent Epistle

> *"Ted Sullivan has issued a brilliant and useful little brochure, entitled, 'Humorous Stories of the Ball Field.' It is replete with sound advice and entertaining tales. Mr. Sullivan displays sound judgment in speaking of the players, though, to be sure, inclined to the usual amount of 'salve'.... The book should be invaluable to young baseball players and young baseball writers and the people who like to be considered well informed on baseball affairs."*
> —*Atlanta Constitution*, April 3, 1903

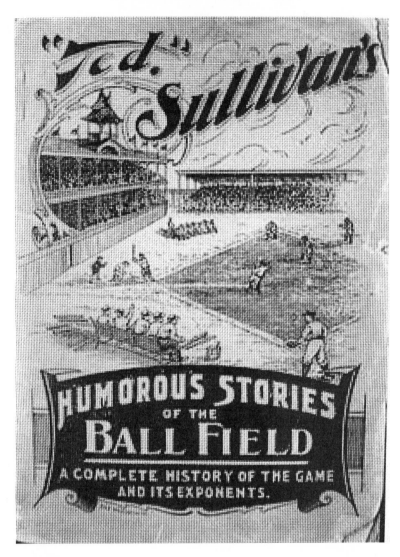

Sullivan's first and most notable book, *Humorous Stories of the Ball Field* (1903) was intended, he said, to illustrate "the sunny side of the men connected to the game," but included a host of cloudy racist jokes and vignettes.

Humorous Stories of the Ball Field, published in 1903, was Ted Sullivan's biggest seller and, according to himself, a favorite read of his most prominent literary fan, the Hero of San Juan Hill, Teddy Roosevelt. In *Humorous Stories*, essayist Sullivan pontificated on the game's rules, its players, its history, its foibles and legends, and, naturally, his own successes as an owner, manager and scout.

"This book," Sullivan wrote in the introduction, "is dedicated to the entire base ball fraternity and the millions of votaries of the great national game. It is intended to be a book of sunshine—not of cyclones and storms— but to the wit and humour, which is the sunnyside of the men connected to the game."

The aim of his "pamphlet," he claimed, was to "give an impartial and unbiased account of the great celebrities of the nation's sport, and not to extol friends or slight enemies—nor to give any vainglorious account of the writer himself."[9]

And, by and large, Sullivan does just that.

He takes the reader through each position on the ball field, citing the now forgotten players he considered the best of their day, dating back to the 1860s, when the game was a barnyard novelty in New York and New England. When the spongy ball was delivered underhand and slow and clubbed with what amounted to a thick, shaved tree branch. When a ball caught after one bounce was an out. When anything hit in front of the plate that veered out of bounds could still be a base hit.

In his 30-some years in the game, Sullivan had seen, first-hand, the play and character of many a future Hall of Famer. In his book, he chronicles the feats and burnishes the legends of his favorites, like George Wright, Charles "Hoss" Radbourn, Hughie Jennings, Buck Ewing, Mike "King" Kelly, Adrian "Cap" Anson, Christy Mathewson, "The Dude" Arlie Latham, Jim Fogarty, William "Wee Willie" Keeler, "The Frenchman" Napoleon Lajoie, John "Muggsy" McGraw, William "Dummy" Hoy, Cornelius "Connie Mack" McGillicuddy, and, of course, Charlie "The Old Roman" Comiskey. He heralds would-be phenoms, like John "Chub" Sullivan and Big Ed Delahanty, who danced with greatness before being carried off by injuries, insanity, consumption, booze, and career-ending brawls.

Copies of *Humorous Stories* were sold at ballparks, and managers like John McGraw purchased copies for each of the players on their teams.

Of course, among the "humorous" stories therein were more vignettes disparaging African Americans. In one, "Satan's plaything" (a baseball) comes through the window of a "darky" church, hits a woman in the head, and inspires her to talk in tongues. In another, a "hoodoo doctor" rubs watermelon juice on injured ballplayers to cure and revive them.

Sullivan soon claimed that he sold more than 40,000 copies of his 25-cent masterpiece, and he announced he was writing another book. "It is hoped he will hire a proofreader this time," quipped an editor at the *Washington Post*.[10]

Shuffles Off to Vaudeville

As early as 1895, when he was guiding the Dallas Steers to an 82–33 finish in the Texas Southern League, Ted Sullivan was telling anyone who would listen that he was just about finished with baseball and was planning, as one newspaper put it, "to enter the giddy-whirl of the playwriting realm."[11]

"Ted is a dramatist and has an innate hankering for things theatrical," said the *Boston Globe*, noting that he'd already written and copyrighted a play, a melodrama called *Biddy Moriarty*.[12]

"Biddy," Sullivan explained to the *Globe*, "was an historic character who lived in the time of the great statesman Daniel O'Connell in Dublin. She was known far and wide as the wittiest woman in Ireland, and it is related that O'Connell, who was a wit himself, once called on Biddy, who kept a stall in the Dublin Market, and entered into a combat of talk with her. O'Donnell's identity wasn't revealed to her till the great statesman left the market, retired a loser."

The *Globe* concluded its account by giving the play a thumbs-up: "Ted read the entire crossfire of Milesian [ancient Irish people] pyrotechnics, in imitation of Daniel and Biddy, and the dialogue is really clever and funny."

Passing through Atlanta in early 1899, Sullivan told a curious scribe that he wasn't in town in the interest of the national game but rather, "I'm in the show business for the present, and I'm on my way to New Orleans to engage talent. 'Coon' shows are all the rage in New York now. There's a mint of money to be made in a first-class vaudeville show composed of Negroes—it's the fad in Gotham, y' know. I'm going to engage one of the best Negro troupes that was ever carried east, and I expect to get my hands on some of the stray coin that's floating around."[13]

No copy of the aspiring playwright's tale of Biddy can be found in the annals of American theater, but it is certain that about 1907 Sullivan did, indeed, turn his starry eyes to vaudeville. Other baseball stars and personalities were picking up big bucks—often double what they were paid to play the National Game—acting, or trying to act, in vaudeville-style plays and skits written expressly for them.

Ballplayers like Cap Anson, Ty Cobb, Christy Mathewson, "Turkey" Mike Donlin, Chief Meyers, and Arlie Lathan, and even the curmudgeonly Muggsy McGraw were lighting up the marquees of vaudeville houses across the country when the aforesaid "famous mime" and master of plantation dialects announced his intention to tread the boards himself.

What very likely put visions of vaudeville into Sullivan's head was the stage success of the Chicago Cubs' popular star shortstop, Joe Tinker. Tin Pan Alley hacks were writing sketches, like "The Home Run Hit," "The

Squeeze Play," and "A Great Catch," just for Tinker to perform in the winter months, and audiences were crying for more. Sullivan couldn't help but notice that Tinker often appeared on stage with popular Caucasian comedienne Sadie Sherman, lauded in playbills of the day as a "singer of coon songs."

In 1909, T.P. Sullivan wrote about "the fallacies and delusions of professional baseball" in the September edition of *Baseball Magazine,* and shortly thereafter announced that he was writing a 30-minute skit for vaudeville called "Touching Second." His play would feature real-life Cubs characters, shortstop Johnnie Evers and second baseman Joe Tinker, along with umpire Hank O'Day. The skit was to re-enact and make comedic fun of a highly controversial play in which Giants rookie Fred Merkle made a boneheaded base-running mistake in the bottom of the ninth and was put out by the Cubs' famous Tinker-to-Evers combination, negating a would-be winning run.

"When Hank O'Day runs up to Evers, substantiating his famous play, we could have the mob dash out on the field and the curtain fall with excitement galore," Sullivan told reporters. "I don't see why it wouldn't take."[14]

It didn't.

Baseball's Ubiquitous Ambassador

Never-Sit-Still Sullivan could well have added "Sports Writer, Will Travel" to his letterhead. Following the first modern (NL vs. AL) World Series in 1903, subway strap-hangers in Pittsburgh and Boston read, cogitated, and argued over Ted Sullivan's copyrighted analyses of the Series, which was rumored to have been tainted by gambling and payoffs.

The old sage disagreed with contentions that the Series had been fixed. He insisted that since the days of winner-take-all gate receipts—which provided a much bigger incentive for cheating—the game had evolved to one of sterling integrity. In late February of 1904, he was in Guthrie, Oklahoma, trying to start a new Southwestern League. In early March he was in Milwaukee, organizing another league in the northern part of the state and the Upper Peninsula of Michigan.[1]

A few days after that, he was in Wichita, Kansas, promising that city a place in the Southwestern League, in which he assured the heartland town's fathers there would be "no rowdyism, no swearing, no drinks, and no cigars."[2]

The local press was, as usual, enamored of the legendary league-starter. "There is no buncombe about Ted Sullivan," the *Topeka Daily Herald* declared. "He asks for no money, and would not take it if it were proffered him. Genial Ted has a heart as big as a bushel basket." Adding, innocently, "Sullivan has never managed a team that was not a success."[3]

Like a man on a pogo stick, throughout March Sullivan bounced back and forth between Kansas, Oklahoma, Milwaukee, Chicago, Cincinnati, and Washington, D.C. But a twister must have blown him back to the East Coast, because he was soon spotted by a correspondent for *Sporting Life* getting off the midnight train in Philadelphia.

Leaning into the teeth of a Nor'easter, a shivering Sullivan told the correspondent that he'd been out west scouting players but made no mention

of a baseball team in Wichita. The correspondent simply noted that Sullivan was "pleased as a boy with new red boots over the showing his Texans
are making with the Brewers. Ted likes Prexy [Charles]) Havenor [the Milwaukee Brewers president]). Quoth Ted: 'Here is a man of his word and a
prince. Just compare him with some of the other magnates, who go about
holding a prayer book in one hand and a scalping knife in the other.' Now,
isn't that Sullivanesque?"[4]

In June, Sullivan popped up in Calumet, Michigan, where he purchased a minor ball club with profits he reportedly made from investments
in another copper mine.

In July, he announced through *The Sporting News* that he was not
presently tied up with any baseball enterprise, saying, "I resolved to
myself last winter that I would keep out of the meshes of the national
game for the World's Fair and Presidential year, at least. I organized two
or three leagues last fall and winter and I could have taken a city in any
one of them if I so desired, but I wanted a vacation or recreation for one
summer, at least."[5]

Like a Duck to Water

Knowing himself, though, Sullivan added the following caveat: "The
utter delusion and illusion of such a resolve would be about the same as if a
duck would claim she was tired of water and in the future would live on dry
land, for when she saw the first sheet of water she couldn't resist the temptation of taking a swim in it."[6]

It was soon reported that Sullivan was, in fact, circulating in the American Association "looking at the ripening fruit" on behalf of the Cincinnati
Reds, and that he had some hot new "phenoms" for sale.[7] "There are some
peaches up there ... and also a fine assortment of gold bricks," said Sullivan
of the nearly decimated minor American Association.[8]

Sullivan had an on-again-off-again relationship with Reds owner
Garry Herrmann. But as the team's accredited scout in 1904 and 1905, he
was Herrmann's darling, bringing the convivial owner a string of solid
young players, including several future greats like pitcher Orval "Orrie"
Overall, who became the ace of the Reds' pitching staff the next year.

Ted also signed catcher Charles "Old Sarge" Street, who didn't hit so
great in the bigs, but managed to gain a modicum of fame for catching a
baseball dropped 555 feet from the top of the Washington Monument.

Sullivan's good work for Herrmann also helped rejuvenate his reputation with the sporting papers. *Sporting Life* maintained, "He [Sullivan]
is too honorable a fellow to recommend anyone in whom he has not the

utmost confidence in his ability to make good in fast company.... President Herrmann is well satisfied with Ted Sullivan's scout work."[9]

Should Be Chloroformed

Of course, back in Wichita, the sports scribes didn't care about Sullivan's good work in Cincinnati. They were still smarting from fast-talking Sully's quick slip out of their town the previous spring. In August, when he stopped in Topeka, fishing for talent, the *Wichita Beacon* harrumphed: "Somebody ought to tell the Topeka sports that Ted Sullivan was a dead one four years ago. He is beginning to be looked upon as a joke." The paper went so far as to connect the aging hustler to famed physician William Osler's cheeky recommendation that men over age 60 be humanely chloroformed.[10]

Ignoring those bitter voices back in the Sunflower State, Sullivan basked in his growing reputation as the big leagues' premier gumshoe. But in the spring of 1906, after he pronounced publicly that the Reds' Cy Seymour, the 1905 NL batting champ, had "asphalt for brains" (which caused the Reds to trade Seymour to the Giants, and then regret it), and after he dropped the ball on signing the future star Joe Nealon, the Reds fired Sir Ted.[11]

Sullivan's "Smoke" League

Even novice scriveners working for papers on the fringe of baseball civilization learned to read the "smoke signals" that wafted oh-so-sensuously from Ted Sullivan's lips. In late 1905, the famous baseball man was again scouring the west for players when he stopped off in Salt Lake to chew the fat with a reporter for the local sheet.[12]

When asked what it would take to get Salt Lake's nine into a league the next year, the old scout looked at a map and reportedly said, with a twinkle in his Irish blues: "I have it my boy! It will make a corker of a league, and I myself will take the Salt Lake franchise. We will form a league with New York, San Francisco, Portland, Oregon, Portland, Maine, and Salt Lake!"[13]

At that point, the atmosphere in the newsroom began to get warm, and Sullivan facetiously boasted that he would give Salt Lake the greatest club they'd ever heard of; he'd sign Christy Mathewson, Cy Young, and Rube Waddell ... and the room got even warmer.

"Oh, there will be nothing small about me when I start," Sullivan boasted. "We will put Lajoie on second base, Wagner at short and Chance at first base." At which point, according to the printed tale, "the wall paper began to smoke, and smoke began curling up from under the door." As Sullivan dropped more names of the great ballplayers he would get for Salt Lake, someone was heard to yell "Fire! Fire!"

Sullivan joked that Salt Lake "certainly was a red hot town when the organization of a league would set a six-story building on fire."

> *"The Father of the Leagues will make all arrangements for the sojourn of the world beaters in Mexico."*—*Rochester (NY) Democrat and Chronicle,* February 6, 1907

Sully's South of the Border Experiment

Pathfinder Ted Sullivan took off on what the *Washington Post* called "a junketing trip through the outlaw league," scoping players to pilfer for the Nationals.[14] Soon after, he was scouting and signing players for Comiskey's Chicago Americans (fast becoming known as the "White Sox"). And before the year was out, at "The Old Roman's" request, Sullivan was making

With Ted Sullivan ahead marking their trail, the White Sox embarked on what was then the longest road trip in the history of the sport, featuring exhibition games throughout the southern U.S. and Mexico (advertisement for Goodrich Tires, 1907).

arrangements to take the Sox (1906 World Series champs) on a spring training mission to Mexico.

In early January of 1907, the *San Antonio Light* reported that Sullivan "intended to make the trip the most pretentious that has ever invaded a foreign country. It is probable that that bunch of huskies will show up here next spring, and in that case Ted Sullivan's beauties will be given a chance to spread themselves a bit."[15]

The *Fairmont West Virginian* predicted, "Mexico City will soon hear of things it never dreamed of in the way of baseball. Ted Sullivan is enroute there to boom the coming of the White Sox."[16]

Indeed, in early February, advance agent Sullivan picked up his always-at-the-ready travel bag and headed for Mexico City to meet with President Porfirio Diaz.

TED SULLIVAN WOULD LURE DIAZ FROM HIS LAIR
Persuasive White Sox Advance Guard
Leaves Today for City of Mexico
Hammond Lake County (IL) Times
February 5, 1907

Ted Sullivan, advance guard, envoy extraordinaire and minister plenipotentiary of the world's champion White Sox, will leave today for the City of Mexico to make plans for the training trip.

Sullivan will take with him a plentiful supply of twelve sheet lithographs showing how the White Sox play ball, pictures of the world's championship series last fall, and autographed photographs of Nick Altrock for the Mexican senoritas.

"I am going to do all I can to make this trip an unqualified success," said Sullivan. "I am going to make the visit of the Sox a 'high-toned festival occasion,' as the southern darkies say. I will stay in the City of Mexico for two weeks and will endeavor to get President Diaz and his cabinet to attend the opening games. I will try and arrange the baseball games so as to avoid conflict with the bull fights, which draw tremendous crowds in the City of Mexico."

Papers across the United States, such as the *Lake County (IL) Times* in Hammond (near Chicago), followed Sullivan's groundbreaking travels and the subsequent tour with uninhibited interest and enthusiasm.

The adventure Sullivan was planning was to be the longest (2,159 miles) and most ambitious "road trip" ever attempted by a baseball team.

In early February, an amused reporter in D.C. wrote, "Down in old Mexico, Ted Sullivan is busy as a 'hot dog' man at a German picnic, booking hotels, calling on senors and handing out the bull in such slices that when the Sox arrive they will be as much at home as if they were raised on chili con carne. If the Mexicans are not impressed ... then Ted is a bum press agent and surely no one ever accused the veteran scout of that affliction."[17]

Knowing Sullivan well, the *Chicago Tribune* quipped: "The toreadors of Mexico will have nothing on Ted Sullivan. Ted is there with the bull, himself."[18]

Blazing a Trail

In updates telegraphed to editors in Chicago and elsewhere, Sullivan reported that he had booked the best hotel in Mexico City and that President Diaz was planning to hold a great reception in the team's honor upon their arrival. The Mexican people, he said, were eagerly awaiting the American champions, and the games he was scheduling would surely draw great crowds.

On March 5, 1907, a jovial party of some 50 tourists, including ball players, dignitaries, and a substantial press contingent, gathered at Chicago's Illinois Central depot and prepared to board a special train decorated with American and Mexican flags; the Sox's oversized championship pennant flapped above the head sleeper car.

The *Boston Sunday Post* heralded the embarkation as "the most spectacular home-leaving ever made by a ball team."[19] The *Washington Post* concurred: "No triumphal tour was ever inaugurated under more auspicious ceremonies than the get-away of the Chicago White Sox, world's champions, from their native heath today. A great crowd was at the depot to see the champions depart. Calls for speeches were made, and the ovation tendered the departing heroes was never equaled in baseball history."[20]

At the outset of the trip, Papa Sullivan offered fatherly advice to the younger ball players, telling them to avoid the worst vice in the land of picante and mescal—bull fights. "I saw one bull fight," he confided to a Chicago reporter on the train, "but I could not stick it out. After one horse and one bull were killed, I left the place. It was too much for me."[21]

"Ted is not a Society for the Prevention of Cruelty to Animals person," wrote another scribe in the entourage, "but his Celtic ire arises to the fine point of explosion when even a bull is mentioned."[22]

After five days on different trains, with delays and stopovers in Memphis and New Orleans, the American entourage finally rolled into Mexico City, where they were greeted by Mexican Vice-President Ramon Corral at the head of a raucous welcoming party.

Plans detailed in Chicago's *Inter Ocean* called for the gringo entourage to stay in Mexico City until St. Patrick's Day, as "Commy says that one of his principal reasons for going to Mexico is to see how the Mexicans celebrate March 17."[23]

Champion Del Mundo

Before playing their first game, the American ballplayers were treated to "a light luncheon" of chili con carne y tortillas washed down with liberal doses of Milwaukee's best cerveza. A crowd of ex-pats was waiting at the ballpark. While their heroes limbered up, the exiled rooters reportedly shouted themselves hoarse and applauded every play.[24]

For that first exhibition, the Sox player were divided into two nines, the Whites and the Blues, and played each other. But the "zumbido" (buzz) in The City of Palaces was about a contest to be played the next day with Mexico's best ball team, called the "Record."

"This old city is baseball crazy," was the lead in a top-of-the-page story printed in American papers. "The arrival of the World's Champion White Sox has awakened every fan, and not the least is a challenge made today by the 'Records,' the champion baseball team of the republic, to a battle royal with the Comiskeyites."[25]

The battle turned out not to be much of a stand-off as the Sox beat the Mexican heroes, 12–2, and earned the right among Mexicans to be called "Champions Del Mundo." The Americans affirmed their status by breezing through additional games against local competition in Vera Cruz and Monterrey.

Along the way, the American ball players complained about the hotel accommodations, lack of hot water, and spotty telegraph service. By then the tour's advance man and PR flack had already returned to Washington, completely unimpressed with the accommodations, the climate (cold), and slow service in the highlands of Old Mexico. "How Commy ever got it in his head to take his champions down there is a mystery to me," he groused.[26]

Despite the complaints about accommodations, Comiskey's young ball players found the senoritas of Mexico to be Five-Star beautiful and most beguiling. The Sox's ace twirler, "Handsome" Nick Altrock, in particular, was a hit with the ladies and was said to be "in a hurry to learn the lingo until he can tell the senoritas what a wonder he is in getting away with games."[27]

On leaving Mexico to play a long series of spring training exhibition games in cities between New Orleans and Indianapolis, reporters—and even Comiskey—questioned the logic and success of baseball's first south of the border tour.

Attendance at the games had not nearly met expectations. Some thought the ticket prices too high for the average Mexican sports fan, and despite a certain press agent's sunny predictions, the tour had not seemed to spark much interest in the idea of starting a Mexican minor league.

The visitors had been well-received and well-treated on their trip south, but it seems the majority of Mexico's citizenry remained confused, if not confounded, by America's bat-and-ball sport. "Judging from the meager attendance at the White Sox games in Mexico City, the swarthy sons of tamales take but little interest in the national game of America," was the *Washington Post's* takeaway.[28]

An Invincible Ignorance

The conclusion of papers like the *Traverse City (MI) Evening Record* was: "most of the team's Latin American hosts possessed an invincible ignorance about the national game and thought that baseball was a gringo variant on the game of Jai Alai."[29]

Had you asked Señor Sullivan, though, he would have told you his Mexican foray was "the best advertising stunt that has ever been pulled off in the history of the great national game," and that he thought old Mexico, with its warm climate and cheap prices, would be a great place to establish spring training camps.[30]

Whereas the training camp thing never happened, Sullivan's 1907 trip across the border would prove fortuitous. As the *Indianapolis Sun* observed: "The White Sox, by going to Mexico City and taking a jaunt over Mexico, make an entirely new departure, which will stand for uniqueness until some enterprising manager takes his team on a European trip."[31]

In a few years, Ted Sullivan would do just that.

In the meantime, it was reported that his old boss, Garry Herrmann, was considering bringing him back to Cincinnati to manage the Reds in 1908.[32] Feigning humility, Sullivan was quoted as saying: "I really prefer to remain my own boss, but now that the matter has been mentioned, I will be candid and say if I entered the major league again Cincinnati would be my choice above all others."[33]

When that didn't happen, baseball's itinerant went back to wandering the West, lassoing players for various National League clients.

In February of 1908, Sullivan pushed his way through deep snow to attend a meeting of Western League magnates in St. Joseph, Missouri. Calling him "the ancient one," the *Omaha Daily Bee* reported that Sullivan had $10,000 in his pocket and was prepared to buy the St. Joe ball club. "But, say honey, here's your money," gibed the *Bee*. "Old Ted Sullivan is here. Ted is there for the goods, too. Sullivan is out for to get St. Joe."[34]

Putting on his country boy hat, Sullivan said he wasn't after the Pony Express town's money. "I've been a scout for the National League these many years, and now I am going to settle down for the quiet life," he purred.[35] His warm charm allowed the snow to melt just enough for him hop a train and light out for warmer climes, with the 10k still warm in his pocket.

The New Papa

When the legendary Henry Chadwick, from whose seminal book on baseball a young Ted Sullivan had first learned the game, passed away in the spring of 1908, a syndicated article under the headline "TED" SULLIVAN BASEBALL GENIUS dubbed him "the most versatile man in baseball and a litterateur of renown" and declared, "now that Henry Chadwick has been struck out by the Eternal hand [Sullivan] has no rival as the Father of Baseball. He's a gem."[36]

Because dead men could tell no tales or challenge Sullivan's authenticity, the little fabulist who had seen it all from the near beginning was now considered the game's unofficial historian, which gave him a license to "elucidate," in his own special Irish way.

At the outset of 1909, the *Dubuque Telegraph-Herald* announced to its readers: "Ted Sullivan, baseball promoter, big league scout, bon vivant, raconteur, is in town … on his way to Dallas, Tex., to personally direct the production of his latest work, a drama bearing the title of *In Ole Virginny*, which has been commented on favorably by such eminent men as Theodore Roosevelt, President of the United States."[37]

The paper noted that the wily scout had enjoyed "a successful fling in copper," which had netted him "a nice bunch of money." Letting bygones be bygones, the Dubuque correspondent wrote that although Sullivan had prospered in recent years, "it hasn't turned his head. He is the same old jovial fellow."

The jovial fellow then wandered down to Kansas City and tried to sell that city's minor league baseball Blues a new "movable baseball electric score board." He even offered to install it and give it the old Sullivan guarantee—good until he was gone.

Come spring, Sullivan was with Charlie Comiskey on the rear platform of the White Sox Special, waving to camp followers and a dozen exploding photographers as the decorated train pulled out of Chicago's Northwestern Station, headed for spring training in San Francisco.[38]

◆ 23 ◆

Show Him the Money

"A most distinguished man, of nationwide renown, is Ted Sullivan, the pride of Ireland and Chicago."—The Abilene Daily Reporter, March 25, 1910

Was Ted Sullivan baseball's first broker/agent?

A catcher breaks a finger. A pitcher throws out his arm. A fielder takes a bad hop to the nose. A left fielder is simply lousy and needs to be replaced. What's a manager to do? In 1910, he could call the American Base Ball Agency—T.P. Sullivan, proprietor.

His reputation as a keen-eyed baseball man having been bolstered by a recent two-part story of his life in *The Sporting News*, Ted Sullivan announced in January that he was opening "a bureau for the supply and demand of players" with an office in the Corn Exchange Bank Building in downtown Chicago.[1]

"It is Sullivan's intention this year to work on a list of independent and unemployed minor or major league players in line for positions," the *Atlanta Georgian and News* reported. "When the list is completed minor or major league clubs in need of material will have only to write Mr. Sullivan and be accommodated."[2]

"Agent" Sullivan acknowledged that his services would not be run for charity. He would expect to charge recruits (rising amateurs, major league washouts, and out-of-work journeymen) $5 each to be on his list of readily available talent. He was, as the *Chicago Tribune* explained, "a broker in baseball aspirants.[3]

"Vacancies are bound to arise among ball clubs during the heat of the pennant races," explained *Sporting Life*. "Players become ill, many are released outright, and others jump their contracts in various ways. The managers of various teams frequently find themselves up an alley for materials. Sullivan's agency will do the work. Ball tossers reared in the smaller circuits need entertain no fears in the future over the whereabouts of their next meals. Sullivan's agency will cater particularly to the finding of jobs for good players who are running at large."[4]

"Just to show that I'm on the square," Sullivan continued, "I would give the club owner a fifteen days' trial of the player. If he still wants the man he can pay me my fee." He added, with his usual confidence, that his broker/agent concept was endorsed by a number of major league magnates.[5]

In short order, it was announced that the management of a minor league franchise in Clinton, Iowa, was looking to Sullivan to furnish it with an entire team. Not surprisingly, the boys back in the Iowa newsrooms were dubious.

This from the *Davenport (IA) Daily Times* of December 3, 1909:

> *S-U-double-L–I–V–A–N spells Sullivan.*
> *If you ever made a hit in your life; if you have ever pilfered a bag, earned an error, or sullied a sacrifice, write to Ted.*
> *He's got job for you.*
> *When the lustre of your batting lamp has been dimmed; when the pedals on which you propelled many a point are feeling like a pair of crooked clothes props; when your back is bent, your liver lazy, and your wing wobbly; don't give up hope.*
> *There's one home left—Ted Sullivan's Haven for Has-Beens.*

Also having a history with Ted Sullivan, the *Hartford Courant* couldn't resist poking a little fun at his intent to provide interested buyers with a biography and list of skill sets for each individual represented by his firm. "It will probably read something like this: 'Can manage a team and act as press agent, as he knows how to write pieces for the paper.'"[6]

"Ted Sullivan's employment bureau is working overtime," added the *Daily Times.* "Clinton wants the veteran to sign up a whole team. It's Ted's first assignment since he opened up his home for cast-offs."[7]

Acknowledging that he was being recruited not only to supply players, but also to manage the new franchise in Clinton, Iowa, Sullivan insisted he was done with managing and was totally focused on his player supply and publishing businesses. He said he was through with the fickle goddess of baseball fortune and not looking for experience … and soon hopped on a train headed for Iowa.

The Clinton "Teddies"

Daddy of Baseball Returns to the Dugout

"The old league did the 'Ted Sullivan'—blew up in July."
—*New York Evening World,* October 20, 1915

At first blush, Ted Sullivan's time in Clinton might seem to be an odd coda to his run of franchise ownership and management. After a quarter of a century of starting, abandoning, and sometimes re-starting teams and leagues across the country, Sullivan had moved into a full-time scouting role for the previous five years or so and had opened his player brokerage business. It appeared that his days of club management were behind him.

But the Clinton Teddies and their 1910 Northern Association season followed an arc consistent with other Ted Sullivan baseball clubs.

Like so many before them, the 25,577 residents of Clinton bit hard on his patented line of blarney once word got around that Sullivan was keen to operate a baseball franchise there during the 1910 season. "Ted Sullivan appears as chubby as young Corbett in his palmy days. Ted is well fed and well groomed," announced a satiated *Dubuque Herald* on the last day of January 1910.

Clinton was ripe for some of that fabled Sullivan magic.

Nonetheless, in 1910, the residents of Clinton were eager for the type of entertainment—"good, clean baseball"—that baseball's bandleader had promised dozens of times to dozens of cities during the previous 30 years.

On March 5, 1910, the *Clinton Daily Herald* announced that a fund-raising committee had received significant contributions to the baseball effort and that Sullivan himself had sent a letter expressing his excitement at running the Clinton franchise. In fact, Sullivan wrote (certainly a stretcher) that he already had the opportunity to move Clinton into the established Three-I league following the 1910 season, and that he had recently signed a pitcher and an infielder to bring in from Comiskey's Chicago club. The letter concluded by saying he expected to be in Clinton on March 20.

Sullivan was actually in El Paso, Texas, sweating spring training details for the White Sox and patronizing eager young reporters. Professing his love for the Lone Star State, he told the *El Paso Times*, "I'm the father of baseball down this way, you know, and I never forget my children. I'm sorry I can't stay here for a month."[8]

His continued absence from Clinton didn't seem to dampen the enthusiasm of that city's boosters. According to the local paper, money was still coming in, and "Fans are Happy" and "Ready for Sullivan." Uncertainty about scheduling and fundraising was shoved aside, and while no one was quite sure where Sullivan was, there was a reassuring rumor that he had departed Los Angeles the previous week, with a plan to stop in Oklahoma City to sign two pitchers while en route to Clinton. Despite the *Daily Herald*'s note "the amount required by Mr. Sullivan's contract with the Clinton club has not yet been secured," local boosterism remained undeterred.

A few days later, in the face of heightening skepticism about Sullivan's purported league, the *Daily Herald* reported that the baseball impresario's arrival could be mere hours away and that public-spirited businessmen were lining up to support the Clinton club. But when Sullivan's silence stretched to a third week, alternatives began to crop up. On March 29, the paper confirmed that Clinton officials had yet to hear a word out of Sullivan, and Malachi Kittridge—a 16-year major league catcher who briefly skippered the 1906 Washington Senators—had offered himself as a managerial option.

By April Fools' Day—nearly a month since Sullivan's initial announcement—Clinton's Northern Association prospects had become increasingly desperate. Under the forlorn headline "TED NOT HERE," the paper reported that $1 Booster Buttons were for sale at various businesses across the area to augment the business community's pledges. Not only had the locals not yet raised enough funds to bring Sullivan to town, they knew nothing of his plans or his whereabouts. There had been reports that he was in Texas setting up a spring training facility for the Chicago White Sox, or that he had left Texas for Oklahoma City, or that he might be on his way to Chicago, but no matter where he actually was, Ted Sullivan *definitely* was on his way to Clinton.[9]

And then it happened. The prayers of the Clinton baseball faithful were answered, and the fans were delivered on April 5 with the arrival of the great Ted Sullivan.

The Fabled Ted Appears

Upon Sullivan's arrival, the longtime promoter set the town abuzz with a flurry of moves and pronouncements. As soon as the matter of his final contract negotiations was handled, he said he planned to sort through the vast number of talented baseball players who were eager to join him in Clinton.

During his first week, Sullivan reportedly kept a frenetic pace. He said he had a full complement of players lined up to arrive in Clinton, though he wasn't prepared to announce their names. The team's first exhibition game would be played on April 17, Sullivan said, but he wasn't in a position to name the opponent. He demanded changes to the upcoming Northern League schedule, and he ordered uniforms for the club, the details of which he kept to himself.

A few days later, Sir Ted announced his roster. Ironically, but not surprisingly, the team was heavily laden with Irish-Catholics—including at least two players named Sullivan, and Paul Hogan, a champion hockey-player-turned-ballplayer from Michigan's Upper Peninsula.

"Ted Sullivan thinks so well of his patronymic that he is scouring the brush for all the Sullivans he can find. He has picked up Jim at Los Angeles and Leo at Erie, Pa. We feel inclined to remark that it is too bad that John L. is abroad and that Billy is in a hospital on the coast. If your name is Sullivan and you're looking for employment, Ted's present address is Clinton, Ioway."
—"The Old Poke," *Davenport Daily Times,* April 10, 1910

If the caliber of Clinton's players didn't generate buzz among the locals, Sullivan still had a few marketing tricks up his sleeve. Concurrent with the arrival of his players, he announced a "Guess the Uniform Color" contest for the young women of Clinton.

The *Daily Herald* observed, "Many of the guesses registered favored green as the color of the Teddies' duds, probably a delicate compliment to the number of sons of Erin enlisted on the team."[10]

By partnering with the newspaper, manager/promoter Sullivan generated the type of pre-season attention he had enjoyed at previous stops with Ladies Days, Fats vs. Leans exhibitions, and even bicycle racks. Ultimately, the season pass prize went to Miss Sadie Amelia Cartwright for her correct guess that the Clinton Teddies (yup, he named the team after himself) would wear black-and-white checked uniforms for the 1910 season. Sadly for Miss Cartwright, by Independence Day her pass would be worthless.

Clinton's Head Teddy continued to work his showman's magic in the run up to the Northern Association season. He let it be known that he just might wear the same uniform as the players and work as an on-field coach during some games, a move that the local paper credited him with originating. He let slip vague promises of gala Opening Day ceremonies the likes of which Clinton had never seen, and the first Clinton Teddies exhibition game on May 1 gave hope that Sullivan's promises might be fulfilled.

Some 1,500 local "fans and fannettes" packed Ringwood Park for Clinton's 11-inning win over the Dubuque "All Professionals." "Every condition was present to make the outlook encouraging. The crowd was so large that it filled all the grandstands and bleachers and fans were lined up along the fences and stretched on the ground in the field," the paper reported.[11]

A few days later, the "Infants" from nearby Sterling "were leisurely slaughtered" by Ted's boys 6–3.[12]

When Clinton's Northern Association schedule opened, however, the local bugs began to savvy what fans from Houston to New Haven had learned after putting their money on a Ted Sullivan-fostered dream.

The town's initial excitement faded fast after a run of mediocre to bad baseball, and Clinton fell deep into the Northern Association cellar with a 10–39 record, drawing barely 200 fans even on a Sunday.

After all Sullivan's hype and promises, Clinton's season continued south in a hurry. Come the middle of May, the *Daily Herald* snarked, "Ted Sullivan now threatens to don a uniform and go on the coaching line. Horrible if true."[13]

Noted a more sympathetic Muscatine news scribe after his town's team had taken its turn drubbing the Teddies: "To Ted: Never in the history of the national pastime, as exploited in Muscatine, has a baseball man in uniform appeared on a local diamond with a history as illustrious as that gray-haired manager who coached yesterday. The fans laughed to see one of his years appearing in baseball togs, but there was a day when the fans of the major leagues cheered when Ted Sullivan came on the field. Take off your hats, boys, to the veteran!"[14]

The intractable Sullivan refused "offers" for him to resign management of the team until he could get them back in the winning column. But calls for his ouster came from all sides. "The Old Poke" in Davenport quipped, "Up in Clinton the popular refrain is 'Slide, Slide, Keep on Sliding,' respectfully dedicated to Ted Sullivan."[15]

The coach's antics sold no tickets. And sure enough, the Teddies, along with the Freeport Pretzels team, disbanded on June 28, but by then the legendary Sullivan was already over the river, through the woods, and gone.

"Clinton simply has refused to support the class of ball furnished," said the nearby *Rock Island Argus* on June 30. "Incidentally, Ted Sullivan, who failed to provide a winning team from the start, is blamed for the present state of affairs."

Clinton wasn't alone with its financial turmoil, however. The league-leading Elgin Kittens and the Kankakee Kays folded on July 11. The Muscatine Pearl Finders, Jacksonville Jacks, and Decatur Commodores soon threw in the towel, and the Northern Association waved the inevitable white flag and disbanded.

Perhaps the Northern Association's most important legacy was the emergence of 19-year-old outfielder Casey Stengel into professional baseball. After signing with his hometown minor league Kansas City Blues of the American Association earlier in 1910, Stengel had been optioned to the Kankakee Kays, where he was batting .251 when the league folded.

Back to Beatin' the Bushes

Fortunately for Ted Sullivan, his tenure in Clinton largely slipped the notice of the national press and quickly became a repressed memory among the locals. But in December of that year (1910), in the generous spirit of the season, the *Washington Post* still insisted that Ted Sullivan was "the most versatile man that was ever connected with the national game ... and no man, no matter how high he is in the councils of baseball, but will consider Ted Sullivan when it comes to the ethics or true knowledge of the game."[16]

Sullivan, of course, agreed with that assessment, saying "I think I am the dean of most persons in the game today and I am under no obligation to any one in baseball. I crave no favors and fear no one's enmity—so far as the national game is concerned."[17]

After a bout with malaria in early 1911, the ubiquitous traveler set out across the continent, planting tall tales and baseball seeds here, there and everywhere. On March 17, he was sitting in the owner's box at Dallas with Charlie and Ann Comiskey. Jim Clarkson of the *Chicago Examiner* noted that Sullivan was celebrating his birthday as well as St. Patrick's Day. "Ted was born on March 17, 1776," Clarkson quipped, "and discovered baseball the following summer."[18]

A Texas League Legend Gets Another Gold Watch

In anticipation of the upcoming annual convention of minor league managers and magnates in San Antonio, Tim Murnane, the former player turned baseball editor of the *Boston Globe*, made a public plea for Ted Sullivan to be recognized for his contributions to baseball.

"I hope the good people of Texas will make a special effort to have present that grand old pioneer scout Ted Sullivan," Murnane wrote. "He has done so much for the national game. In fact, Ted is a real national character, and no big baseball gathering should find him missing."[19]

Indeed, Sullivan was a keynote speaker at a 25th annual gathering of the National Association of Base Ball Clubs of America and was presented with a gold watch for his contributions to the Texas League. Although limited to 10 minutes at the dais for his acceptance speech, fast-talking Sullivan managed to invoke the blood-stained walls of the Alamo, Roman chariot races, the ancient Olympics, and Caesar Augustus before praising his fellow minor league magnates and predicting that Texas would never again be divided geographically or "Base Ballically."[20]

Calls Draft "Root of all baseball evils"

Echoing the sentiments of many of his fellow minor league "magnates," Sullivan railed against what he called "the root of all baseball evils"—the draft. He condemned the major league clubs' often-misused practice of drafting and locking up the better players on struggling, second-tier minor league clubs.

"To think that any major league club should draft players from those poor struggling minors and put them on the counters to resell back, either to the clubs they were drafted from or to the higher minor leagues is a travesty on the whole system of draft," Sullivan complained to reporters.[21]

"There are today in the major leagues a couple of magpie hucksters … that should be forced to go back to their natural and real vocation in life—dealing in short weights in the retail grocery or coal trade. I am in a position to know those jackdaws of base ball, and also the grand and broad men that have controlled the game, and I mark the difference. To me, an ass is an ass, no matter how many bags of gold he has on his back."

Addressing the major league owners directly, he said, "It is a wrongful thing, gentlemen, that good-sized cities in the class C or D leagues should have the foundations of their teams torn from under them every year by losing three or four or five of their good players."[22]

"Remember," he reminded them, "the minors have to draw on the raw material, while you draw on the finished article, even if you have to send some of them back to their seats of baseball learning to get better versed in their baseball algebra."

In February 1912, *Washington Post* news hawk Joe S. Jackson reported that Sullivan, "who is not hooked up at the present," was in line to become president of the upstart Outlaw League: "It is said that Ted Sullivan, known from coast to coast, and at present in Washington, is the man some of the magnates have in mind. No man is better known both in minors and majors. Sullivan has organized more leagues than any man in history."[23]

The appointment never came, but Sullivan was already bouncing around the country, giving his History of Baseball lectures to college students and hunting talent for Comiskey. In fact, he was about to make one of his biggest scores ever for the Sox by finding and bringing forth a barely 20-year-old ballplayer who had been working winters as a linotype machinists' apprentice. On Sullivan's insistence, the normally parsimonious Comiskey bought the young, 5'7", 144-pound backstop, Ray Schalk, for $10,000. The smart, likable, hard-working Schalk would go on to catch a spot in the Hall of Fame—and carry Ted Sullivan's coffin when the time came.[24]

"Commy's Kindergarten"

Sullivan could bring prospects to the table, but he couldn't guarantee they'd play well enough in fast company to make the professional grade. The old scout typically found and prepared spring training grounds for the Sox, then hung around a while to see how his "kids" fared.

Covering spring training for *Collier's* in 1912, Will Irwin—under the headline "Being a Report of a Rambling Hibernian Conversation on

Nothing in General and Everything in Particular"—called the encampment Sullivan had set up in Waco, Texas, "Commy's Kindergarten." He described the "first council of war," the evaluation of young players that took place among "cigars and some 20-year-old stuff" in the privacy of Comiskey's personal rail car.[25]

Among the advice-givers on hand were Scout Ted Sullivan ; Sox manager Nixie Callahan; the *Chicago Tribune's* official booster, Joe Farrell; and one C.J. Quille. Monsignor Quille, head of the Newsboys Home in Chicago, took his annual vacation to help out at Comiskey's training camps, hitting fungos and shagging balls. But his real job was analyzing the heart, spirit, and character of Sullivan prospects.

When Comiskey tapped the ash from his custom-rolled stogie and asked the group, "Well, what do you think of the little ones?" Father Quille was the first to give his opinion, followed by Callahan and Sullivan, who spoke to the aspiring young players' strengths and weaknesses on the ballfield. "Ball players," Sullivan pontificated (while Big Ed Walsh hummed "Roamin' in the Gloamin" in the background), "are not made to order. Some of them haven't the brains to hold on in the big leagues, while possessing natural ability. It's a hard matter to find a man who is up to all the requirements."[26]

On "Puritanical" Frat Boys

As educated, articulate and well-read as he was, "Sir Tedford" wasn't wild about what he called "pharisaical, hypocritical and puritanical college athletes" in professional baseball, especially when frat boys played for minor league teams in the summer and collected paychecks under assumed names in order to protect their amateur status.[27]

"There is many a struggling student who finds the summer money paid to him for his skill very convenient to pay his tuition at school for each coming year," he told the *Washington Evening Star.* "No penalty or stigma should be placed on a young man for receiving money for such a commendable purpose. It is only a class of students who come from the hothouse of college snobbery that have hidden pockets themselves to receive this supposed tainted money."[28]

Crossing Linguistic Swords

In a series of dueling letters in which a University of Pennsylvania law student tried to verbally bully him into hiring a bunch of his college ballplayer friends for the summer, Sullivan crossed scholarly swords by telling the erudite young man, "I am going to have an investigation into how you got your diploma from the University of Pennsylvania, as your letters to me have violated all the laws of syntax, your tenses were one month apart, your rhetoric would shame a prep schooler and your orthography was so bad it would make Noah Webster turn over in his grave."

In December 1912, Comiskey's ecumenical envoy signed three young pitchers and explained how he did it under a headline that read: "Ted Sullivan Selects Swede, German and Irishman for Sox."[29]

◆ 24 ◆

Next Stop: The World

Create a show. Take it on the road. Heck, take it all around the planet. Get the world hooked on America's game. And make a buck.

So whose idea was it? Ted Sullivan, of course, claimed it was his, that he pitched the notion of a World's Tour to the often-disagreeable-but-friend-of-the-Harp manager of the New York Giants, John McGraw, whom he knew had been thinking about such a thing ever since the American sporting goods czar Al Spalding took an antiquated version of baseball around the globe in 1888–1889.

"Why not make it a joint affair," Sullivan said he said, "as it would be bigger in the eyes of the world in having the great teams from the two largest cities in America."[1]

The story goes that McGraw ("The Little Napoleon") and Charlie Comiskey ("The Old Roman") met sometime around the Christmas holidays in 1912 at "Smiley" Mike Corbett's Chicago saloon, and that, after a spirits-infused discussion, the two baseball titans toasted to Sullivan's excellent idea.

In early February 1913, correspondence (almost certainly written by Sullivan) to national news editors and sports writers announced the plan, under the headline: "TED SULLIVAN TO MANAGE WORLD TOUR."

T. P.'s DNA was all over the initial announcement, to wit:

> This circuit of the globe by those two major league clubs, led by the game's two greatest leaders and sportsmen, namely, Charles Comiskey, president of the CWS, and John McGraw, leader of the NYGs, is a tour that is not a money making affair.
>
> Mr. Comiskey stands ready to shoulder any losses incurred on the trip. He wants to make the trip a triumphal march through foreign countries just for the pleasure of travel and to show the world what a great game baseball is.[2]

In his 2003 book, *The Tour to End All Tours,* author and historian James E. Elfers notes: "Both Comiskey and McGraw entrusted Sullivan with their portion of the capital for the tour. Sullivan, perpetually circumspect, made an excellent friend and blind trust, one unlikely to betray either man's confidence."[3]

It was decided that, as soon as the 1913 World Series was concluded, the Sox and Giants would make a barnstorming run through some key American cities, sell some tickets, raise some travel money, and build excitement for the global gallop.

In mid–February, as word of the World's Tour was passed from newspaper to newspaper around the country, Sullivan was aboard Comiskey's private rail car, heading for the Sox spring training camp in Paso Robles, California. Among the scribes, bards, and baseball men sipping brandy and blowing smoke with the Old Roman was "Admiral" John Agnew, a builder of ballparks and the group's official bartender and cigar-clipper.

Bored during a long pull through the middle of Nebraska, the group elected "Senators" from their midst. According to one of the attendant scribes: "It was the sentence of the court that Mr. Sullivan enlighten the inhabitants of every nation to be visited on the world's tour, and he cheerfully agreed to make good."[4]

By early summer of 1913, there were rumors and speculation that Sullivan's much-hyped world's tour was D.O.A.—that the players were being asked to put up a big chunk of their annual salaries for the opportunity to travel to and play ball in foreign lands, and they weren't happy about it.

The young magnate Comiskey was up for just about any new adventures contrived by his favorite scout and counselor (Library of Congress).

As it turned out, the level of investment required by participating players was greatly exaggerated. The participants were required to put up only a couple of hundred bucks each to take the trip of a lifetime, and at least one report had them recouping their money, and then some, before they ever left America's western shore.

In addition to most of their own players, for the World's Tour the two managers, Comiskey and McGraw, salted their squads with high-profile ringers who would draw more interest in the tour and more money at the gates. Among the other-team stars that signed on for the tour were Tris Speaker, Mike Donlin, Germany Schaefer, Christy Mathewson, spit-baller Urban "Red" Faber, and the Native American Olympian, Jim Thorpe, whom one scribbler called "the aborigine who is just now the talk of the entire world."[5]

Thorpe couldn't hit nearly as well as he could run, jump, pole vault, or throw the javelin, but he got paid $6,000 to take a trip to Europe and play baseball for the Giants for a few months.

The White Sox had a less than stellar season in 1913, finishing 17½ games behind Philadelphia, but McGraw's Giants stomped their way to the National League pennant before losing the World Series to the Athletics in five games.

Sox and Giants Go on a Tour of the Wide World
Chicago Examiner
October 18, 1913

All aboard. They're off. The biggest event in the life of a big man—Charles A. Comiskey—had its beginning last night when five handsome Pullman cars, all brand new and supplied with the latest of conveniences, pulled out of the Polk Street station…. Aside from the athletes there were many others in the party, among them Ban B. Johnson, president of the American League; Ted Sullivan, general director and advance agent, and a large gathering of south side fans….

"General Director and Advance Agent" Ted Sullivan beamed when The World's Tour he had long dreamed of headed for the West Coast on October 17, 1913.

As the Old Roman stood under the shed in the Polk Street station last night and saw his athletes, guests, newspaper men and faithful fans step aboard the palatial train he was probably the happiest man in Chicago. His ambition and dream of many years had finally become a reality.

Barnstorming Through the Boonies

Within a week of the last out of the season, the Giants were back in uniform, along with their new sparring partners, the mixed-and-matched White Sox, taking the field before 5,000 baseball fanatics in Cincinnati. The baseball tourists played before big and enthusiastic crowds everywhere they went: Chicago, Ottumwa, Muskogee, Bisbee, Portland ... 31 exhibition games in more than two dozen cities in 34 days (a few additional scheduled games were rained out). For many a small-town baseball fan, it would be the only time they'd see big league ballplayers, in person, playing a big league game.

Sliding west one step ahead of oncoming winter, the travelers played on many a cold, wet day, but that did not stop the crowds from coming.

In Kansas City, for instance, freezing rain and snow had left the field a soggy mess, yet on October 26, 3,300 of Sullivan's stubborn Missouri "fans"—including several who brought oil stoves into the stands to keep warm—turned out for a game of "rather wobbly" baseball. Boasted one local sportswriter: "Their presence was a distinct sign of bravery and a healthy tribute to baseball."[6]

Whereas Ted Sullivan knew his way around his old Cowboys' town, Giants manager McGraw did not. The *Kansas City Journal* reported that "the little Napoleon tarried a bit too long in the club offices getting the world tour's share of the kale," causing him to miss the bus back to the hotel. One of the 200 or so fans waiting outside the ballpark offered to take McGraw to the hotel in his automobile, which, the fan said, was parked just down the street a ways. After following the Good Sam fan for about eight blocks, a mad and sweaty Muggsy sat down in the middle of the road, refused to go any farther, shook his fists, and threatened to "wipe the dirt" with the throng of baseball fans, who were having a hoot of a time watching and making fun of the famous manager sitting on a suitcase, stewing in the middle of the street.[7]

For all their differences in dress, demeanor and elocution (the *Washington Post* once called McGraw "that mild-mannered assassin of the English language and of umpires' sensitive feelings"), Sullivan and McGraw were lifelong pals and partners in various travel-for-profit schemes.[8]

Sullivan loved the 5'7" McGraw's Irish spirit and his banty rooster strut. "I do think," Sullivan once said, "there is so much life, ginger, magnetism and fiery spirit in John McGraw that if he touched a corpse he would make it move."[9]

In Tulsa a few days later, fans pushing into the right field bleachers caused the structure to collapse, crushing one young man to death and injuring scores more. The players helped tend to the wounded, but the crowd insisted that the game go on, and, a half an hour later, it did.

After a long regular season, the "World's Tour" was a chance for the players to have a little fun and take an exotic vacation. Early on, not everyone behaved to Ted Sullivan's expectations. Germany Schaefer, whom John McGraw called one of baseball's "most delightful and whimsical of characters," drew the serious-minded (some called him "sanctimonious") tour manager's ire. In late November, papers around the country reported that "Ted Sullivan, managing director of the world's baseball tour, is said to be disgusted with Steve Evans and Germany Schaefer because they lack dignity and are not taking the trip seriously enough. Ted's goat is the pet of the party."[10]

MC GRAW, N. Y. NAT'L

Took a Spill in Colorado

The tourists were traveling through Colorado, working their way toward the West Coast and departure for Japan, when their deluxe chartered passenger train was struck

In Kansas City, the generally dyspeptic Giants skipper "Muggsy" McGraw tangled with fans who offered to give him a ride to his hotel but left him sitting on his suitcase at the curb. American Tobacco Company souvenir card, 1909–1911 (Library of Congress).

by a passing freight near the town of Palmer Lake. The impact derailed the observation car and disrupted the peace of Sullivan, Comiskey, Ban Johnson, and others who were enjoying the elixir of cigar smoke and mirth in the buffet car.

Thankfully, there were no fatalities. Only minor losses. Those, according to the *Chicago Examiner*, included:

"Johnson B.B.—Lost part of a good story"
And "Comiskey C.A.—Lost one highball"

As the tourists grew closer to the coast and embarkation for foreign lands, at least one observer estimated that "when Charlie Comiskey has returned from the world tour he will be able to say, 'Let's have another,' in fourteen languages."[11]

Beer for Breakfast

Sullivan's tourists were admired, coddled, and fussed over by fans and dignitaries all the way to California. Prior to a game at Oxnard, that city's mayor hosted the team owners, managers, and players at a morning barbecue, the menu for which included slow-roasted ox and a barrel of beer.[12]

"That was our breakfast!" recalled third base tender Hans Lobert. "Did you ever try roasted ox and beer for breakfast? Puts hair on your chest, to say the least."

Once all were well-fed and sufficiently buzzed, the mayor threw down a wager—that the speedy Lobert couldn't beat a racehorse in a run around the bases.

Knowing the wager would be settled that day, some 5,000 fans came out to the ballpark early to watch. A Mexican caballero trotted out a coal-black, rodeo-savvy cow pony trained to make sharp turns.

"So, I got off and, bingo! I led to first base by at least 10 feet, and at second I was 20 feet ahead," Lobert told the author and historian Lawrence Ritter. "All of a sudden that Mexican came around second base and shot right in to short stop, and just missed me by that far. I had to dodge to get clear, but I picked up immediately and I was still in front going into third. When I pulled up to the finish, I said to Klem, the referee, I said 'How about it.?' He said the horse won by a nose. I said, listen, don't tell me that. No horse could beat ME by a nose!"

Sullivan's and Lobert's teammates agreed, saying it was impossible for the horse to have won by a nose, given the sizable proportions of Lobert's proboscis.

The "Fair Reserves"

A number of women, including five honeymooning newlyweds, and a few small children were along for all or parts of the tour. The writer G. W. Axelson (who later penned Comiskey's biography) referred to the wives of the players as "the fair reserves." Mrs. Jim Thorpe, Mrs. "Chief" Meyers, and Mrs. Larry Doyle were the tomboys of the ladies' contingent and sometimes liked to join the boys in fielding practice.[13]

"Mrs. Doyle has the distinction of being the only one among the women who has been knocked out during the practice," Axelson wrote. "The other day she was catching batted balls, missed one and the ball hit her in the head, and she was out for a couple of minutes. Now she sticks to the suffrage end of the game, which is not quite as exciting, but safer."[14]

Besides their occasional forays onto the practice fields, the spouses of players and team officials were also seen in the stands during most exhibition games. However, they were typically excluded from stag-only receptions, smokers, and banquets.[15]

After drawing some 12,000 fans to an exhibition in San Francisco, the tourists moved up the coast to Oregon. In Portland, Sullivan made it clear that he was the "Chief Tourist."

"Just tell the people I am not the White Sox scout," he instructed reporters. "I am the managing director of this tour. And if you don't believe it, look at this."[16]

"Thereupon," the press reported, "Mr. Sullivan produced a letter of introduction from William H. Taft when that fat rascal was President of these United States."[17]

On their trek through big- and small-town America, Sullivan's baseball road show played before more than 140,000 fans, racked up a reported $97,240 in revenue, and showed a profit of some $10,000 above expenses.[18]

Finally, in late November at Victoria, British Columbia, two dozen ballplayers (including six future Hall of Famers) and managers, along with a hefty entourage of owners, wives and two children (Callahan's), sportswriters, equipment handlers, two umpires, and one mother hen tour manager boarded the 5,900-ton, Canadian-owned *Empress of Japan*. The entourage gathered on the top deck for a parting photo in which Ted Sullivan, front and center, waved a large American flag given the tourists by the baseball fans of Portland. It was reported that umpire Jack Sheridan waved so hard, his false teeth fell out.[19]

Leaving an oompah band and a cheering crowd behind, the tourists settled into their first-class berths and set out across the Pacific Ocean. Thirteen of Europe's and the Middle and Far East's greatest cities lay ahead. First stop, Tokyo.

Homage to Neptune

MISS CALLAHAN
ENJOYING HERSELF

Sure enough, the tourists had barely settled into their upscale berths when the *Empress* was spun about in the heart of a late-season typhoon, losing a boiler and its bearings. Everyone from the captain of the ship to the captains of the two ball teams became painfully sick and disoriented as the *Empress* was nearly swamped under 60-foot-high waves.

"Neptune was on 'a tear' for six or seven days of the first part of the voyage," Sullivan recalled, "and showed his mean disposition by exacting more than one tribute off some of the passengers in the way of a disagreeable stomach."[20]

"The propellers were up in the air 1001 times ...

Just hours out to sea on their way to Japan, Ted and his World's Tourists found themselves being tossed about like scarecrows in a fierce late-season typhoon. While the adults aboard fed their lunches to the fish, White Sox manager Nixie Callahan's kids continued to play (*Boston Globe* December 28, 1913).

and Wingo's [Cardinals catcher Ivey Wingo] hair stood straight up for ten days," added Chicago's Joe "The Rooter" Farrell, who rode the swells with the tourists.[21]

Passenger John O. Seys, a sportswriter for the *Chicago Daily News*, wrote, finger-in-throat:

> We were crowded in the cabins.
> Not a player was asleep.
> There was breakfast in the waters.
> There was luncheon in the deep.

On the third day a cable was sent to the Chicago press: "All's well except the passengers."

According to an accounting in the *Boston Globe*, some of the tourists were so violently seasick, "they were asking in feeble whispers to be cast overboard. No names shall be mentioned, but not a few had made their peace with the world and were ready to make the long journey to the beyond."[22]

When the storm finally subsided a bit, the players were ordered into their uniforms and practiced throwing into nets erected on the leeward deck. Germany Schaefer proceeded to demonstrate for the Royal Navy officers aboard the throwing of a curve ball, which the skeptical Brits had heard of but considered "a bit of the usual American bunk."[23]

When weather confined them below decks, the tourists killed time by "fanning" (telling stories), creating their own vaudeville skits, dancing, playing practical jokes, and betting on human horse races (players on hands and knees, carrying Nixie Callahan's kids across the dining room).

Gossip Aboard

As the tour's official communicant, manager Sullivan served as the on-board editor of a typewritten daily newspaper he conceived called *The Sea Gull Express*. News, including celebrity tidbits and rumors, was to be received "by wireless and seagulls" and dispensed by Sullivan. But *The Sea Gull Express* was quickly sunk by what Sullivan called "Gossip Row," a group of chin-wagging passengers, including "Mr. and Mrs. Highbrow" and a suffragette he called "The Duchess of Loud Talk," who spread the juice faster than Sullivan could type it.[24]

Giants manager McGraw, in one of his regular cable dispatches to the *Boston Post*, wrote that Ted Sullivan's entertainment was a show in itself: "It consists of a lecture on the origin and evolution of baseball. He has a number of lantern sides of old players and incidents of the game which are intensely interesting."[25]

Gus Axelson was kind but more honest: "Ted expatiated on the rise of the national games until his hearers were groggy."[26]

Buttoned-up Sullivan was not one for horseplay and avoided the smoking room, which the card sharks aboard called "gambling hell." "The Chicago crowd has been having a lot of fun with Sullivan," wrote McGraw in his dispatch to stateside readers. "He is very serious and cannot see any 'kidding,' the result being that they make him the object of numerous jokes and play all kinds of tricks on him."[27]

In one incident, the players goosed Sullivan's shirt-sleeve patriotism by changing out all the American flags decorating the dining room with British Union Jacks.

"It was all done for his [Sullivan's] discomfiture," reported McGraw, "and had the desired effect."[28]

"The twentieth century tourists were to exhibit before the little brown men of the Mikado's kingdom, the almond-eyed celestials and before the reformed head hunters of Uncle Sam's island possessions."
—G. W. Axelson[29]

Hucksters and Rickshaws

Arriving in port at Yokohama, Japan, the tourists were taken aback by the unusual sights and smells and the cloying throngs of hucksters and rickshaws. "If you did not ride in one of those wagonettes, those Japs would follow after you and call you cheap," the tour manager groused.[30]

The "human horses," as Sullivan called them, twice fooled the 300-plus pound fan, contractor, and Comiskey pal, Tom Lynch, into paying for faked damage to their rickshaws, claiming his American-size bulk had led to axle breaks.

SCHAEFER, Detroit

A goofball on and off the field, Germany Schaefer gave a nonsensical speech to an enthusiastic crowd of confused Japanese fans (American Tobacco card series, 1909–1911, Library of Congress).

"American fish in the shape of the gullible man or woman may not bite at everything in their own waters," complained Sullivan. "But in foreign waters they will not bite the bait only, but the hook and line and even the man that is holding the rod."[31]

Veteran Cubs executive James A. Hart had warned the tourists before they left America's more tolerant shores that "Deportment of players on and off the field will be most important, as the people in the countries to be visited hardly will understand that quarreling with the umpire and some of the tricks that are here regarded as legitimate."[32]

Arriving shaky-legged in Tokyo, the tourists barely had time to change into their uniforms before taking the field for the first of three scheduled exhibitions.

Afterward they were treated to a feast, complete with entrancing geishas. And the following day, McGraw and Callahan combined their squads to take on Japan's best ball team from Keio University before a reported crowd of 10,000 curious and enthusiastic Japanese.

Much to the embarrassment of serious Sullivan, baseball's Clown Prince, Germany Schaefer, proceeded to doff his hat to the Japanese crowd and babble out a long-winded greeting in a language entirely of his own making.[33]

The bigger, more powerful Americans overwhelmed the Keios with blur pitching and long knocks over the outfield wall, winning the game, 16–3.

Meanwhile, Sullivan delivered an illustrated lecture on America's national sport to students and ball players at rival Waseda University and cabled reports back home saying that baseball was driving the Japanese mad with interest and uncontainable enthusiasm. Sullivan's claim, via trans-oceanic cable reports, that "our game has been adopted as the national pastime in Japan" would prove not only accurate, but prophetic.[34]

Shanghai-ed

Entering the crowded, steamy port of Shanghai, the tourists at the rail of the *Empress* found themselves surrounded by a flotilla of little boats and rafts filled with shouting men, women and children, who extended long poles with baskets on the ends, into which they begged the visitors to deposit coins.

But rains washed out any hopes for a game in Shanghai, and the entourage had to settle for more feasts and long-winded (Sullivan) after-dinner speeches. Few or none of the players could identify what they had for dinner, but each one left with the now rarest of souvenirs, a silver-headed cane with "Shanghai 1913" etched upon it.

Full as a tick after one such dinner, McGraw reportedly declined an offer from a street vendor to try a sample of fresh-grilled rat and high-tailed it back to the ship, while a few of the bachelor boys were reported late getting back aboard, having "got lost" in Chinatown, home of Shanghai's famous brothels.

Remembering the Maine

In Manila, the tourists were welcomed by American military bands. Awaiting them on shore was McGraw's old teammate from the Baltimore Orioles of the 1890s, Arlie Pond, who had served in the Spanish-American

War and stayed on the islands to practice medicine among the Filipinos. An American Navy admiral gave an impassioned speech welcoming the baseball emissaries, and Ted Sullivan, of course, gave an extended oratorical response that dredged up every detail of Admiral Dewey's military accomplishments, decorations, and dietary considerations.

The two games played in Manila drew some 14,000 spectators, many of them American Army and Navy personnel, who paid the highest ticket prices—as much as $3.50 apiece—of the entire World's Tour.

A Feast for Cannibals

Puffed up and well-fed once again, the tourists steamed out of Manila to the strains of a band playing the *Star Spangled Banner* and headed for Australia. Rumors that cannibals still inhabited some of the outer islands caused no little trepidation among the ladies of the entourage. According to Sullivan, the gargantuan but gallant tourist, Tom Lynch, allayed the fair ones' fears by saying he would offer himself as a feast to any cannibals who might board the ship, reasoning that "after they get through eating me they will have no appetite for anyone else."[35]

Christmas Down Under

Steaming toward Australia, the tourists celebrated Christmas aboard ship. Hans Lobert dressed up as Santa Claus and handed out gifts of toys to the Callahan kids. For Mr. Sullivan, he had a diamond pin, compliments of the manager's friends and fans back in Chicago.[36]

The tourists were enamored of what Sullivan called "the open-hearted and magnetic people of Australia," who greeted them at Brisbane on New Year's Day 1914. After a quick ball game at the Brisbane Driving Park, the entourage was off to Sydney to demonstrate the American game to 6,000 cricket fans. Sullivan called the Australians "the most sport loving people in the world, especially manly outdoor sport."[37]

Tracking the tourists on nearly a daily basis, papers back home called erudite Sullivan "a student of men, a keen observer, a pleasant entertainer and a gifted orator. Mr. Sullivan was selected as the official speechmaker for the world's tour."[38]

In Melbourne, following yet another grand reception and fully winded welcoming speeches by distinguished scholars and statesmen of Australia, Ted Sullivan humbly spoke on behalf of the touring party and for 20 minutes or so managed to deliver, at least according to one yawning chronicler, "odes to baseball, Captain Cook, Waterloo, the War of the Roses, the Panama Canal and the Battle of Gettysburg."

"Baseball," Sullivan carefully explained to the gentry Down Under,

Is the creation of American temperament and genius and it is co-existent with the growth of American youth…. It has enabled the farmer's son to help his father to lift an old mortgage off his farm or help him buy a new one. It has placed the struggling student in a position to pay his way through college and it has taken the humble boy from the city lots and gave him a chance to gain a little knowledge and culture of the outside world.[39]

While Sullivan droned on, many in the ball-playing entourage were no doubt daydreaming about the casinos at Monte Carlo and the cabaret ladies at the Moulin Rouge that lay ahead.

Leaving Australia, Ambassador Sullivan sent a confessional missive to the *Washington Times*: "The Englishman [in Australia] will no more give up his national game of cricket than he will stop eating roast beef and plum pudding."[40]

Hustled at the Pyramids

After stops in Adelaide, Freemantle, Perth, and Colombo in Ceylon (where the baseball tourists slurped tea with none other than the Irish baronet, Sir Thomas J. Lipton, then one of, if not *the* richest man in the world), the entourage arrived in Suez, anxious to see the sights in the Cradle of Civilization. There, however, there were no dignitaries waiting to grant their every wish. "At Suez," snorted Sullivan, "we met the advance guard of Ali Baba and his forty thieves from Cairo in the shape of card sellers, cap sellers, and any other wares they could sell. They would begin at ten dollars and then come down to ten cents."[41]

The tourists hired camels to take them to the Sphinx and pyramids at Cairo. "Mr. Tom Lynch, our three-hundred pounder, had a hard time with Ali Baba and his henchmen," recalled Sullivan. "They wanted two dollars for helping him get on the camel and then wanted a dollar more for helping him off."[42]

In Cairo, the Americans played two games before Egypt's exalted and last Khedive (the head of state under Turkish rule). Comiskey would later jokingly recall that "the Bedouin removed himself to a safe distance, squatted on his haunches and silently awaited the finish."[43]

McGraw wrote in his book, *My 30 Years in Baseball*, that every time he looked up to Khedive Abba II's box, the ruler had his back to the ballgame. McGraw claimed to have plucked Germany Schaefer off the bench and sent him up into the stands to get the skinny.[44]

The World's Tourists were lionized in Sydney, Melbourne and Brisbane, where those cities' Lord Mayors gave lengthy welcoming speeches and Ted (front row, second from left in the ice cream suit) declaimed in kind, waxing for more than 20 minutes on the history of the planet and the world's greatest sport, baseball, "the creation of American temperament and genius" (from Ted Sullivan's book, *History of World's Tour*, 1914).

Returning a few minutes later, Schaefer reportedly assured McGraw that it was all right: "I just talked to one of them fellows with the funny hats. He said the Khedive means no disrespect to our game, but he's got to look toward home. With so many American ballplayers here the Khedive figures he'd better keep an eye on his harem."[45]

Spin Doctor Ted Sullivan, on the other hand, claimed that he had met the Khedive personally and that "his Majesty enjoyed the games very much. He told me his subjects were thinking of taking up our game, and he hoped they would."[46]

Given the Boot

After some of the boys having caused a public row at a pool hall in Nagasaki and strayed from the moral path in Shanghai's China Town, Sullivan was nervous about the bachelor tourists' social inclinations upon reaching Italy, the heart of Catholicism. "Ted Sullivan tells us we should remember that we are now in 'Christian Country' and that we should begin to behave," recalled future Hall of Famer Tris Speaker.[47]

The tourists were entertained on arrival by what Sullivan described as "the vaudeville talent of Naples"—performers balancing on flatboats, singing, dancing tangos, and diving after coins tossed by the tourists. At Rome, the entourage was greeted by posters and banners announcing "*Grandi Match Baseball Stadium Nazionale Pomoreggio Mercoldi*." But once again, the scheduled game had to be called off due to rain, which gave the tourists time to take in the Coliseum (where Thorpe, "The Indian Apollo," pinned fellow diamond gladiator Fred Merkle in a mock wrestling match), the Catacombs and cathedrals, and a chance to meet Pope Pius X.[48]

Not coincidentally, the organizers of the tour—Comiskey, McGraw, Sullivan, and Sox manager Jimmy "Nixie" Callahan—as well as a good many of the players were Irish-Catholics.

"Nothing was more imposing to us all, irrespective of the creed of members of the party than the entrance, to the room in which we were seated, of this grand old man of the Roman Catholic Church," Sullivan—who had arranged the audience with the pontiff—recalled in his account of the trip. "His beautiful, classic face, his manner of giving us his blessing, impressed all very much."[49]

The tourists, Catholic and non–Catholic alike, left the Vatican awed and carrying pockets and purses full of religious trinkets blessed by Pope Pius X.

When it came time to leave Rome and head for France, Comiskey

GIANTS & WHITE SOX. AT THE VATICAN - FEB. 1914.

A highlight for many of the Catholics in the entourage was having an audience with Pope Pius X at the Vatican. Ted Sullivan is in the center of the second row, slightly behind and to the left of Nixie Callahan, the man with his hand on little girl's shoulder (from Ted Sullivan's *History of World's Tour,* **1914).**

was too ill to travel. Sullivan stayed behind while an Italian doctor treated the Old Roman for, ironically, "Roman Fever." The doc's prescription: He told Comiskey to refrain from drinking ice water. And it actually worked.

Dicey in France

In Nice, the ballplayers donned their colorful World Tour uniforms and rode in a parade before slipping off to the casino at Monte Carlo, where McGraw reportedly dropped $500 and several of the lesser earners lost their lunch money before returning to town to play an afternoon ballgame.

"The French were somewhat puzzled by the intricacies of the play, which they found difficult to understand," reported *Sporting Life,* "but they showed much enthusiasm when the ball was hit hard to the outfield."[50]

Less confusing, and much more fascinating to the French, was Jim Thorpe putting on a side show of running, throwing the javelin, and other Olympic-style feats while a French aviator did daring loops in the sky above.

In the "Long-Sought City" at Last

The insistent rain that had washed away many a game along the way followed the tour to Paris (Sullivan called Gay Paree "the cynosure of all eyes"), snuffing any chance for one last game before the tour had to leave for London, its final stop before returning home to the United States.[51]

Reporting from Paris, the great sportswriter Damon Runyon said the rain was so heavy that, if there was a bottom to the field, nobody could find it. With little else to write about, reporters naturally gravitated to the tour's storyteller emeritus. Runyon joked that "Ted Sullivan gives out an interview every few seconds and every one is different."[52]

But it was Paris, after all. The high-, middle- and would-be brows wandered the Louvre, while the ballplayers smoked cigarettes and whistled at French women, and Ted Sullivan went up to Waterloo to admire paintings of his hero, Napoleon. At a luncheon in their honor, the tourists shook hands and/or exchanged cheek kisses with French President Raymond Poincaré.

Last Stop: "Swelldom"

Sullivan initially hoped and had announced that the final contest of the World's Tour would be in Dublin on George Washington's birthday. But somewhere along the way plans changed, and it was on to London for the last hurrah. As a product of Eire, the manager of the world tour was less than eager to deal with the self-possessed British, but anxious to make a show of his and the tour's success.

Damon Runyon joked that the real purpose of the tour was "to convince Herman Schaefer and the rest of the heathens included on the roster of the two clubs that Ireland, one of the stopping points, is the greatest country in the atlas." He pretended to observe "great unrest in the Hibernian contingent over the rumor that Fred Merkle, Hans Lobert and other 'Germans' had voted to cut out Dublin and descend upon Berlin." Evans had reportedly drawn Sullivan aside and in a conspiratorial tone asked him, "What right do the Dutchmen with this party have to hold a meeting by themselves and vote that we go to play in Germany instead of Ireland?"[53]

That, reported Lardner, garnered "an explosion" from Sullivan.

Behind his hand, Sullivan regularly referred to English King George's domain as "Swelldom," and believed that the Americans, "with their magnetic gingery temperament," would never be able to assimilate with the English, given the latter's "frigid-zone temperament."[54]

The Giants' third base coach, Arlie Latham, a.k.a. "the freshest man on earth," recalled, "We took to Ted Sullivan, a pillar of the baseball world in the United States, who said of the British aristocracy: 'The definition of the word gentlemen in England is a man who was never guilty of the crime of soiling his hands with honest toil.'"[55]

A bored Runyon sat through a stiff-shirt luncheon sponsored by American businessmen in London, where he reported that "His Gracious Majesty, King George, the Ban Johnson of all England, will give baseball one glare tomorrow afternoon."[56]

Runyon noted that the attendees all drank to the health of King George and Woodrow Wilson, and that "Old Ted Sullivan closed with an oratorical effort that sounded like a combination of 'The Star Spangled Banner' and Marc Anthony's outburst over the late J. Caesar set to tango music. Only it was longer."[57]

In fact, King George V *had* agreed to attend the baseball game—to be his first appearance ever at Chelsea Stadium, causing Promoter and Head-Cash-Counter Ted to envision a ravenous crowd of 30,000 or more.

Here's Mutton in Your Eye

McGraw, in his recounting of the game, recalled that Sullivan had cut a catering deal with an Englishman who'd been hanging around the stadium.

> Several times while I sat on the bench, he [the caterer] came to me all a-flutter, wanting to know when the intermission would take place. "Why, what's the matter with you?" I asked. "Don't you know that baseball does not have any intermissions?"[58]
> "My God," he [the caterer] cried, putting his hands to his head. "I'm ruined! What am I going to do with my mutton pies?"

Said McGraw with a straight face: "You can bring me one if you want to."

Ultimately, Ted Sullivan's London show came off without a hitch. In deference to the king and with a nod to political ecumenism, Irish pitchers were, as "Hotspur," a.k.a. Albert Feist of Britain's *Daily Telegraph*, put it, "taboo for the day."[59]

Nonetheless, the Brits were fascinated by the American twirlers' curious menu of pitches, particularly Christy Mathewson's fade-away. Asked how Mathewson did it, only-the-facts Sullivan told onlookers the pitch was legally patented by the hurler and that no one else could throw it without his permission.

At least 25,000 Brits, including one mystified sovereign, saw the Sox beat the Giants, 5–4, in extra innings. A polite British press reported that the king and his subjects found America's game "quite interesting."

The view from *Harper's Weekly* was much more upbeat, claiming that

"Though he [King George] might not have imbibed much wisdom, he was certainly entertained, as the royal smile never faded, from the first inning to the last."[60]

Once the globe-girdling entourage was safely ensconced on the ship that would take them home, the Americans traded jokes about the stoic English men and women who had politely clapped during the game, even though less interested in America's silly version of rounders than catching a glimpse of their Majesty.

At a safe distance from the Liverpool pier, Sullivan proclaimed the English so dull that American comedians in London had to give free matinees every day at 2 p.m. to allow the audiences to laugh at the jokes they told the night before, as it took them 18 hours to digest the point of the gibes.

Tris Speaker, Boston's star center fielder, who had played for the White Sox on the tour, and who Sullivan considered one of the most cordial and jovial players on board, concluded that "The trip would have been a great success if we had only dropped the umpires overboard in the middle of the Pacific."[61]

The Americans were all surely in good humor as they crossed the Atlantic, headed for home on the smooth-sailing *Lusitania*. In a final on-board celebration, Ted Sullivan reportedly told Irish stories to the captive populace.

Home Again, Home Again....

The legendary descriptor Runyon was present with pen in hand to describe the tourists' arrival in New York harbor:

> When the ferryboat Niagara, listing slightly under a load of shrieking White Sox fans, and breathing ragtime music from every port hole, crept up out of the haze, its passengers saw a short, pudgy old gentleman leaning far over the rail of the Lusitania, one hand clamping his derby hat to his brow and the other swinging an American flag ... indubitably Ted Sullivan, patriarch of our national pastime.[62]

Although it had clearly not set the world on fire for baseball, the 35,000-mile tour was considered a public relations success—despite the fact that coverage by the foreign press had been largely overshadowed by the darkening cloud that was about to rain World War I.

Waiting to pounce on the baseball tourists as they disembarked at Pier 56 were agents from the upstart Federal League. They made a mad dash for stars like Tris Speaker, who were unsigned for the coming year, and their offers of higher salaries and benefits were not subtle.

New York reporters noted, with evident traces of sarcasm, that Manager Sullivan (whom Runyon had recently dubbed "The Barnacle of Baseball") was the first passenger to lean over the rail of the *Lusitania,* wave the American flag and hail the press when the thought-to-be-unsinkable pride of the Cunard line was tugged to its moorings at New York on March 6, 1914. Illustration by Wallace Carlson, *Inter Ocean* (Chicago).

The world's tourists returned to what papers claimed was one of the greatest welcomes New York had ever seen. There were dinners, banquets, and proclamations galore. At Chicago, 700 cheering baseball fans crowded into the ballroom of the Congress Hotel to welcome Comiskey and his entourage home. The *Chicago Examiner* observed: "American League and National League sat side by side. On either side of them were represented the old American Association and the Brotherhood, while Ted Sullivan was a living reminder of the days when he gave 'Commy' his first job as a professional ball player."[63]

Among the after-dinner speakers was, of course, the uber-patriotic Ted Sullivan, who concluded that "The Europeans know now if they never knew it before that America would be a hard country to lick in time of war."[64]

Still beatific from the trip around the globe, Rooter Farrell declared: "Let all prejudices against other lands die. It's a wonderful world filled with wonderful people. They're all nice if you let them, and best of all they like Americans."[65]

The murder of Archduke Franz Ferdinand in Sarajevo some 14 weeks later would trigger the most murderous conflict the "wonderful world" had ever seen.

Finally—to the Bank

Ever the shrewd businessman, Charles Comiskey managed to dodge any questions regarding how much profit was made from the tour. The ball players had each put up $250 of their own money to participate (and stay in nice hotels, see the world, and eat like kings along the way), and at the tour's end were reimbursed their $250 and given an additional $250 to take home.

Author Timothy M. Gay, in a book about baseball legend and tour participant Tris Speaker, concludes that "for Commy it was money well invested; he more than recouped it in the end. The other two principal investors, McGraw and minor league impresario Ted Sullivan, also made out handsomely."[66]

Reports in papers around the country put the tour's end-game profit at more than $70,000.

While the other baseball men proceeded to hustle home, kiss their wives, and do their laundry before rushing off to their respective spring training camps, Ted Sullivan, according to the *Calumet News* of March 17, 1914, spent a week visiting his brother Dennis in Wisconsin.

Baseball's wily pioneer scout offered the *News* a grand and prophetic observation before he "packed his typewriter and hiked away south to look for promising players."

The paper concluded its story with: "Ted says in Japan our game has been adopted as the national pastime and it is being played on lots, on the school grounds and on the college campuses. He thinks this will prove to cement the friendship of these two countries more than anything else could."

Another scribbler quipped: "Now that he is been around the world, Ted can be expected to put on the market next year a few Hawaiians, a couple of Australians, a Chinese coolie, a Japanese juggler and some natives of India, Egypt and Turkey."[67]

Lost to History

Throughout the tour, the antics and on-field performances of the ball players were recorded on film by a small crew from the Pathé Eclectic Film

Company. Their moving picture camera captured not only the boys showing boys on the four continents how to play baseball, but the reactions of the foreign dignitaries who attended the games, the spectators who threw coconuts at the players in New Guinea, the entourage's meeting with the Pope, the wrestling match between Thorpe and Merkle on the floor of the Colosseum—and even Hans Lobert's race with a horse around the bases in California.

Within weeks of the tourist's return home, Pathé Eclectic Film Company had produced and released an animated, hour-long travelogue called, simply enough, "The Giants-White Sox World Tour." The silent film was enlivened by the comedic actions of "the world's greatest baseball fan," a made-up character, a stowaway played by the film's director, Frank McGlynn.

Ted Sullivan, of course, waxed endlessly about the trip for months. "We saw the Sphinx and the Pyramids, the sculpture and paintings of Angelo and Raphael in the galleries of Naples, Rome and Paris," he would say, hand over heart, "but the statue of statues that roused all the Americanism in us is a piece of art that stands at the portals of Manhattan Isle called 'the Statue of Liberty.'"[68]

By the middle of May, Sullivan had written and published an 89-page *History of World's Tour* and was making plans for a cross-country, lecture-with-pictures peregrination.

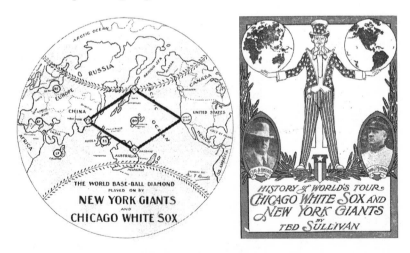

The picture of cheering throngs and Lady Liberty still fresh in his mind, in May of 1914, Sullivan cranked out a small book of personal observations and bloviations dedicated to the players who "reflected credit not only on themselves as the exponents of America's National Game but also on American citizenship" (*History of World's Tour*, May 1914).

20,000 Words—Give or Take....

"The book is a story of the world's tour. It is more than that," wrote R.W. "Ring" Lardner in a book review for the *Chicago Tribune*. "It is an insight into the life and habits of that grand old man, its author, and of Napoleon Bonaparte, who was to France what Mr. Sullivan is to and has been to baseball. It is not our custom to advise our readers to buy the books which are reviewed here in these columns. But in the case of Mr. Sullivan's volume we must at least recommend that you borrow it."[69]

But then there was Ted Sullivan's abiding wish to see true-blue American baseball played on the Emerald Isle. "I am thinking of hitting two birds with one stone," he told the press, "by giving the great national game of America and at the same time celebrating the institution of the new 'Home Rule' of Ireland."[70]

Within weeks of his return to the British Isles, one headline back home read: "WAR STOPS BALL TOUR—TED SULLIVAN MAROONED ON WRONG SIDE OF OCEAN."[71] It was reported that trans-Atlantic steamer sailing had been suspended, and plans for a European tour by all German (-American) and all-Irish (-American) baseball teams had been called off. "I was in London the night England declared war on Germany," said Sullivan. "The scenes it brought on—in the way of excitement will ever be impressed upon my mind."[72]

In a cable sent back to reporters in America, Sullivan quipped that, when he had asked the European powers to take up America's national game, "they got into a war as to who would adopt it first."[73]

Carrying a letter from President Wilson sanctioning his travels, the glib Sullivan was able to, as he put it, "frisk the bank of England for enough gold to get me home," and he booked passage on an English liner with 2,499 other souls seeking safety in still-neutral America. English navy cruisers shadowed the liner to protect it from being sunk by German U-boats, and the vessel's stacks were painted several times while at sea to reflect the colors of different (neutral) nations—including the colors of Japan and Sweden.[74]

The ship went unmolested, but a war of words broke out onboard. In a letter to his pals in the press, Sullivan wrote: "The English passengers and members of the crew hate the Germans aboard to such an extent that if you order a bottle of Pabst or Schlitz beer you would be under suspicion of a being a German spy."[75]

And he made no bones about favoring Germany over the British, whom he despised.

Writing in the third person, he said: "Ted Sullivan's teachers were German. The playmates of his youth were German, and Ted is with the Germans in sentiment to a finish, and so should every one of the right Irish blood be with the Germans, whether they like the Kaiser or not."[76]

◆ 25 ◆

Ted's Magic Lantern Show

"America's great newspapers select from their staffs their brightest writers and cleverest artists to adorn the 'pink sheet' with story and pictures of the nation's game, and the magazines, recognizing base ball's tremendous hold on the public, compete for the services of the game's ablest exponents as contributors of special articles, but it has remained for that unique character who has done so much for base ball, in the fields and in its councils, Ted Sullivan, to be the pioneer in showing the possibilities of the game as the subject of an illustrated lecture that as entertainment and instruction marks an epoch."
—*The Sporting News*, April 18, 1912

He couldn't help it. It was in his genes. More than scouting, managing and promoting, Ted Sullivan loved to tell stories. Well-read and inventive, he was, by all accounts, very good at it.

Said sports writing pioneer Al Spink: "His travel and brisk acquaintance have added to his natural fund of Irish wit and made him delightful as a raconteur. No man in the baseball world can compare with Sullivan as a storyteller."[1]

By 1912, after more than four decades in the game, Sir Ted had become baseball's de facto historian and best-known bon vivant. When baseball went into its winter hibernation, the old Samaritan took his stories, remembrances, and collection of historic photographs on the road.

Lugging a trunk full of lantern slides, Sullivan gave illustrated lectures in town square theaters across the United States, paying tribute to baseball pioneers including Abner Doubleday and Ban Johnson and many of the stars of his yesteryear.

Ads in advance of his appearance promised that "For 10 cents, Ted Sullivan will take you around the world."

218

Baseball Lecture
Hartford Courant
January 27, 1913

A treat for the fans is promised at the Park Casino Wednesday night when Ted Sullivan, known as a great genius of the game, will give an illustrated baseball lecture that is not only a novelty, but is educational, historical and humorous. The illustrations number over 100 pictures, taking in every angle of the game, from its inception down to the present day, winding up with pictures of the late World Series between the New York Giants and the Boston Red Sox. Some of the old clubs that will be shown on the canvas include the original Knickerbockers of New York, the first organized team to play the game.

During the past week, Mr. Sullivan gave his lecture in Washington, attracting big crowds. He has the quality of being a witty talker and is full of baseball facts. He makes the entertainment enjoyable in every detail, and all loyal baseball fans will be highly interested in the old-time teams and players. The lecture will begin at 8 o'clock, and the vast enclosure of the Park Casino will accommodate a big crowd.

Between scouting and spring training commitments, "Professor" Sullivan presented his "World's Tour of Baseball Pictures" at movie and playhouses throughout America (advertisement from the *Muscatine (IA) News-Tribune*, April 23, 1915).

At St. Louis University, where he had once prepped for a minute, Sullivan's "shafts of Irish wit" aimed at the English and their "deliberate" (slow) game of cricket garnered guffaws and applause. "The result was one of the finest treats that could be laid before a body of young Americans who have a love of base ball," wrote Spink, "and where can a body of young Americans be gathered that doesn't love it?"[2]

Sullivan told the students he felt there was room in the popular game for yet another professional league. A few weeks later it was reported that he was in line to become president of the new, "outlaw" United States League, although that did not happen.

From Saint Louis U, he took his lecture and slide presentation to Yale, Brown, and Holy Cross. At Catholic University in D.C. he spoke in Carroll Hall of St. Patrick's Church as guest of the Catholic University Athletic Association.

"HOW THEY LOVE IT!" was the *Topeka Journal's* headline following Sullivan's lecture at St. Louis. "The lecture made such a hit, and there was so much interest shown that the 'movie men' saw a new opportunity to give the public just what it wants."[3]

"A Witty Talker Full of Baseball Facts"

The veteran promoter siphoned lots of good ink from the wells of his old pals, the knights of small-town newsrooms. They ballyhooed his lectures at every stop. In the spring of 1916, the *Arkansas Democrat* informed its readers that "the most well-known baseball man and manager in the country today will bring his ten thousand dollar six reels of Pathe films to the Kempner Theatre for a continuous performance."[4]

"Ted Sullivan, the celebrated baseball seer, who arranged the tour, will explain every part of the journey," promised the *Dubuque Telegraph-Herald*, calling his motion pictures "amusing, entertaining and an educational treat."[5]

As Sullivan headed back to the burning fields of his college days, the *Topeka State Journal* announced: "Ted Sullivan, the Grand Old Man of baseball … one of baseball's most unique characters and as brainy as was ever connected with the national game, will be in Topeka from today until the end of the week.… The pictures are entertaining and instructive, and Mr. Sullivan's talks are well worth the price. Mr. Sullivan has continued to make a hit wherever he has appeared … the stories he tells off stage, even a German could get a laugh out of them."[6]

Over the years, ballplayers, particularly those playing and traveling with the White Sox, heard and saw Ted Sullivan's lecture and stereopticon slide show so many times, they began to joke about it among themselves.

Sports columnist Hugh S. Fullerton recalled that at spring training in El Paso, a couple of the boys switched out the slides in Sullivan's carousel. When he began his lecture with a flowery tribute to Big Ed Walsh, the photo that came up was of a lop-eared burro eating cactus. When he unleashed one of his rousing patriotic diatribes, the picture that came up—which was supposed to be the American flag—was one of the great pitcher and pinch-hitter Nick Altrock "cutting up didos" (clowning).[7]

"Ted struggled through it, with every picture wrong," wrote Fullerton, "but it was a riot."[8]

Newspapers continued to report the whereabouts of Sullivan (Damon Runyon had taken to calling him "the celebrated carpetbagger of baseball") throughout the 1915 season. Although he was only on the periphery of the game at that point—scouting and lecturing—his name was still part of sportswriters' lexicon.[9]

Writing about a young player that the Yankees had just acquired, the *New York Evening World's* Bozeman Bulger noted that the kid had been setting the Nebraska State League on fire before that league "did the old Ted Sullivan" and blew up in mid-year the previous season.[10]

Sullivan's plan to take baseball to Ireland in 1914 having been torpedoed by the outbreak of the Great War in Europe, he began casting longing looks at South America. Attending the Pan American Congress in D.C. in late December of 1915, he announced that he would take a band of star ballplayers to Panama, Argentina, Brazil, and Chile to "spread the gospel of base ball south of the equator."[11]

The Gospel According to Ted

Comiskey and McGraw let it be known that they were on board with Sullivan's latest travel scheme. McGraw claimed that the trip around the world that Sullivan had orchestrated in 1913–1914 "was one of the best things that ever happened for baseball," and that this one would be even more successful in developing baseball outside the states.[12]

Sullivan believed a swing through the southern continent made perfect sense, as multinational men working on construction of the Panama Canal already were forming leagues and playing ball. "Who knows," he said, "but that in due time the winner of the big league in that country would play the winner of the championship of our major leagues for the world title."[13]

The wits in Chicago feigned alarm, saying: "If Ted Sullivan carries out his threat to conduct another world's tour, we fear he will start international complications unless he refrains from inflicting that baseball lecture on the natives."[14]

Throughout 1916, Sullivan and McGraw talked up their imaginative plan for a full-on South American tour. In November, Sullivan applied for a passport to travel to Rio de Janeiro, Buenos Aires, and Panama, listing his home as Chicago and his occupation as "Writer and Baseball Magnate." And in the early spring of 1917, armed with a letter of introduction and support from President Woodrow Wilson, the traveler was busy making arrangements for ball fields and accommodations in Argentina and Brazil, when Wilson declared war on Germany, shooting down Sullivan's dream of a foreign baseball tour once again.

The *Washington Times* reported that "Ted wanted to take two more teams to South America, spreading the good word, but Kaiser Bill thought different, started a lot of foolish fighting with real weapons and Ted has been compelled to stick to dreaming of that tour in South America."[15] Responded Sullivan: "I promised the people in South America cities that I would return within six months and perhaps sooner."

Following the war, he actually attempted to keep that promise.

Sox and Saints

Hall of Famers Slay St. Mary's

Some 679,923 fans paid to see the White Sox play at Comiskey Park in 1916, but only a few hundred merchants and farmers saw them slay the St. Mary's Saints back in Kansas on April 6, 1916.

The boys on St. Mary's College baseball team, many of them still lacking chin whiskers, were warming up for their first practice of the year on a cold and clammy March day in 1916 when they found out who their first opponent would be: The White Sox. The famous and soon-to-be world champion Chicago White Sox.

The *St. Marys Star* had casually reported that White Sox owner and St. Mary's College alum, Charlie Comiskey, had recently passed through Topeka, some 25 miles to southeast, on his way to the team's spring training camp at Mineral Wells, Texas, and told a reporter he'd like to see the old college campus again. The Old Roman, a former Saints pitcher, promised to stop there on the way back to Chicago. "And, say," Comiskey said, "wouldn't it be fun to get up a little game" on the ballfield of his youth?

And, sure enough, he did, and they did.

On April 6, 1916, Comiskey and his baseball mentor, scout and fellow S.M.C. alum, Ted Sullivan, rousted the White Sox off their chartered train at Topeka and caravanned up to St. Marys, Kansas, population 1,775, where they were met by a crowd of Jesuit priests, religious brothers, and awestruck college boys.

The spring edition of the college's student publication, *The Dial*, excitedly chronicled the historic event: "The big leaguers on their way home from the training camp stopped off at St. Mary's to display their prowess and to demonstrate just how the game should be played. Big Ed Walsh began the battle for the boys from the big show and lasted until the fifth when the locals smashed out four hits and tied the score."

The euphoria that came with going tit-for-tat with the professional

St. Mary's Saints baseball team. When returning to Chicago from spring training camp down south, nostalgic alums Comiskey and Sullivan often brought the
White Sox to their old alma mater for exhibition contests with the college's ball
teams. In 1916, the Sox featured no fewer than four future Hall of Famers—who
toyed with the young Saints for a few innings before taking them to the proverbial woodshed (courtesy *Kansas State Historical Society*).

ball club that would win the World Series the following year didn't last long.
The pros socked 17 singles, and Eddie Collins, Red Faber, Jack Lapp, Fred
McMullin, and Nemo Leibold hit for extra bases. The big league barrage,
against a dozen errors committed by the nervous college boys, saw the contest end in a 17–5 victory for the men from Chicago.

It seems that any time spring training took them anywhere near old
St. Mary's, Sullivan and Comiskey made a point to stop in and see the
Saints. "Comiskey has never lost his love for St. Mary's College, where
he took his first real step in baseball," waxed the *Chicago Tribune*. "And
every season since he has managed the White Sox he has included the
college in the spring schedule whenever he had a team in that part of the
country."[1]

Records at the college show that, one year, when stormy weather
forced a looked-forward-to contest with the big leaguers to be cancelled,

BASE BALL

Only chance to see the famous

CHICAGO WHITE SOX

(American League)

VS

ST. MARY'S COLLEGE
St. Marys, Kansas

COLLEGE CAMPUS, APRIL 6, 1916

AT 1:30 P.M.

ADMISSION 50 Cents

Chas. Comiskey, Manager of the White Sox, was a student at S.M.C. in the early Seventies. He will be here with his team.

Business houses will close during the game

The *St. Marys Star* of April 3, 1916, ran this advertisement touting the biggest sporting event in the small town's history but didn't bother to cover the game. Fortunately, the St. Mary's College paper, *The Dial*, covered it like the proverbial glove.

the boys had to settle for an interminably long lecture by Sullivan on the importance of baseball and the legacy of St. Patrick.

Wartime at "Fort Sullivan"

Back in America after his plans for a South American tour had been shot down, Ted Sullivan invested in a lumber operation and turned his attention to building a waterfront bungalow on a small plantation he had purchased alongside the Pasquotank River near Elizabeth City on the

North Carolina coast. But in July 1917, when General "Black Jack" Pershing's Expeditionary Forces set sail for France to stop the Kaiser's mob, Sullivan felt compelled to march down to Washington and see Secretary of War Newton Baker. Citizen Sullivan thereupon offered the War Department his property as an ideal spot for stopping any German U-boats from sneaking up the Pasquotank.

Shortly after Woodrow Wilson had declared war on Germany in April of 1917, the *Brooklyn Eagle* said, "Ted has certainly been seized with patriotic fever, and if Uncle Sam will cause Fort Sullivan to exist and mount cannon there he will not only donate the land, but will agree to run the fort for the government. The War Department has assured Ted that it will keep his magnanimous offer in mind and that if it decides to establish a fort on the Pasquotank it will name it Fort Sullivan and put him in charge."[2]

The Crippled Wrecks of War

Between July 1917 and Armistice Day, November 11, 1918, more than a million American men and boys were sent onto the contested high seas of Europe or into the claustrophobic and deadly trenches of eastern France. More than 120,000 were killed, but almost twice that many came home limbless, battered, bandaged, and shell-shocked, overwhelming U.S. military hospitals and convalescence facilities.

Ted Sullivan's illustrated lectures on and personal stories about the history of baseball, the world's tour and the game's famous stars—including Eddie Collins, Tris Speaker, Christy Mathewson, Red Faber, Rube Marquard, Grover Alexander, and Ty Cobb, who had all served in the war—took on a new interest and life.

Sullivan entertained wounded sailors and soldiers, whom he called "the crippled wrecks of war," with his illustrated baseball lectures at veteran reconstruction hospitals up and down the South Atlantic Coast.[3]

While traveling, he maintained his habit of sending regular "letters" to newspapers, keeping them up to date on his patriotic activities and good deeds. He wrote in a dispatch to *The Sporting News*:

> Wounded boys are arriving by hundreds and being sequestered in hospitals, where the government means to put them in some kind of shape before permitting them to return to civilian life. It touches one's heart to see the gatherings of young fellows with legs, arms, even faces gone, but they are displaying splendid spirit in their misfortune. Boys with one leg or one arm gone stamp and clap the remaining members of their bodies when any great player or team is thrown upon the screen. The enthusiasm of these boys for something that takes their mind off their sorrows shows how eager they are for the game to come back.

When the conflict to end all conflicts finally ended in late 1918, Ted took America's beloved game to what he called "the crippled wrecks of war," in the form of personal stories, pictures and film clips. Baseball was found to be an effective therapy for depressed and wounded soldiers (National Archives)

> I met their [soldiers'] relatives and friends. In short, the whole American people are anxious for the relaxation and diversion that baseball furnishes … the change from the awfulness of real war to the bloodless combat of the diamond.[4]

As for the future of America's game, Sullivan was his usual optimistic self. In 1919, tens of thousands of still healthy young men were gradually being released from service, and he was sure that there would be plenty of new young talent to infuse baseball with fresh vigor and vitality. Hand over heart, baseball's Barnacle reminded reporters that "even if the old-time stars do not come back to the game," there would be scores of youngsters developed in the army and navy well worthy of trials.[5] "The present war of our country has shaken the old baseball ship to its center, but the game will go on forever, as it is inherent in American youth and inseparable from the hearts of the American people."

In late 1918, Sullivan was on his way to the minor leagues' winter meeting in Peoria, Illinois, "loaded to the gunwales with live, bright ideas for the moguls and will gladly get rid of his load. Ted thinks baseball is coming back with a loud noise."[6]

Once the crippled wrecks of war were safely home or housed in nurs-
ing homes and asylums, America turned its attention back to baseball. In
October 1919, the ever-rambling Sullivan popped up in Raleigh, North Carolina, titillating the hopes and imagination of yet another chamber of commerce with talk of a new North Carolina League.

Reporting that "the grand old man of baseball lectures" had spoken
at Camp Green in North Carolina in early January of 1919, the *Charlotte
Observer* noted that Sullivan, "though well along the path of life, is still as
full of pep and ginger as he was when 'balling' out the umpires in his playing days."[7]

A few days later the *Observer* expressed hope that

> The grand old man of American baseball, known the world over as one of the
> chief exponents of America's great national pastime, may take up the work of
> organizing a North Carolina-Virginia baseball league.
> If he could be prevailed upon to accept the presidency once it is formed, the
> league would be assured of a fair and efficient leadership, by a man who knows
> the game from Alpha to Omega and then back again.[8]

Unfortunately, Sullivan was probably gone before he had a chance to
read this latest litany of his praises. He had moved to a suburb outside Chicago, scouting players for Comiskey, giving his lectures, and dreaming up
yet another global excursion.

> *"There has been more ugly talk and more suspicion among
> the fans than there ever has been in any world series. The
> rumors of crookedness, of fixed games and plots, are thick."*
> —Hugh Fullerton, *New York World*,
> following Game Four of the 1919 World Series

Ever-loyal Sullivan was still the go-to scout for Charlie Comiskey
when the infamous "Black Sox" scandal twisted the face of the game
to a villainous look. Eight White Sox players, including at least one of
Sullivan's discoveries, were accused of conspiring with gamblers to
throw the 1919 World Series to their underdog opponents, the Cincinnati Reds.

Sports hacks and rumor mongers also pointed suspicious fingers at the
players' boss. The beleaguered magnate was constantly fending off allegations that it was his notoriously cheap ways that forced his players to take
money from gamblers in the first place.

Screeds and parables in defense of his friend flew from Sullivan's
well-worn typewriter. He debunked Comiskey's longtime reputation as
a tightwad and insisted that the idea of players having "fixed" the Series
was "pure nonsense."[9] "The talk of crookedness and dishonesty which

FIX THESE FACES IN YOUR MEMORY

'CHICK' GANDIL

"HAP" FELSCH

JOE JACKSON

EDDIE CICOTTE

CLAUDE WILLIAMS

FRED McMULLIN

SWEDE RISBERG

'BUCK' WEAVER

EIGHT MEN CHARGED WITH SELLING OUT BASEBALL

Among the Chicago White Sox who were banned for throwing the 1919 World Series was Sullivan discovery Chick Gandil (Bain News Service, 1913, Library of Congress).

followed in the wake of the recent world series ... is laughed at by the veteran," wrote J. J. FitzGerald, editor of the (New York) *Daily Sports Bulletin*.[10]

Still, many a speculator in the sporting press insisted that Comiskey's miserly attitude pushed those eight players to seek cash from gamblers and vengeance against their owner. Proof of that view, it has been argued, is the fact that the "Black Sox" label had been well established prior to 1919 because of Comiskey's refusal to pay to have uniforms regularly laundered. That apocryphal story has been debunked time and again over the decades, yet it hangs on in popular culture.

Over the decades, the mythology of Comiskey's tightness has been thoroughly discredited. According to John Thorn, the official historian for

Major League Baseball, Comiskey's White Sox opened the 1919 season with the highest payroll in the American League. The move to throw the World Series originated with the players as a simple crime of opportunity.[11]

Even though all eight White Sox players were acquitted in court of all charges in 1921, they were ultimately banned from the game for life, and Comiskey spent the rest of his life under the shadow of those dark stockings.

A century later, the reasons behind the players' decision to throw the Series remain in dispute, but one reality is crystal clear: the 1919 scandal was the zenith of baseball's long connection to gambling. It immediately followed World War I, during which President Woodrow Wilson had ordered racetracks closed, causing wagering railbirds to flock to ballparks and become bleacher buzzards. By 1919, more money was being bet on the outcome of games than ever before.

Though Sullivan steadfastly hailed America's pastime as wholesome and incorruptible, he acknowledged that there was "such talk and considerable betting" around the fall extravaganza, and he even publicly called for having the World Series abolished altogether.

FitzGerald of the *Daily Sports Bulletin* reported that "the genial old-timer"—now into his 70s—proposed to shorten the two eight-team leagues' individual seasons; then, in mid-summer, have all 16 teams come together and each play each other three times. The winner in this race, he reasoned, would, without question be the championship club of the major leagues.[12]

One way or the other, Comiskey was ready to kick dirt over the topic of gambling and talk about brighter days ahead. While the once-powerful White Sox had staggered through the 1920 and 1921 seasons with mix-and-match rosters and measly crowds, the Old Roman predicted a re-energized White Sox team in 1922, with steadier fielders and more muscle on the mound.

"I have men out everywhere keeping an eye open for pitching talent," he told Al Spink. "Among the many scouting for a good pitcher is Ted Sullivan, the best judge of a baseball player in the world. Ted makes his headquarters in Washington and keeps a close eye on the International League and all the pitching talent there is down there."[13]

◆ 27 ◆

Twilight of a Colorful Career

"Ted Sullivan is known throughout the land as 'The Builder of Baseball.... There is perhaps no one quite as familiar with baseball in foreign lands as Ted Sullivan ... he is one of the most popular men identified with baseball."

—*New York Evening World*, May 3, 1922

Applying for a passport to go to South America in 1920 to try and make good on the promise he made in 1917, Ted Sullivan cited his purpose as "arranging for the games of two American League teams" and listed his occupation as "Writer, Baseball Magnate, Capitalist."

While in South America drumming up interest in baseball, he thought he might also introduce the boys of that continent to a sport called "soccer." "Soccer will go with a boom in South America," declared Sullivan. "The rules are so simple that he who runs may read. There is no reason why it should not become the great winter game of South America."[1]

Add "prophet" to the man's resume.

Announcing a banquet at which Ted Sullivan and Ban Johnson were to speak, papers like the *Tampa Times* of February 22, 1921, carried a story that said, "Ted Sullivan is about the oldest baseball man in the country, but you would never know it to look at him. Bright as a new dime, mentally and physically."

For a month in the early spring of 1921, the old manager camped out with the boys of the Wake Forest college baseball team to advise them on what he called "the high mathematics of the game." "With Ted Sullivan on the 'inside' coaching line, the Baptist boys will put out a strong baseball team this year," predicted the *Winston-Salem Journal*.[2]

Another Swing at Ireland

In early 1922, old T.P. Sullivan seemed to have finally slowed down a bit, having purchased and settled into a new a home on Chesapeake Bay. But apparently the respite just gave him more time to conjure up a new scheme.

Before the grass turned green in the spring, Sir Ted was cultivating a plan to take Washington's "Griffmen" and McGraw's Giants to Ireland for a series of exhibition games in Dublin and Cork.

The previous year, a ceasefire had been declared in Ireland's festering War of Independence against England, and an agreement was in place to allow southern Ireland to become a semi-autonomous, self-ruling province of the Commonwealth. Ted Sullivan thought it would be a great time to take America's peaceful pastime to the fractured and contentious little green isle. He told the *Washington Times*:

Although still working as a "pinch picket" spotting minor league prospects for Comiskey's White Sox, by the 1920s Ted was being referred to in the press as "one of the quaint old figures of baseball" *Kansas City Star*, June 15, 1915.

> The appearance of the two ball clubs in the Irish Free State will certainly bring out thousands of real fans, for the liberation of Ireland is sending many Irishmen home from this country.... Here they have learned all the fine points of baseball and will appreciate all they see when the two clubs get together. Now that Irishmen are free I look for a wonderful growth of baseball in that country.
>
> We'll be pioneers in Ireland in the real sense [note—capitalized, the word 'Pioneer' is used in Ireland to refer to a non-drinker]. Of course, baseball is known now to many Irishmen who have been here. We shall give them a concrete demonstration of the game which, I sincerely hope, will one day be Ireland's national game, just as it is ours.[3]

As the baseball season of 1922 got under way, Sullivan's scheme grew ever larger and more ambitious. He would take Clark Griffith's and McGraw's boys (maybe even the Yankees, with the fast-becoming-legend Babe Ruth) to Dublin to put on an exhibition or two as part of festivities commemorating the establishment of the Irish Free State. The American stars would meet the newly anointed leaders of Ireland, then travel on to London and Paris, and maybe even Rome, Belgium, Germany, and Japan.[4]

On May 6, Sullivan boarded the USS *George Washington* and headed across the pond to begin making arrangements. In Paris, he met with the French Olympic Committee and reserved the use of Colombes Stadium, which was being readied for the World Games of 1924. In Dublin, he booked Croke Park, the center of Irish sporting events that would accommodate 40,000 fans, and in London, he toured parks with the King's Counsel.[5]

In transatlantic telegrams, advance man Sullivan ballyhooed the interest and excitement of European officials and sports fans. "You can fancy how great is the enthusiasm when I tell you how even the girls [in France] play baseball on Sunday and take part in other forms of sport," he reported. "I find that the French have advanced considerably in the matter of outdoor games, and I have no doubt whatever that the arrival in Paris next October of the two ball teams will be hailed with the greatest enthusiasm."[6]

The trip, he promised, would be a once-in-a-lifetime experience for the American players who would travel first-class all the way, going and coming, and be entertained by the officials of every city they visited. Side tours would be arranged for them in Ireland, England and France. "There will be no hanging around hotel lobbies," he said confidently. "Things of interest will occupy each day."[7]

Troubles Brewing

Ted Sullivan felt the tour would be especially educational and of interest to the people of Ireland, saying:

> It is well known that England claims that their game of "rounders" is the original of the ball game of America. On the other hand, Ireland claims that rounders was essentially a Gaelic game, and they point to the great part played in America by Irishmen in building up America's national game. In October when the two ball teams of America appear at Croke Park the Gaels of Dublin and of Ireland will have a rare opportunity of seeing their old game of rounders coming back to them from America in dress suit form.[8]

But come summer, Ireland wasn't in the mood to talk about rounders *or* baseball. A vehement disagreement over the Free State agreement with England (one of the provisions being that Irish people living in the "free" southern "republic" would have to swear loyalty to the crown), fractured the Republican movement and led to a violent, confusing civil war. As a consequence, the tour Ted Sullivan had planned for the fall had to be cancelled.

Lost in this and his many other plans and failures to take baseball to all corners of the world is his prescience as to the future of baseball.

In promoting his European barnstorming tour in 1922, Sullivan talked about the likely emergence of world-class baseball teams and major league-caliber players from Japan and South America. It made sense, he said, because "Japanese colleges have produced nines that have played on par with the best in the United States."[9]

"It may so happen," he predicted, "that a world's championship in the future will see but one American team in it." The other team, he thought, might come from Ireland, Japan, or South America. "Then the title would mean far more than it does now. That will take years of effort, however, and we are but pioneers today in the movement for the spread of baseball."[10]

Retirement, Sullivan–style

For the next couple of years, the aging Sullivan pretty much stayed out of the headlines, dividing his time between D.C. and a rural "plantation" near Elizabeth City, North Carolina. He carried VIP passes to all American and National league parks and was occasionally noticed by a like-aged newspaper man.

But even in his late 70s, Sullivan was still out-hustling and out-traveling many a man half his age. His fame in the game preceded him and continued to open doors for him just about everywhere he went.

Asked about the aging Sullivan in 1923, Baseball Commissioner Kenesaw Mountain Landis said with all sincerity, "the game will never be able to repay him for what he has done for it."[11] Al Spink agreed, writing: "Ted always moves quietly and without ostentation. He never boasts of his deeds, or the great players he has unearthed, and all that, but he keeps moving all the same."[12]

As for Sullivan "moving quietly," most sportswriters of the day might have chuckled at that notion.

"It is reported that Ted Sullivan is in New York getting some dope on the Giants," read one typically tongue-in-cheek sports page blurb. "The report goes on to say that Ted is silent as a sphinx. Is somebody kidding the public or has Mr. Sullivan lost his voice?"[13]

Writing about a magnetic young catcher for the Cubs named Charles Leo "Gabby" Hartnett, columnist John B. Sheridan wrote in the spring of 1925 that the future Hall of Famer reminded him of the old-time Irish ballplayers of the late 19th century—"the great, rosy faced, white toothed, fair skinned, dark haired, blue eyed athletes who went at baseball as if it was the greatest fun in the world. Rollicking, dashing, eyeful, fun loving Irish boys who made baseball a delight to watch and more delightful, still, to listen to ... men like Mike Kelly, Mickey Welch, Tim Keefe, Ted Sullivan, Hugh Jennings, Joe Kelly, John McGraw, Jimmy Callahan, Tom McCarthy, Jack O'Connor and Jack Doyle"[14]

Although out of field-level baseball, with the exception of an occasional scouting foray for Comiskey and his White Sox, Sullivan kept his hand in the game as a freelance writer, covering the 1924 World Series.

The Washington Senators were facing John McGraw's Giants. The 1924 Series went down as one of the most dramatic in the history of the game, with the Senators, pitching Walter "Big Train" Johnson in relief, coming from behind to win Game 7 and the title in a 12-inning heart-stopper.

From his newfound spot in the press box, Sullivan wrote of the underdog Senators: "I have seen championship teams come and go—disintegrate and pass on to baseball oblivion and obscurity—but I'll emphatically state I never saw a collection of players banded together in one team who came from such humble sources, unheralded as stars."[15]

Sullivan continued to pen guest columns for the *Washington Post* under a banner labeling him "The Dean of Pro Baseball." On allegations that a ballplayer had intentionally thrown a game in 1924, he wrote: "Any man who is a student of the game knows that no one man can throw a game by himself ... unless the winning run was on third base and a defender deliberately allows a passed ball." He maintained that professional baseball had cleaned itself up since the days when it was "in the hands of gamblers and sure-thing men" back in the 1870s.[16]

The old scout might have had amnesia when he wrote that, as he seems to have developed repressed memory syndrome with regard to the Black Sox scandal.

Dawn of Big Bucks in Baseball

Having played ball for a buck a game back in his day, old Ted Sullivan was aghast in 1925 when it was rumored that Connie Mack was offering the princely sum of $100,000 for a starting pitcher. He recalled having once instructed Chris Van der Ahe to sign Giants catcher (and future Hall of Famer) Buck Ewing for St. Louis for whatever Ewing asked for, and that he had had the audacity to ask for $5,000 a year. According to the *Dubuque Herald* of July 5, 1925, the conversation between Van der Ahe and Ewing, Sullivan said, went something like this:

> Von der Ahe: "What kind of man are you Buck? Are you a whole team? If I sign you I won't need anyone else? My whole team now, you know, doesn't cost me $5,000."

"So that settles it?" asked Buck.

"Yes, that settles it," said Chris. "I wonder, Buck, do you know when the next train leaves for St. Louis?"

By 1926 (the year St. Louis won a World Series for the first time since 1888), Sullivan was mostly out of the public eye, relegated to visiting past haunts and retelling old tales at banquets and reunions. When he was seen, *The Sporting News* admitted, "No one dare ask him his age."[17]

"The Papa of the Pastime likes to talk baseball, of its changes since he was a participant," said the *Dubuque Telegraph-Herald* when the aging Sullivan returned to the Key City for a visit. "Nearly half a century ago, a sturdy, red-faced Irishman conducted a news agency in a shanty close to the Illinois Central station, by a vacant lot where he and his associates played ball when not selling papers. Today, this same red-faced Irishman is known to millions as the 'Father of Baseball.'"[18]

All his life, Sullivan avoided telling anyone the actual year of his birth, believed now to be 1848, making him about 75 when baseball's minor league magnates gathered for their 25th annual convocation in Asheville, North Carolina, to talk business and honor their own.

Al Spink's ever-supportive *Sporting News* made a case for recognizing Sullivan at that august gathering: "Baseball quickly forgets its pioneers, but on the occasion of the anniversary of a quarter century existence of the National Association, we are inclined to resurrect Ted Sullivan as the man who laid the foundation years before."[19] That quote was followed by a retrospective of Ted Sullivan's career, which, of course, could not tell the whole story because his story wasn't finished. He had one more big scheme up his sleeve.

The Old Man in the Stands

By the mid–1920s, Ted Sullivan was unquestionably long in the tooth, particularly for his day, when the average lifespan of an American male was 58 years. He was at least 70-something when, in a preview of a baseball banquet in Washington, D.C., the *Washington Herald* jokingly referred to attendee Sullivan as "the oldest man in captivity."[20]

By then a great many of the boys and young men that Sullivan had discovered, signed or managed were gone, taken at early ages by hard living, alcohol and diseases du jour. "Occasionally I get very lonesome," he once admitted, "and then I have to pull out and visit the ball men in New York, St. Louis, Cincinnati, Washington, or Chicago with whom I have been associated all my life."[21]

"Ted Sullivan, one of the quaint old figures of baseball, was an interested spectator at yesterday's double-headers at Fans Field," observed a reporter sitting nearby in the summer of 1923. "Sullivan, though well along in his 70s, and not as lithe of step as a few years back, is still mixed up in the game as a scout, and an interesting old character, well worth a hearing."[22]

"He's still just as enthusiastic over the thrilling game as any schoolboy," noted an admiring scribe from the *Richmond Times Dispatch*.[23]

"His hair is white and his hands are shaky," wrote a correspondent for Baltimore's *Evening Sun*. "But his mind is as keen as when he directed the destinies of the White Stockings. Old Ted Sullivan is still in love with baseball."[24]

Graying Ted Sullivan made few concessions to his advancing age, but once drew considerable titters and stares when he showed up at a stylish Washington affair in evening dress, wearing a pair of bright green carpet slippers because his feet hurt.[25]

A Lost Soul

One night at "an old timers' feed" at the Great Northern Hotel in St. Louis, Ted Sullivan was asked whatever happened to young Tom Sullivan, Old Hoss Radbourn's catcher on that famous Rabbits team of 1879. They all knew Tom had gone on to play a few years with the Cincinnati Reds.

"Tom's a croppy [term to describe an Irish rebel]," said Sullivan, sadly. "He struck out one New Year's night." And he proceeded to regale the men with this story:

> One Christmas Eve in old St. Louis, Tom started over the hills to the St. Louis poor house. Tom lived in Kerry Patch and it was a seven-mile walk over the hills to the big city institution. The night, too, was fearsome cold and the snow was flying. But Tom's old friend, Jack Cullinane, was out there, and Tom had promised him a bottle of the real juice on the Christmas Eve. Tom was one of those who would have laid down his life for his old pal Jack, and set out on his long journey. He reached the poor house all right, and presented Jack with his bottle, but he froze his hands and ears in the journey and received such injuries that he died from the effects the following New Year's day. Tom was not only a great player but he had a great heart. God rest his soul.[26]

◆ 28 ◆

Ted's Last Hurrah

As far back as 1888, Ted Sullivan had announced plans to promote traveling teams—sometimes even leagues—across Europe. Newspapers routinely published dispatches from across the Atlantic Ocean in which he gave updates on his efforts to introduce "the national game" in Ireland, England and France.

One of his most fervent and recurring dreams was to take a couple of American ball teams to Ireland for a series of exhibitions and demonstrations. He believed young Irishmen, schooled in the ancient sport of hurling (or "shinty," as he called it), made natural baseball players and that once they saw and learned the game, they'd follow the rainbow to paycheck gold in America.

After many trips and many tries, Sullivan gave up on the idea of an Ireland tour. His kinsmen just weren't fans of his ball-and-stick game. But less than two years before his death, nearing 80, yet still indefatigable, Ted Sullivan concocted and brought off one last great scheme.

Sullivan reportedly first took an interest in Gaelic football during the Giants-White Sox world tour, and he remained intrigued at the idea of bringing Ireland's game to American sports fans.[1] Discussions regarding a possible American tour for the County Kerry GAA champions began in 1925 when Sullivan was among a group of American tourists who watched the champion County Kerry team play Dublin. The baseball magnate's host was the Rev. Edward Fitzgerald, brother of Dick Fitzgerald, a native of Killarney who won five all-Ireland medals during his legendary football career. A committed Republican, Dick Fitzgerald was interned twice following the 1916 Easter Rising. The Gaelic football legend—identified in the American press as "The Irish Red Grange" and "the most popular and famous man in all Ireland"[2]—worked through a dispute regarding the size of the traveling party, and the particulars of the tour were announced at the close of 1926.[3]

Ancient Order of Hibernians "football" club, ca. 1927. After the unrest of a civil war, Ireland was mad for the game of Gaelic football, described in the American press as a cross between soccer, rugby and basketball. In 1927, Ted conspired to bring Ireland's champion footballers from County Kerry to the U.S. for a series of exhibitions against newly formed American club teams. He likely never suspected that one of his partners in the venture was the Irish Republican Army (author's collection).

A Tour Built on Big Dreams, Big Talk

Sullivan convinced the Fitzgeralds and the Board of the Kerry Gaelic Athletic Association that America's huge Irish immigrant population was hungry for a tour by the famous Kerrymen, and would eat it up.

He worked out a straightforward deal with Kerry's "Fabulous Fifteen." As promoter, he would be on the hook for all expenses, and at the end of the tour he would hand over 40 percent of net profit to the Irish.[4]

The Reverend Fitzgerald traveled to America to meet with Sullivan and oversee arrangements on behalf of the Kerry group. And in late May of 1927, the touring party left Queenstown (now called Cobh) in the south of Ireland aboard the White Star liner Baltic. Sullivan met the group at quarantine in New York, and they set off for a welcoming event at City Hall, the first stop on a journey designed to heighten Gaelic football's profile in America while raising funds for facilities and programs back home in Ireland.[5]

Overseas,
Overmatched
and Abandoned

From the earliest indi-
cations, the tour was set to
be a booming success. The
Irish stars were feted at a
massive reception with a
crowd reported at 1,000
people. Attendees included
political leaders, business
chieftains, and high-profile
members of New York's
Irish immigrant commu-
nity. While Prohibition was
then the law of the land in
America, the law apparently
didn't extend into the ballroom of the Commodore Hotel.[6]

Sullivan To Bring Gaelic Football Champs to U. S.

NEW YORK—Ted Sullivan who piloted the Giants and White Sox around the world in 1914, is now turning his attention to exhibiting Gaelic football in America. He has arranged to have the champion Kerry team visit America and play a team of picked stars who will come over from Ireland to furnish formidable opposition. An itinerary is now being arranged.

Sullivan had repeatedly announced plans to promote baseball in Ireland since 1888, but in 1927 the Irish came to him, when he directed the County Kerry Gaelic football tour of Amer- ica. It didn't end well (*Madison Capital Times*, March 17, 1926).

After all the toasts and speeches—Sullivan waxed eloquent and often—the time came for the Kerry champions to dominate the local side and amaze American spectators. Sullivan and his heroes quickly learned that New York was filled with recent Irish immigrants who also happened to be experienced, world-class Gaelic footballers. To the promoter's shock and dismay, the "New York All Stars" defeated the Celtic invaders, 3 goals 11 points to 1 goal 7 points, in front of a Polo Grounds crowd of 30,000— less than half the attendance organizers anticipated. Nevertheless, a larger crowd was predicted for the scheduled rematch, with Sullivan declaring, "We will come back and wipe the field with them."[7]

That first game made it clear to Fitzgerald and the Kerrymen that Sul- livan had no intention of spending any money on advertising and market- ing the exhibitions throughout the tour. To make matters worse, American newspapers uniformly boycotted the Irish invasion, and many refused to publicize upcoming games.[8]

But the most deadly fallout came after Father Fitzgerald sent a cable to Ireland explaining the team's loss of their first game in America. The cable cited heat, high humidity, blistering sunshine, a small, rock-hard field, and dirty play by the New Yorkers as causes of the unexpected defeat. The per- ceived whiny tone of the cable received a venomous reception from the powers-that-be back home.[9]

Following the New York debacle, the Kerry team headed out for Sullivan-arranged exhibitions in Boston, Springfield, Hartford, and New Haven. Those stops served to reset the group's original expectations for their American experience.

According to Irish newspaper correspondent Patrick Foley, the Kerrymen were treated like visiting potentates by enthusiastic but disappointingly small crowds in Massachusetts and Connecticut. At each stop, the traveling party received a boisterous welcome at a train station and were paraded to their hotel by bands and the local Irish diaspora.

The football grounds, however, were merely local baseball fields, and at each site the Kerrymen routed the locals in front of crowds that ranged from disappointingly small to outright pitiful. Sullivan maintained his refusal to spend money on advertising and other promotional activities.

While the celebrations and events were plenty lively, revenues from the Massachusetts and Connecticut exhibitions barely covered expenses.[10]

The party then traveled to Chicago, putting nearly 900 miles between them and the Polo Grounds. The team was met at the train and delivered to City Hall, where they received an enthusiastic welcome, were given the run of the town, and were placed in the care of Sgt. Lynch of the Chicago PD, a native of Ballybunion, who supervised all the arrangements for their time in Chicago.

Kerry played an exhibition at Comiskey's White Sox Park on June 12 against a local selection and won easily, performing before an estimated crowd of 8,000 before their return to the Polo Grounds, the scene of their only defeat. As bad as the shocking initial result was, the second effort was worse. The New York Selected again dominated the visitors, this time with decidedly less pomp, fanfare, and excitement. The media blackout of the tour remained in force, advertising and promotion remained sparse, and the game was subject to boycott calls from New York GAA officials still angry about the content of Father Fitzgerald's infamous telegram. The July 4 return game drew an estimated 15,000 fans, about half the size of the previous (and disappointingly small) New York crowd.[11]

Sullivan and the Irish delegation were scheduled to meet the following morning to settle up. But when July 5 dawned, the Kerry crew learned that Sullivan was long gone, and their 40 percent cut with him.[12]

After learning that Sullivan had absconded with their $4,500 share (the equivalent of more than $115,000 today),[13] the Kerry group met with attorney Bill O'Dwyer, a Mayo man and later mayor of New York City. He explained that Sullivan could drag out the case and force costly return trips from Ireland for numerous court appearances. He advised they drop the matter of their 40 percent and move on. They did.

But the matter would flare up in late August during an accounting of the American tour before the Kerry County Board GAA.

IRA Eyes Ted's Stash

Ted Sullivan hadn't been the only party to view the Kerry football tour as a money-making opportunity: the Irish Republican Army (IRA) had been equally keen on tapping the tour till.

In 1927, Connie Neenan was the IRA's official representative in the United States, and he was in regular contact with John Joe Sheehy, the captain of the Kerry team and a staunch Republican. Neenan was determined to loosen Sullivan's grip on the cash.

> "Kerry's tour of America on 1927 was organised secretly by the IRA as a fund raising exercise by the IRA even though the non–Republicans on the team had no idea of this."
> —Richard McElligott, Terrace Talk interview,
> Radio Kerry, October 17, 2013

An American "Martyr"

According to authors Tom Mahon and James J. Gillogly, "Neenan regarded Sullivan's support as 'private enterprise where exploitation of [the] champions is indulged for personal gain' and sent word to the Kerry captain, John Joe Sheehy, that Sullivan 'is not to be trusted.' Neenan added: 'Sullivan pretends to be a martyr to philanthropic motives. I doubt [this] very much.'"[14]

Neenan had attempted to minimize the number of Sullivan's events while mounting a separate series of football exhibitions to benefit the IRA, with an emphasis on games in the immigrant-laden cities of Boston, Chicago, and New York City.

After Sullivan gave his Irish partners the ditch in early July, seven of the Kerry players headed back home, while 18 (mostly Republican) players stayed in the states and played games to benefit an unnamed "friend."[15]

According to Irish newspaper accounts, "one friend who provided most of the expenses of the team … has been let down badly by those who controlled the purse-strings at the other side and that the team seeing their position decided to promote other contests so as to make good the loss to their patron."[16]

"As with all trips, gifts have to be brought to the folks back home," Mahon and Gillogly noted. "And on the return voyage on the Baltic some of the players smuggled Thompson submachine guns in their luggage. These weapons belonged to the IRA."[17]

When the entire team had made it back home to County Kerry and the details of the tour were known, Ted Sullivan had become the target of withering criticism. Even his supporters in the New York *Irish American Advocate* newspaper had turned against him, demanding that he "make good" on the 40 percent of tour proceeds owed to his Kerry partners.[18]

Sheehy decried that Father Fitzgerald was the "victim of foolish trust" in a crooked promoter and presented the priest with a check to reimburse his expenses incurred during his dealings with Sullivan. On the whole, the American experience was a good one for the team, Sheehy contended, but nobody, it seemed, had a good word to say about the "sinister" and "mean" Ted Sullivan.[19]

At the conclusion of the meeting, the GAA Board approved a resolution that read, in part:

> That having heard the reports of our members who visited America, we heartily congratulate the Kerry team on the success of the tour despite the promoter, Mr. Ted Sullivan, of whose actions in the matter we hereby express our wholehearted condemnation; we also congratulate the Governing Body of the G.A.A. in America upon the great success they have achieved in connection with the Gaelic games there, and we offer our sincere and hearty congratulations to the New York team on the victories over our team.[20]

In response, Sullivan attempted to defend his reputation in a letter to correspondent Foley.[21]

Sullivan alleged that he had mortgaged property to raise cash to pay for steamship transportation for the 26-member touring party. Once the Kerry team had arrived, Sullivan said he was subjected to ongoing acts of "smallness and meanness" by Irish immigrant communities, which sought to either block or cash in on various tour stops.[22] "But the climax of all was the act of the Kerry team," Sullivan wrote, "after I treated them so well, and that was to go to a lawyer to compel me to show the revenue taken in and paid out on the trip."[23]

THE KERRY TOUR

WHAT HAPPENED IN THE STATES?

After the Kerry football team returned home, the Gaelic Athletic Association excoriated Ted Sullivan for abandoning the tourists and absconding with their 40 percent of the gate receipts. One reporter summed up the situation by noting, "we had reckoned without our host" (*Irish Independent*, July 27, 1927).

He acknowledged that his contract with his Irish partners required him to hand over 40 percent of the tour's net proceeds to Father Fitzgerald, which Sullivan refused to do. Instead, he said he would travel to Ireland, acquire property, and deed the parcel to County Kerry to "use it as they see fit for football, hurling or anything. As I was good enough to bring out the team, I'll be good enough to give a playing field to the county I was born in," Sullivan concluded.[24]

As was often the case when it came to his age and place of birth, Ted Sullivan was conveniently struck with episodic amnesia. He was born in County Clare, not in County Kerry.

◆ 29 ◆

The Third Strike

*"Sullivan says he would not trade his experiences in base-
ball for any amount of money. He has enjoyed many a
laugh at the expense of ball players and bugs and is said to
have been the originator of the expression 'baseball fan.'"*
—*The Cincinnati Enquirer,* December 25, 1921

As he neared 80 (still claiming he was much younger), Ted Sullivan
grew grumpy about the state of his beloved game. He harrumphed at what
he called the "mollycoddling" of modern ball players. "If a star player has
a corn on his little toe or any minor blemish it is watched by the trainer
with all the care given a prima donna's vocal cords," he said sarcastically. "If
things keep going on this way, the club will soon have to provide a valet for
each player to carry his glove out to him."[1]

In February of 1929, in a column that ran in papers across the country,
the *United Press* staff correspondent Alfred P. Reck wrote that Sullivan had
become soured on organized ball, that "The Builder of Baseball" felt the
day's club owners—"the big bugs," he called them—were debasing the game
with their petty rivalries and penurious ways; that they were all about business, not baseball; that they hadn't come up in the game, and simply didn't
understand or appreciate the nation's love of, and need for the pureness and
simplicity of the sport.[2]

"The grand old man of baseball knows the game from A to Z," wrote
Reck. "But he has confidence that the country will never lose interest in
baseball for it is in the blood of the American people."[3]

In April, returning to Chicago from what was to be his last spring
training trip with the White Sox, Sullivan reiterated his concerns to another
UP correspondent, who called him "the aged man" and "The Grandfather
of Baseball," and quoted him as saying: "Something is wrong with the game.
It's not what it used to be. It appears to me that the trouble is in the higher
ups. To be sure some of the players are a bit radical, but, well, it isn't what it

was when I was years younger. I don't mean the game is fading out, but I do mean that something should be done to bind the friendship of the 16 big league managers instead of trying to make them all enemies."[4]

The onetime instigator of the game-changing American League predicted yet another professional league would emerge to challenge the American and the National associations "if some of these so called experts don't spoil it by souring the entire country on our national pastime."[5]

Sullivan blamed the decline of pure-hearted baseball on greedy, egotistic team owners and the demise of sandlot teams, where kids and young men played simply for fun and local glory: "What this country needs is public baseball parks where the children can play and learn the game. Wellington once wisely remarked that the Battle of Waterloo was won on the cricket fields of Eton. Many of America's future battles can be won years in advance if this country will awaken to the necessity for more playgrounds and baseball parks for children."[6]

Over his 50-plus years in baseball, Ted Sullivan accumulated wealth and property but, most important to him, a reputation as one of the great builders of the game (*Spink Sport Stories*, by Al Spink, Dean of Sporting Writers, 1921).

Sullivan was prescient once again in that just a few years later, in the thin-soup 1930s, cities and towns across America built public ball diamonds with backstops and bleachers as a way to keep young men occupied and fit, and communities socially connected and cheaply entertained.

> *"When Ted Sullivan promoted the first minor league back in 1879 ... he started something that has cost hometown boosters a lot of money, but which has provided a lot of wholesome recreation and entertainment in towns that otherwise would have been dead as the proverbial doornail."*
> —Jim Nasium, *The Sporting News*, January 12, 1928

Not many of the old baseball scribes were still around when Ted Sullivan took his last strike on July 5, 1929.

The man whom a generation of sports writers called "The Daddy of the Game" died alone and largely unnoticed on July 5, 1929, in Gallinger Hospital in Washington, D.C. Even the *Washington Post* missed the news, the hospital having filed Sullivan's death notice under his real name: Timothy Paul Sullivan. Not Ted.

He was 72, 76, or 78 years old, depending on which obit you read. He had given so many fictitious birthdates over the years that no one—perhaps not even he—was quite certain. But carved into his now broken and crumbling headstone at Calvary Catholic Cemetery in Milwaukee (with Miller Park, home of the modern Milwaukee Brewers, visible just beyond the graveyard fence) is "1848." Which would put him somewhere near 81 the day he finally ran out of stories, jokes, schemes and ideas.

Young sportswriters who likely had never heard of the Grandfather of Baseball cobbled together obituary tributes that were often rendered comical by their inaccuracies and convoluted accounts of Ted Sullivan's career. Their stories were, well, very Ted-like.

Finally, on July 14, 1929, the *Washington Post* got Ted Sullivan's story, and got it mostly right, under the headline:

Irish Immigrant, Known as Pioneer of Baseball, Dies Out of Public Notice;
Developed Anson in Rough and Ready Days

His adopted hometown's paper acknowledged that Sullivan's fame was national, that he had enjoyed the title of scout, but was better known as the sport's "ambassador," who "preached the gospel of baseball wherever his travels took him," and who had made serious attempts to establish the game in foreign countries.

The *Washington Post*'s obituary recounted:

Sullivan's own baseball days were the days of the rough and ready element. There were no 65,000 baseball crowds or $75,000 salaries when he managed the St. Louis Browns ... that probably came close to being the payroll for the entire league and 65,000 persons came close to being the attendance of the home season in St. Louis in the early eighties.

There were no luxuries in those early days of baseball campaigning with Sullivan. Players got off at stations for their 25-cent breakfasts and their 50-cent dinners. If one of Sullivan's teams made an overnight jump, the players curled in their seats using their carpet bags for pillows. When the club was on the road, players slept two in a bed. There were no pampered athletes in that era of baseball.

The *Milwaukee Sentinel*'s top-of-the-page story led with "The Father of Inside Baseball and Former Milwaukeean, Dies," and cited his friendship with Charles Comiskey, his coining of the term "fan," his role in the World's Tour in 1913–1914, his feat of organizing and financing the Gaelic football team tour in 1927, and the fact that he had written a number of plays and books. And added, "for some time he had been at work on a new book on baseball, which was really to have been his memoirs."[7]

The *Milwaukee Journal's* account referred to Sullivan as "a prominent character in baseball history" and called him "an author of note" who had written many books and plays, including a tome—apparently now lost to the ages—called *"Sullivan's History of Ireland."*[8]

Half a century as a baseball nomad had, no doubt, distanced Ted Sullivan's connections to family. It is not known how many Sullivans and former players, managers, umps, bugs, croaks, cranks or fans attended his funeral, held at St. John's Cathedral in Milwaukee on July 11, 1929.

Among Ted Sullivan's pallbearers were future Hall of Famer Ray Schalk (above) and Chick Gandil. Schalk and Gandil both played on the infamous "Black Sox" team of 1919. Gandil was indicted as a participant in the scheme to throw the World Series. Schalk was credited with blowing the whistle on his crooked teammates (Library of Congress).

Ted Sullivan's grave in Milwaukee's Calvary Catholic Cemetery is marked only by a worn and broken headstone. But it finally and definitively reveals the year he was born. If his birthday wasn't on St. Patrick's Day, as he always said, it was close. And, as if he ordered it, the Brewers' ballfield, Miller Park, can be seen just over the cemetery fence (courtesy Sam Gazdziak of *RIP Baseball,* www. ripbaseball.com).

Many years earlier, Ted Sullivan lamented that he had "helped players in my life that were not known—that nobody cared for; they were as blank on the baseball market as if they never existed. In their obscurity they were pulled out of mines, off drays, and other humble positions. I pushed them to the front with no gain for myself, but with sympathetic heart, and I never in my life heard one of those people say 'Thank you.'"[9]

But in the end, at least some of those players came to pay their respects and pray their thank-yous to Ted Sullivan. Among his pallbearers were Arnold "Chick" Gandil, the star first baseman implicated in the Black Sox Scandal, and Ray "Cracker" Schalk, another popular—and innocent— member of that infamous team. A future Hall of Famer, Schalk was one of the many great players Sullivan had discovered and signed for Comiskey and other team owners over the years.

"They buried Ted Sullivan in Milwaukee Monday morning—Ted Sullivan, that kindly old man of baseball fame … the last surviving member of the small group that made baseball the great American sport," wrote the columnist A. T. Baum. "A cheerful personality and a thorough knowledge

"This friendship of the two men is one of the finest things of the game"—*Pittsburgh Press*, December 26, 1909. Comiskey (left) and Sullivan (right).

of baseball from every angle made Ted Sullivan a favorite wherever he went and that is every place baseball was played."[10]

It appears that, by the time of his death, Ted Sullivan had sold off much of the property he was said to have owned in and around Washington—perhaps for money to live on in his final years. His last will and testament, written just months before he died, bequeathed $500 to his beloved St. Mary's College, and $300 to the Rev. Father Edward Fitzgerald, of Kinsale, Ireland; the latter very likely was offered as atonement for a long-festering sin connected to the contentious Gaelic Football tour of 1927.[11]

Father Fitzgerald, the brother of Gaelic football legend Dick Fitzgerald, had helped Sullivan organize and promote the Kerry team's tour of the states in 1927. Toward the conclusion of the tour, Irish tempers had flared, with many, including the priest, feeling that hustling Sullivan had picked the team's pocket by palming more than his share of the gate receipts. Ninety-two years later, the slight still festers in the late clergyman's bio on the official website of the Diocese of Cork & Ross (Ireland): "In 1927, he organized an American tour for the Kerry team. He traveled out ahead of the team. Unfortunately, he had very few happy memories of this historic event, as a member [whose initials were likely T.P. S.] of the organizing committee misappropriated most of the funds, from which upset he never fully recovered."

Father Fitzgerald died in 1930. The $300 check from the Sullivan estate apparently didn't absolve Sullivan of the sin of 1927, but it may have been Sullivan's nod to penance.

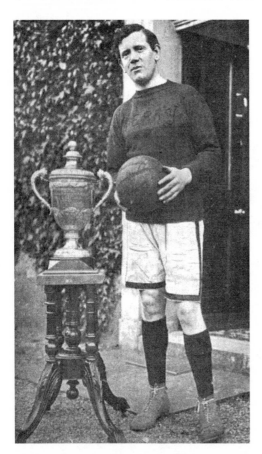

Dick Fitzgerald, County Kerry's Gaelic football legend, worked with Ted Sullivan to organize his team's 1927 tour of America.

Sullivan also left $1,000 to his grand-nephew, John Sullivan, Jr., of Milwaukee, with the stipulation that any remaining money or property be divided among his three surviving nieces to "share and share alike."

And with that, America and baseball proceeded to forget all about Timothy Paul "Ted" Sullivan, the oft-acknowledged "Daddy" of the modern game.

Sporting Editor's Notes

Column head used by the Ted-following editor who called himself "Old Poke" in the *Davenport (IA) Daily Times* in the early 1900s.

Ted Sullivan on
HOW TO SCHMOOZE A SCRIBE:

"Ted gives advice to managers as follows: 'The next thing is your reporter. You will meet him at night. Be sure you have a good cigar with you. If you ever give a bad cigar to a reporter it will settle you in his estimation. Tell the reporter about all the players you brought out, but be careful. Don't tackle any of those practical base ball reporters and give them any of those hayloft stories or you are gone. Catch one of those fellows who think they are nice and tell them all about your signs and how this player did this or that. Then if you look wise and have a half smile on your countenance everything great will be imputed to you.'"
—*Fort Wayne News*, March 18, 1899

"Mr. Sullivan occupied a seat on the press bench during the game and kept the scribes in roars of laughter by his witty sallies. What he does not know about baseball is not worth knowing."
—*Edmonton (Canada) Journal,* August 3, 1911

"Every time Ted sees a reporter, another 'pipe story' is added to the world's stock of mystic nothings."
—*Dubuque Daily Times,* September 20, 1898

"Ted Sullivan must have kissed the Blarney Stone, for he can throw the most exquisite bouquets of anyone in the business."
—*Kansas City Star,* December 29, 1905

"(Ted Sullivan) is one of the most delightful stringers in the game whose stories need to be taken with a great big grain of salt."
—*Philadelphia Enquirer,* August 27, 1897

"Ted Sullivan, author, baseball magnate, promoter of leagues, expert in judging 'phenoms,' financier and inimitable storyteller...."
—*Baltimore Sun,* November 8, 1903

"Ted Sullivan is considered by veteran baseball men the greatest hustler and genius the game has ever produced."
—*The Sporting News,* December 1909

"When Ted lights he can always tell the natives a story they've never heard before."
—*Baltimore Sun,* February 7, 1895

"We regret to note incidentally that our good gossip, Ted Sullivan, is somewhat of a shine as a vicarious soothsayer."
—Columnist HEK, *Chicago Tribune,* April 25, 1909

"What Ted says in regard to base-ball of signing of players always goes with anybody that knows him—with 90 per cent off."
—*Cincinnati Enquirer* October 13, 1891

"The most painful thing that the old votaries of the game have to endure is the obtuseness and illiteracy of the average provincial writer, who once in a while gains a position on the metropolitan press. He knows nothing of the

antecedents of the game or the history of its exponents or promoters. If he is a collegian, he has nothing in stock at first but conceit and freshness."

—"Ted Tells Ball Tales," *Sporting Times*
(reprinted in the *Chattanooga Daily Times,*
January 23, 1910)

Chapter Notes

Preface

1. From article "Dooks and Luds" dispatched from London to Hearst papers in America, Feb. 25, 1914.
2. Alfred H. Spink, *The National Game*, Southern Illinois University Press, 2000, first published 1910 by The National Game Publishing Co., 288.
3. John B. Foster in the *Rock Island Argus*, Jan. 26, 1932.
4. *Sporting Life* article reprinted in the *Buffalo Courier*, Dec. 18, 1891.
5. Al Spink, *Sports Stories: 1000 Big and Little Ones*, The Spink Sport Stories Co., 1921, 432.
6. Spink, *The National Game*.
7. Jerrold Casway, *The Culture and Ethnicity of Nineteenth Century Baseball*, McFarland, 2017, 22.
8. *Ibid*, 55, 64.
9. Ted Sullivan, *Humorous Stories of the Ball Field*, M.A. Donohue & Co. Printers and Binders, Chicago (1903); and *History of World's Tour: Chicago White Sox/New York Giants* (1914).
10. *Los Angeles Herald*, Feb. 6, 1905.
11. *The Sporting News*, Dec. 23, 1909.

Chapter 1

1. Ted Sullivan, *Humorous Stories of the Ball Field: A Complete History of the Game and Its Exponents*, M.A. Donohue & Co. Printers and Binders, Chicago (1903), 107.
2. *Sioux City (IA) Herald*, Feb. 29, 1912.
3. Ted Sullivan, *Humorous Stories*, 139.
4. *Ibid.*, 37.
5. *Ibid.*, 110–111.
6. *The Sporting News*, Jan. 24, 1918.

Chapter 2

1. Ted Sullivan, *Humorous Stories of the Ball Field: A Complete History of the Game and Its Exponents*, M.A. Donohue & Co. Printers and Binders, Chicago, 116.
2. *Ibid*, 117.
3. *Ibid*, 118–119.
4. George S. Robbins, *Chicago Daily News*, Dec. 28, 1916.
5. G.W. Axelson, *Commy: The Life Story of Charles A. Comiskey*, told by, 1919, The Reilly & Co. publishers. (reprinted in paperback, 2003, The McFarland Historical Baseball Library #2) 26.
6. Hugh Fullerton, *Chicago Examiner*, Feb. 9, 1908.
7. Ted Sullivan, *Humorous Stories*, 233.
8. *Ibid*, 234–235.
9. *Ogden Standard*, Sept. 29, 1917.
10. *Topeka Daily Capital*, Oct. 8, 1917.
11. Axelson *Commy*, 40, 41.
12. George S. Robbins, *Chicago Daily News*, Dec. 28, 1916.
13. Axelson *Commy*, 10, 11.
14. *Ibid*, 4.
15. Bozeman Bulger, *Des Moines Register*, March 20, 1924.
16. Axelson, *Commy*, 42, 43.
17. *Buffalo Enquirer*, March 7, 1898.

Chapter 3

1. *Dubuque Daily Times*, Jan. 23, 1881.
2. *The Sporting News*, Jan. 24, 1918.
3. *Rock Island Argus*, Jan. 26, 1932.
4. *Racine (Wisc) Journal*, Retrospective Feb. 28, 1930.
5. Ted Sullivan, *Humorous Stories*, 235.

6. *Dubuque Telegraph-Herald*, July 8, 1923.
7. *Dubuque Telegraph-Herald*, Nov. 2, 1913.
8. *Vancouver Sun*, Nov. 1, 1913.
9. *Chicago Daily Tribune*, Feb. 15, 1903.
10. *Pittsburgh Press*, Dec. 26, 1909.
11. Ted Sullivan, *Humorous Stories*, 27.
12. *Washington Times*, Jan. 8, 1922.
13. *Buffalo Enquirer*, March 1, 1897.
14. *Ibid.*
15. *Chicago Examiner*, Feb. 4, 1912.

Chapter 4

1. *Washington Times*, Jan. 8, 1922.
2. *Chicago Tribune*, Feb. 3, 1903.
3. Crooked Ball story is a composite of numerous versions of the tale presented in dozens of newspapers over a dozen years, including *The Sporting News*, March 19, 1898, *Decatur (IL) Herald*, Feb. 18, 1912, *Buffalo (NY) Times*, March 15, 1903.
4. *Chicago Daily Tribune*, Feb. 15, 1903.
5. *Council Bluffs (IA) Nonpareil*, May 13, 1879.
6. *Anaconda (MT) Standard*, June 1, 1913.
7. Ted Sullivan, *Humorous Stories of the Ball Field*, M.A. Donohue & Co. Printers and Binders, Chicago (1903), 51–58.
8. *Buffalo (NY) Times* of March 15, 1903.
9. *Dubuque Telegraph Herald*, March 21, 1912.

Chapter 5

1. *Dubuque Daily Times*, Jan. 23, 1881.
2. *Dubuque Daily Times* Aug. 5, 1906.
3. *New Castle (PA) News*, Jan. 10, 1918; and *Salt Lake Tribune* Feb. 6, 1920.
4. *New Castle News*, Jan. 10, 1918.
5. *St. Louis Globe-Democrat* July 17, 1881.
6. *Ogden Standard*, Sept. 29, 1917.
7. *The Cincinnati Enquirer*, May 8, 1890.
8. *Sporting Life*, June 24, 1911.
9. Ted Sullivan, *Humorous Stories of the Ball Field*, M.A. Donohue & Co. Printers and Binders, Chicago (1903), 238.
10. *Dubuque Telegraph Herald*, Dec. 26, 1909.
11. *Washington Post*, Jan. 9, 1896, Baseball Notes.
12. Sullivan, *Humorous Stories*, 207.

13. *St. Louis Globe-Democrat*, April 10, 1884.
14. Ted Sullivan, *Humorous Stories*, 115.
15. *Buffalo Enquirer*, March 7, 1898.
16. *Sporting Life*, June 14, 1913; and *St. Louis Star and Times*, June 9. 1913.
17. *Alaska Daily Empire*, Feb. 5, 1915.
18. *Sporting Life*, April 15, 1911.
19. *Sporting Life*, Nov. 23, 1887.
20. *Sporting Life*, April 15. 1911.
21. *Nashville Tennessean*, Dec. 10, 1907.
22. "Ted Tells Ball Tales," *Sporting Times* reprinted in *Chattanooga Daily Times*, Jan. 23, 1910.
23. *Washington Sunday Star*, Jan. 21, 1906.
24. *St. Louis Post-Dispatch*, Nov. 3, 1883.
25. *Washington Sunday Star*, Jan. 21, 1906.
26. *Sheboygan Press-Telegram*, Dec. 27, 1922.
27. *Winnipeg Tribune*, March 22, 1906.
28. *Lawrence (KS) Daily Journal*, Nov. 9, 1883.
29. *Ibid.*
30. *Cairo (IL) Bulletin*, Nov. 10, 1883.
31. *Washington Sunday Star*, Jan. 21, 1906.
32. *Ibid.*

Chapter 6

1. *St. Louis Post-Dispatch*, Feb. 18, 1884.
2. *St. Louis Post-Dispatch*, June 14, 1884.
3. *Kansas City Times*, July 23, 1884.
4. *Kansas City Journal*, July 17, 1884.
5. *The Dickson Baseball Dictionary*, W.W. Norton Company (2009).
6. *Ibid.*
7. *Indianapolis News*, March 18, 1905.
8. *Kansas City Daily Times*, Aug. 16, 1884.
9. *Kansas City Times*, Aug. 11, 1884.
10. *Kansas City Star*, Jan. 6, 1913, "Baseball in the Old Days."
11. *Indianapolis News*, March 18, 1905.
12. *Kansas City Evening Star*, Aug. 23, 1884.
13. *Kansas City Times*, Aug. 19, 1884.
14. *Kansas City Star*, Sept. 4, 1884.
15. *Kansas City Star*, Aug. 23, 1884.
16. *San Antonio Gazette*, March 23, 1906.
17. *Ibid.*
18. *Richmond (MO) Democrat*, Aug. 28, 1884.

19. *Indianapolis News*, March 18, 1905.
20. *Kansas City Journal*, Oct. 2, 1884.
21. *The New Bill James Historical Abstract*, Free Press, New York (2003).

Chapter 7

1. *Philadelphia Times*, July 25, 1886.
2. *Kansas City Evening Star*, April 14, 1885.
3. *Cincinnati Enquirer*, June 22, 1890.
4. *Kansas City Star*, April 14–15, 1885; and a 30-year retrospective, Jan. 24, 1915.
5. *The Kansas City Evening Star*, June 1, 1885.
6. *The Kansas City Journal*, May 5, 1885.
7. *Kansas City Journal*, May 7, 1885.
8. *St. Louis Republic*, Feb. 7, 1901.
9. Ted Sullivan, *Humorous Stories of the Ball Field*, M.A. Donohue & Co. Printers and Binders, Chicago (1903), 195.
10. William Walter Veach, *The Sporting News*, reprinted in *St. Louis Republic*, Feb. 7, 1901.
11. *Chattanooga Daily Times*, Jan. 3, 1910.
12. *Sporting Life*, June 3, 1885.
13. *St. Louis Post-Dispatch*, May 28, 1885.
14. *St. Louis Republic*, Feb. 7, 1901.
15. Sullivan, *Humorous Stories*, 59–62.
16. *Kansas City Evening Star*, June 8, 1885.
17. *Kansas City Evening Star*, June 11, 1885.
18. *Kansas City Evening Star*, June 13, 1885.
19. *Buffalo Enquirer*, March 2, 1905.
20. *Dubuque Daily Herald*, June 14, 1885.
21. *Sporting Life*, Jan. 27, 1886.
22. *St. Louis Post-Dispatch*, Aug. 8, 1885.
23. *Sporting Life*, Jan. 27, 1886.
24. *Sporting Life*, Nov. 11, 1885.
25. *Monticello (IA) Express*, Feb. 11, 1886.

Chapter 8

1. *Milwaukee Sentinel*, June 28, 1886.
2. *The Sporting News*, reprinted in *Buffalo Enquirer*, March 31, 1899.
3. *Ibid.*
4. *St. Louis Post-Dispatch*, Aug. 28, 1886.
5. *Ibid.*

6. *Sporting Life*, July 14, 1886, and *Minneapolis Tribune* July 16, 1886.
7. *Sporting Life*, Aug. 18, 1886.
8. *St. Louis Star and Times*, March 4, 1912.
9. *Ibid.*
10. Dougherty's story is a composite of articles in *Racine (WI) Journal Times*, May 21, 1913, and *Washington Herald*, Feb. 21, 1921.
11. *St. Paul Daily Globe*, July 29, 1886.
12. *Milwaukee Sentinel*, Sept. 21, 1886.
13. *Sporting Times*, reprinted in *Lincoln (NE) Star*, Jan. 16, 1910, and *Chattanooga Daily Times*, Jan. 23, 1910.
14. *Indianapolis News*, March 18, 1905.
15. *St. Louis Post-Dispatch*, Aug. 28. 1886.
16. *The Sporting News*, Dec. 4, 1886.

Chapter 9

1. *Buffalo Enquirer*, Dec. 28, 1905.
2. *Philadelphia Times*, July 31, 1887.
3. *Boston Daily Globe*, July 29, 1887.
4. *Baltimore Sun*, Aug. 9, 1887.
5. *Philadelphia Times*, Aug. 14, 1887.
6. *New York Clipper*, Aug. 13, 1887.

Chapter 10

1. *New York Sun*, Oct. 31, 1887.
2. *Warren County (VA) Democrat*, Nov. 24, 1887.
3. *Memphis Daily Appeal*, Dec. 9, 1887.
4. *Washington Post*, Dec. 4, 1887.
5. *Washington Post*, Dec. 11, 1887.
6. *Ibid.*
7. From various versions of Connie Mack, *My 50 Years in Baseball: Connie Mack Recalls First Southern Trip* that appeared in many publications of the day, including: *Boston Daily Globe*, Dec. 9, 1930; *Syracuse (NY) Herald*, Sept. 17, 1930; and *Key West Citizen*, Sept. 17, 1930.
8. *Ibid.*
9. *New York Sun*, Jan. 15, 1888.
10. Mack, *My 50 Years In Baseball*.
11. *Ibid.*
12. *Ibid.*
13. *The Sporting News*, Feb. 4, 1899.
14. *The Deaf-Mutes Journal*, July 8, 1897.
15. *Washington Evening Star*, July 31, 1898.
16. Mack, *My 50 Years in Baseball*.

17. Williamson's quote reprinted in John Thorn, *Baseball in the Garden of Eden: The Secret History of the Early Game*, Simon & Schuster, New York, 2011, 188.

18. Weldy Walker's reaction to league's all-white rule is included in Dorothy Seymour Mills and Harold Seymour, *Baseball: The People's Game*, Oxford University Press, New York, 1990, 554.

19. Christy Mathewson, *Pitching in a Pinch: Or, Baseball from the Inside*, Gossett & Dunlap, New York, 1912, 245.

20. *Washington Evening Star*, April 2, 1888.

21. *Washington Evening Star*, April 8, 1890.

22. *Sporting Life*, Nov. 13, 1887.

23. Ted Sullivan, *Humorous Stories of the Ball Field*, M.A. Donohue & Co. Printers and Binders, Chicago (1903), 65.

24. *Washington Post*, April 19, 1888.

25. *Washington Post*, June 12, 1888.

26. *Washington Evening Star*, April 8, 1890.

27. *Atlanta Constitution*, July 29, 1888.

28. *Escanaba (MI) Daily Press*, April 1914.

29. *St. Bernard (LA) Voice*, April 14, 1914.

30. *Ibid.*

31. *Ibid.*

32. *The Sporting News*, Nov. 21, 1907.

33. *Ibid.*

34. *New York Evening World*, Sept. 25, 1888.

35. *Sporting Life*, Oct. 17. 1888.

36. W.W. Aulick, *Pittsburgh Press*, Feb. 24, 1911.

37. *New York Daily Clipper*, Oct. 27, 1888.

38. *The Sporting News*, Dec. 30, 1909.

Chapter 11

1. *St. Louis Post-Dispatch*, Nov. 7, 1888, and Dec. 21, 1888.

2. *Kansas City Star*, Dec. 22, 1888.

3. *Wisconsin (Madison) State Journal*, Dec. 27, 1888.

4. *(Chicago) Inter Ocean*, Dec. 29, 1888.

5. *Washington Post*, Dec. 25, 1904.

6. Ted Sullivan, *Humorous Stories of the Ball Field*, M.A. Donohue & Co. Printers and Binders, Chicago (1903), 82.

7. Sullivan, *Humorous Stories*, 83.

8. *Ibid.*

9. *Pittsburgh (PA) Daily Post*, Aug. 10, 1889 6.

10. *Sporting Life*, June 11, 1889.

11. *Sporting Life*, July 3, 1889.

12. Sullivan, *Humorous Stories*, 82.

13. *Sporting Life*, arch 13, 1889.

14. *Omaha Daily Bee*, August 25, 1889.

15. *St. Paul Daily Globe*, Nov. 10, 1889.

16. *St. Paul Daily Globe*, March 31, 1888.

17. Lawrence S. Ritter, *The Glory of Their Times*, William Morrow, New York (1966).

18. *Pittsburgh Dispatch*, March 22, 1889.

19. *Washington Post*, Feb. 12, 1890.

20. *Sunday Herald & Weekly National Intelligencer*, April 13, 1890.

21. *Sporting Life*, July 27, 1890.

22. Sullivan, *Humorous Stories*, 74.

23. *Chicago Tribune*, April 1, 1900.

24. *Washington Evening Star*, May 13, 1890.

25. *Washington Post*, May 28, 1890.

26. *Washington Evening Star*, May 7, 1890.

27. Sullivan, *Humorous Stories*, 120.

28. *Cincinnati Enquirer*, May 16, 1890.

29. *Sunday Herald and Weekly National Intelligencer*, June 1, 1890.

30. *Washington Evening Star*, July 30, 1890.

31. *Washington Evening Star*, Aug. 4, 1890.

32. *Baltimore Sun*, Aug. 9, 1890.

33. *Sunday Herald and Weekly National Intelligencer*, Aug. 10, 1890.

34. *Pittsburgh Dispatch*, Aug. 12, 1890.

35. *Washington Post*, Sept. 28, 1890.

36. *Waterbury (CT) Evening Democrat*, Oct. 6, 1890.

37. *Sporting Life*, July 15, 1891.

38. *Cincinnati Enquirer*, Oct. 13, 1891.

39. *New York Sun*, Oct. 14, 1891.

Chapter 12

1. *Sporting Life*, February 27, 1892.

2. *Atlanta Constitution*, March 1, 1892.

3. *Daily Nebraska State Journal (Lincoln)*, July 3, 1892.

4. *Boston Daily Globe*, June 9, 1892.

5. *Richmond Dispatch*, July 22, 1892.

6. *Daily Nebraska State Journal*, September 11, 1892 ("During the New Orleans series of slaughters, Ted Sullivan implored the Chattanoogas to wake up. From the catcher's box the Irish baron

pleaded—'Boys, you aren't playing croquet.'").

7. *Boston Daily Globe*, August 15, 1892.
8. *Evening Star (Washington, D.C.)*, August 6, 1892.
9. *Boston Daily Globe*, September 9, 1892.
10. *Atlanta Constitution*, September 10, 1892.
11. *Atlanta Constitution*, September 25, 1892.
12. *Pittsburgh Dispatch*, October 4, 1892.
13. *Sporting Life*, November 5, 1892.
14. *Times-Democrat (New Orleans)*, June 29, 1893.
15. *Wichita Daily Eagle*, December 17, 1892.
16. *Sporting Life*, January 7, 1893.
17. *Times-Picayune*, May 23, 1894.
18. *(Chicago) Inter Ocean*, July 17, 1893.
19. *Times-Picayune*, July 19, 1893.
20. *Times Democrat (New Orleans)*, July 28, 1893.
21. *Sporting Life*, August 12, 1893.
22. *The St. Louis Sporting News*, Aug. 19, 1893.
23. *Sporting Life*, August 5, 1893.
24. *Richmond (VA) Times*, Oct. 1, 1893.
25. *Atlanta Constitution*, January 21, 1894.
26. *Sporting Life*, March 19, 1894.
27. *Sporting Life*, April 14, 1894.
28. *Boston Globe*, March 6, 1894.
29. *Atlanta Constitution*, May 27, 1894.
30. *Times-Picayune*, May 23, 1894.
31. *(Chicago) Inter Ocean*, Dec. 16, 1906.
32. *Ibid.*
33. *Savannah Morning News*, June 25, 1894.
34. *Atlanta Constitution*, June 26, 1894.
35. *Jersey City News*, August 21, 1894.

Chapter 13

1. Ted Sullivan, *Humorous Stories of the Ball Field*, M.A. Donohue & Co. Printers and Binders, Chicago (1903), 214.
2. *Ibid.*
3. *Ibid.*, 221.
4. *Ibid.*, 227.
5. *Ibid.*
6. *Kansas City Journal*, Feb. 6, 1897.
7. *Fort Worth Gazette*, Dec. 31, 1895.
8. *Athens (GA) Daily Banner*, March 10, 1901.

9. *Bloomington (IL) Pantograph*, Aug. 30, 1901.
10. *Washington Post*, Nov. 12, 1894.
11. Sullivan, *Humorous Stories*, 246.
12. *Ibid.*
13. *Washington Post*, Nov. 12, 1894.
14. *Reno Gazette-Journal*, Aug. 5, 1919.
15. *Ibid.*

Chapter 14

1. *Atlanta Constitution*, April 8, 1895.
2. *Morning News (Savannah, GA)*, June 27, 1894.
3. *Fort Worth Gazette*, March 8, 1895.
4. *Austin Weekly Statesman*, March 14, 1895.
5. *Houston Post*, March 1, 1914.
6. *Fort Worth Gazette*, April 3, 1895.
7. *Buffalo Enquirer*, Dec. 23, 1898.
8. *Atlanta Constitution*, April 8, 1895.
9. *Atlanta Constitution*, April 8, 1895.
10. *Atlanta Constitution*, April 9, 1895.
11. *Buffalo (NY) Enquirer*, Oct. 4, 1906.
12. *Galveston Daily News*, March 15, 1912.
13. *Galveston Daily News*, May 19, 1895.
14. *Galveston Daily News*, July 14, 1895.
15. Reprinted in dozens of newspapers, including the *Buffalo Times*, April 3, 1904.
16. *Galveston Daily News*, September 7, 1895.
17. *Galveston Daily News*, September 8, 1895.
18. In a column published in the Dec. 7, 1895 edition of *Sporting Life*, league secretary James Nolan praised Sullivan for his role in the 1895 season's successes: "Ted was the brains and backbone of the League magnates last season. I know it to be a fact that he spent a big sum of money to boost this league along that he never asked or expected to be repaid to him, and that was more than anyone else did. He gave me less trouble than any other manager did, too. I never had him to make a kick of any kind, to protest against umpires or to wrangle with other clubs, and he was always the most prompt in money matters. Tedrick is all right...."
19. *Sporting Life*, August 10, 1895.
20. *Houston Post*, January 11, 1914.
21. *Houston Daily Post*, Jan. 17, 1896.
22. *Ibid.*

Chapter 15

1. *Sporting Life* and *Boston Globe*, Aug. 9, 1899.
2. *Pittsburgh Herald*, Feb. 27, 1896.
3. *New Haven Daily Morning Journal and Courier*, Dec. 30, 1895; *Houston Daily Post*, Jan. 5, 1896.
4. *Washington Times*, Feb. 5, 1899.
5. *Wilmington (DE) Evening Journal*, April 10, 1896.
6. *Sporting Life*, Jan. 18, 1896.
7. *New York Sun*, Feb. 1896.
8. *Baltimore Sun*, April 11, 1896.
9. *New Haven Morning Journal-Courier*, April 1, 1896.
10. *New Haven (CT) Morning Journal and Courier*, April 20, 1896.
11. *Washington Morning Times*, April 6, 1896.
12. *Ibid.*
13. *Sporting Life*, May 2, 1896.
14. *San Antonio (TX) Sunday Light*, June 5, 1896.
15. *Macon (GA) Telegraph*, Sept. 28, 1896.
16. *Baltimore Sun*, Oct. 31, 1896.
17. *Washington Evening Times*, Nov. 21, 1896.
18. *Times of Washington*, Aug. 22, 1897.
19. *Cincinnati Enquirer*, Feb. 28, 1897.
20. *St. Louis Post-Dispatch*, Nov. 5, 1897.

Chapter 16

1. Special to the *Baltimore Sun*, Feb. 18, 1898.
2. *Burlington (IA) Gazette*, Feb. 24, 1898.
3. *Burlington (IA) Hawkeye*, Feb. 25, 1898, reprinted from *Dubuque Times*, Feb. 24, 1898. A version of the story also ran in *The Sporting News*, under the byline "Old Timer," March 26, 1898.
4. *The Sporting News*, April 9, 1898.
5. *The Sporting News*, March 26, 1898.
6. *Dubuque Herald*, Feb. 25, 1898.
7. *The Sporting News*, April 9, 1898.
8. Per the *Dubuque Daily Herald*, March 19, 1898.
9. *Dubuque Herald*, May 25, 1898.
10. *Dubuque Herald*, May 29, 1898.
11. *Dubuque Daily Herald*, June 2, 1898.
12. *Dubuque Daily Times*, June 22, 1898.
13. *Cincinnati Enquirer*, June 21, 1898.
14. *Washington Post*, Sept. 18. 1898; and *Chicago Tribune*, Sept. 27, 1898.

15. *Lincoln (Neb.) State Journal*, Feb. 19, 1899.
16. *Washington Time*, Feb. 2, 1899.
17. *Ibid.*
18. *Dubuque Daily Herald*, Sept. 28, 1898.
19. *Dubuque Daily Herald*, Oct. 16, 1898.
20. *Kansas City Journal*, Jan. 19, 1899.
21. *Baltimore Sun*, Feb. 3, 1899.
22. *Pittsburg Morning Sun*, June 29, 2013.
23. *Chicago Journal*, Feb. 8, 1904, the *Spokesman-Review* (Spokane, WA) Feb. 28, 1904, and dozens of other papers throughout the country carried the same article.
24. *Ibid.*

Chaper 17

1. *Montgomery (Alabama) Advertiser*, January 20, 1899.
2. *San Antonio Light*, Feb. 19, 1899.
3. *Advertiser*, March 30, 1899.
4. *Dubuque Herald*, April 30, 1899.
5. *Advertiser*, March 1, 1906.
6. *Advertiser*, April 28, 1899.
7. *Times-Picayune*, May 5, 1899.
8. *Advertiser*, March 1, 1906.
9. *Times-Picayune*, May 2, 1899.
10. *Times-Picayune*, May 5, 1899.
11. *Advertiser*, April 28, 1899.
12. *Chattanooga Daily Times*, May 24, 1899.
13. *Ibid.*
14. *St. Louis Post-Dispatch*, June 2, 1899.
15. *(Chicago) Daily Inter Ocean*, Sept. 27, 1899.
16. *Spokane Daily Chronicle*, March 5 and March 13, 1900.
17. *Salt Lake Herald*, March 18, 1900.

Chapter 18

1. Alfred H. Spink, *The National Game*, Southern Illinois University Press, 2000; first published 1910 by The National Game Publishing Co.
2. *Ibid.*
3. *Sporting Life*, Jan. 20, 1900.
4. *Watertown (NY) News*, July 11, 1899.
5. *Boston Globe*, July 24, 1899.
6. *St. Louis Post-Dispatch*, July 17, 1899.
7. *Topeka State Journal*, Sept. 18, 1899.
8. *St. Louis Post-Dispatch*, Aug. 4, 1899.

9. *Leadville (CO) Herald-Democrat*, Sept. 12, 1899.
10. *(Chicago) Inter Ocean*, Sept. 18, 1899.
11. *San Francisco Examiner*, Jan 5, 1919.
12. *Brooklyn Daily Eagle*, Sept. 19, 1899.
13. *Ibid.*
14. *Scranton Republican*, Nov 27, 1899.
15. *Chicago Tribune*, Oct. 1, 1899.
16. *Wilkes-Barre (PA) Record*, Nov. 24, 1899.
17. *Indianapolis Journal*, March 5, 1900.
18. *Detroit Free Press*, April 9, 1900.
19. *Detroit Free Press*, Aug. 26, 1900.
20. *Buffalo (NY) Times*, Aug. 24, 1900.
21. *Detroit Free Press*, Aug. 26, 1900.
22. *Buffalo Times*, Aug. 24, 1900.
23. *Louisville (KY) Courier Times-Journal*, Dec. 30, 1900.
24. *Buffalo (NY) Times*, Aug. 24, 1900.
25. *Louisville (KY) Courier-Journal*, March 17, 1901.
26. *Washington Post*, Aug. 18, 1901.
27. *Dayton (OH) Herald*, March 14, 1901.
28. *Buffalo (NY) Courier*, Dec. 18, 1891.
29. *Ibid.*
30. *Baltimore Sun*, Feb. 22, 1901.
31. *Washington Post*, Aug. 18, 1901.
32. *Ibid.*
33. *Buffalo Courier*, Feb. 4, 1902.
34. *Buffalo) Enquirer*, Dec. 16, 1901.
35. *Buffalo Enquirer*, Jan. 11, 1902.
36. *Pittsburgh Press*, Dec. 22, 1901.
37. *Ibid.*

Chapter 19

1. *Houston Post*, March 1, 1914.
2. *Fort Worth Gazette*, April 3, 1895.
3. *Houston Post*, March 1, 1914.
4. Kris Rutherford, *Baseball on the Prairie: How Seven Small-Town Teams Shaped Texas League History*, The History Press, South Carolina (2014), 107–110.
5. Rutherford, *Baseball on the Prairie*, 110.
6. *Daily Arkansas (Little Rock) Gazette*, May 30, 1903.
7. *Houston Daily Post*, September 29, 1902.
8. *Austin Daily Statesman*, October 14, 1902.
9. *Houston Daily Post*, November 4, 1902.
10. *Bryan Morning Eagle*, March 12, 1905.

11. *Paris News*, July 12, 1951.
12. *Austin Stateman*, June 7, 1903.
13. Rutherford, *Baseball on the Prairie*, 116.
14. *Waxahachie Daily Light*, January 18, 1904.
15. *Salt Lake Tribune*, April 23, 1905.
16. *San Francisco Examiner*, Jan 2, 1905.

Chapter 20

1. *Washington Post*, Aug. 18, 1901.
2. *Sporting Life*, Jan. 20, 1894.
3. *Cincinnati Enquirer*, Oct. 13, 1891.
4. *Butte (MT) Miner*, April 20, 1908.
5. *St. Joseph (MO) Gazette*, Aug. 10, 1905.
6. *Cincinnati Enquirer*, March 24, 1904.
7. *The Sporting News*, Sept 12, 1891, and Jan. 30, 1919.
8. *Washington Post*, March 10, 1907.
9. *Chicago Daily Tribune*, Feb. 4, 1900.
10. *Muskogee (OK) Times Democrat*, October 16, 1911.
11. *Pittsburgh Press*, June 17, 1902.
12. *Washington Evening Star*, April 17, 1907.
13. *Minneapolis Morning Tribune*, Aug. 17, 1910.
14. Ted Sullivan, *Humorous Stories of the Ball Field*, M.A. Donohue & Co. Printers and Binders, Chicago (1903), 95.
15. *Humorous Stories*, 153.
16. *Humorous Stories*, 153.
17. William G. Weart, *Pittsburgh Press*, Feb. 6, 1913.
18. *Washington Post*, July 2, 1905.
19. *Cincinnati Commercial-Tribune*, Jan. 28, 1898.
20. *Des Moines Register*, June 25, 1911.
21. *Washington Post*, June 26, 1913; and Sullivan, *Humorous Stories.*
22. *Rochester (NY) Democrat and Chronicle*, Dec. 16, 1900.
23. *Washington Post*, June 26, 1913, and Sullivan, *Humorous Stories*, 67.
24. Sullivan, *Humorous Stories*, 77.
25. *Decatur (IL) Herald*, Aug. 7, 1904.
26. *The Daily Review (Decatur, IL)*, Aug. 7, 1904.
27. *Omaha Bee*, April 19, 1886.
28. *St. Louis Post-Dispatch*, April 12, 1886.
29. *Omaha Bee*, April 19, 1886.
30. *Chicago Tribune*, Sept. 24, 1899.

31. Tim Murnane column, *Buffalo (NY) Enquirer*, Dec. 18, 1907.

32. *Chicago Tribune*, Aug. 18, 1907.

33. *Chicago Tribune*, Aug. 5, 1900.

34. *Decatur Review*, Aug. 7, 1904.

35. *Washington Post*, June 17, 1906.

36. *Dubuque Daily Times*, Aug. 5, 1906.

37. *Baltimore Sun*, Dec. 29, 1916.

38. *St. Louis Post*, Jan. 8, 1911.

39. *The Sporting News*, Jan. 30, 1919.

40. *Winnipeg Tribune*, July 13, 1906.

41. *St. Louis Post-Dispatch*, Jan. 8, 1911.

42. *Dubuque Daily Times*, Jan. 10, 1909.

43. *Dubuque Telegraph-Herald*, Aug. 3, 1906.

44. *Washington Post*, Sept. 9, 1904.

45. *St. Louis Post-Dispatch*, Jan. 8, 1911.

46. *Sporting Life*, June 2, 1894.

Chapter 21

1. *Atlanta Constitution*, Jan. 27, 1896.

2. *The Sporting News*, July 1, 1899.

3. *Ogden (UT) Standard*, March 16, 1900.

4. *New York Clipper*, March 17, 1902; and *Sporting Life*, Feb. 20, 1904.

5. *Washington Post*, June 18, 1906.

6. Tim Murnane, *Cincinnati Enquirer*, Dec. 3, 1906.

7. *The Sporting News*, Dec. 12, 1918.

8. *Dubuque Times-Journal*, July 8, 1923.

9. *Humorous Stories*, 112–113.

10. *Washington Post*, July 2, 1904.

11. *Calumet (IL) News*, Jan. 17, 1910.

12. *Boston Globe*, Dec. 15, 1895.

13. *Atlanta Constitution*, Feb. 28, 1899.

14. *Chicago Examiner*, Jan. 1, 1910.

Chapter 22

1. *Cincinnati Enquirer*, March 24, 1904.

2. *Wichita Eagle*, March 17, 1904.

3. *Topeka (KS) Daily Herald*, March 17, 1904.

4. *Sporting Life*, May 21, 1904.

5. *The Sporting News*, reprinted in *Washington Post*, July 10, 1904.

6. *Ibid.*

7. *Washington Post*, July 7, 1904.

8. *Sporting Life*, Aug. 4, 1904.

9. *Sporting Life*, Sept. 3, 1904.

10. *Wichita Beacon*, referenced in *Topeka State Journal*, Aug. 11, 1905.

11. David Nemec (ed.), *Major League Baseball Profiles 1871–1900*, Vol. 2, University of Nebraska Press, Lincoln and London (2011), 147.

12. *Salt Lake Herald*, Nov. 29, 1905; and *The Sporting News*, Dec. 9, 1905.

13. *Ibid.*

14. *Washington Post*, June 18, 1906.

15. *San Antonio Light*, Jan. 6, 1907.

16. *Fairmont West Virginian*, Feb. 13, 1907.

17. *The Washington Post*, March 3, 1907.

18. *Chicago Tribune*, Feb. 10, 1907.

19. *Boston Sunday Post*, March 10, 1907.

20. *Washington Post*, March 6, 1907.

21. *The (Chicago) Inter Ocean*, March 5, 1907.

22. *Washington Post*, March 10, 1907.

23. *The (Chicago) Inter Ocean*, Jan. 6, 1907.

24. *Roswell (NM) Daily Record*, March 4, 1907; and *Dubuque Daily Journal*, March 11, 1907.

25. *Lake County (IN) Times*, March 13, 1907.

26. *Washington Post*, March 10, 1907.

27. *Boston Sunday Post*, March 10, 1907.

28. *Washington Post*, March 23, 1907.

29. *Traverse City (MI) Evening Record*, March 13, 1907.

30. *Washington Times*, March 12, 1907.

31. *Indianapolis Sun*, Feb. 13, 1907.

32. *Atlanta Constitution*, Dec. 4, 1907.

33. *Trenton (NJ) Evening Times*, Dec. 2, 1907.

34. *Omaha Daily Bee*, Feb. 20, 1908.

35. *Ibid.*

36. Article appeared in papers throughout the U.S. and Canada, including the *Winnipeg Tribune*, May 27, 1911.

37. *Dubuque Telegraph-Herald*, Jan. 10, 1909.

38. *Chicago Examiner*, Feb. 27, 1909.

Chapter 23

1. *The Sporting News*, Dec. 26, 1909.

2. *Atlanta Georgian and News*, Dec. 29, 1909.

3. *Chicago Tribune*, Jan. 30, 1910.

4. *Sporting Life*, Jan. 22, 1910.

5. *Ibid.*

6. *Hartford Courant*, Dec. 18, 1909.

7. *Davenport (IA) Daily Times*, Jan. 19, 1910.

8. *El Paso Morning Times* March 25, 1910.

9. *Clinton Daily Herald*, April 1, 1910.
10. *Clinton Daily Herald*, May 2, 1910.
11. *Clinton Daily Herald*, May 7, 1910.
12. *Clinton Daily Herald*, May 12, 1910.
13. *Clinton Daily Herald*, May 16, 1910.
14. *Muscatine (IA) Journal*, May 31, 1910.
15. *Davenport (IA) Daily Time*, June 4, 1910.
16. *Washington Post*, Dec. 11, 1910.
17. *Minneapolis Star Tribune*, April 3, 1910.
18. *Chicago Examiner*, March 18, 1911.
19. *Cincinnati Enquirer*, Sept. 13, 1911.
20. *Official Guide of the National Association of Professional Baseball Leagues 1912*, T.H. Murnane, Editor, American Sports Publishing Company, New York, 46–49.
21. *Saskatoon (CA) Star Phoenix*, Oct. 27, 1911.
22. *Butte (MT) Miner*, Oct. 30, 1911.
23. *Washington Post*, Feb. 14, 1912.
24. *New York Sun*, July 29, 1912.
25. *Collier's*, April 20, 1912.
26. *Ibid.*; and *Sporting Life*, Aug. 4, 1904.
27. *Washington Evening Star*, Feb. 4, 1912.
28. *Ibid.*
29. *The (Chicago) Inter Ocean*, Dec. 12, 1912.

Chapter 24

1. Retrospective article by Tom Handley, *Chicago Tribune*, Nov. 2, 2005.
2. *New York Times*, Feb. 2, 1913.
3. James E. Elfers, *The Tour to End All Tours: The Story of Major League Baseball World Tour, 1913–1914*, University of Nebraska Press, Lincoln (2003).
4. *Davenport Daily Times*, Feb. 22, 1913.
5. *Lincoln (Neb) Star*, Feb. 16, 1913.
6. *Kansas City Journal*, Oct. 26, 1913.
7. *Kansas City Journal*, Oct. 28, 1913.
8. *Washington Post*, Aug. 21, 1897.
9. *Washington Post*, July 10, 1904.
10. *Cairo (IL) Bulletin*, Nov. 26, 1913.
11. *Salem (OR) Capitol Journal*, Nov. 7, 1913.
12. Lawrence S. Ritter, *The Glory of Their Times: The Story of the Early Days of Baseball Told by the Men Who Played It*, Macmillan, New York (1966), 187–189.
13. *Sunday Oregonian*, Nov. 16, 1914.
14. *Anaconda (MT) Standard*, Nov. 23. 1913.
15. *Morning Oregonian*, Nov. 19, 1914.
16. *Ibid.*
17. *Ibid.*
18. *Davenport (IA) Daily Times*, Nov. 20, 1913; and *Oregon (Portland) Daily Journal*, Nov. 30, 1913.
19. John J. McGraw, "Special Correspondent" for *Boston Post*," Dec. 4, 1913.
20. *History of World's Tour*, 23.
21. *Chicago Tribune*, Dec. 27, 1913.
22. *Boston Globe*, Dec. 27, 1913.
23. John J. McGraw, Special Correspondent for the *Boston Post*, Dec. 28, 1913.
24. *History of World's Tour*, 31, 55.
25. John J. McGraw, Special Correspondent for *Boston Post*, Dec. 4, 1913.
26. *Boston Globe*, Dec. 29, 1913.
27. John J. McGraw, Special Correspondent for *Boston Post*, Dec. 4, 1913.
28. *Ibid.*
29. Axelson, *Commy*, 221.
30. *History of World's Tour*, 15 & 16.
31. *Ibid.*, 47.
32. *Kansas City Star*, June 17, 1913.
33. Malcolm Bingay, *Chicago Tribune*, June 24, 1940.
34. *Calumet (MI) News*, March 17, 1914.
35. *History of World's Tour*, 21.
36. Joe Farrell, *Chicago Tribune*, Feb. 3, 1914.
37. *History of World's Tour*, 22.
38. *Topeka State Journal*, March 18, 1914.
39. *History of World's Tour*, 29.
40. *Washington Times*, Feb. 9, 1914.
41. *History of World's Tour*, 28.
42. *History of World's Tour*, 33.
43. Axelson, *Commy*, 159.
44. *My 30 Years in Baseball*, Boni & Liveright, Inc. Publishers, 1923, by arrangement with the Christy Walsh Syndicate and *The New York Times*, Feb. 2, 1914.
45. *Ibid.*
46. *History of World's Tour*, 34.
47. *The Tour to End All Tours: The Story of Major League Baseball's 1913–14 World Tour*, by James E. Elfers, University of Nebraska Press 2003, 200.
48. *Sporting Life*, Feb. 21, 1914.
49. *History of World's Tour*, 39.
50. *Sporting Life* Feb. 21, 1914.
51. *History of World's Tour*, 40.
52. Damon Runyon dispatch from London, Feb. 22, 1914, from *Guys, Dolls, and Curveballs—Damon Ruynyon on Baseball*,

Jim Reisler, Editor, Carroll & Graf Publishers, 2005.
53. *St. Louis Star and Times*, May 12, 1914.
54. *History of the World's Tour*, 52 and 30.
55. L.M. Sutter, *Arlie Latham: A Baseball Biography of the Freshest Man on Earth*, McFarland (2012), 218.
56. *Chicago Examiner*, Feb. 26, 1914. Also reprinted in Jim Reisler (ed.), *Guys, Dolls, and Curveballs: Damon Runyon on Baseball*, Carroll & Graf Publishers, New York, 2005.
57. *Ibid.*
58. *Shreveport (LA) Journal*, Feb. 28, 1923.
59. Hotspur, *Buffalo Courier*, Feb. 26, 1914.
60. *Harper's Weekly*, April 4, 1914, Vols. 58–59, 24–26.
61. *History of World's Tour*, 62.
62. *Chicago Examiner*, March 7, 1914.
63. *Chicago Examiner*, March 11, 1914.
64. *Ibid.*
65. *The (Chicago) Inter Ocean*, March 11, 1914.
66. Timothy M. Gray, *Tris Speaker: The Rough-and-Tumble Life of a Baseball Legend*, University of Nebraska Press, Lincoln, (2005).
67. *Pittsburgh Press*, Feb. 6, 1913.
68. *History of World's Tour*, 5.
69. *Chicago Tribune*, May 8, 1914.
70. *Calumet (MI) News*, June 22, 1914.
71. *New York Tribune*, Aug. 2, 1914.
72. *Escabana (MI) Morning Press*, Aug. 23, 1914.
73. *Ibid.*
74. *Billings (MT) Daily Tribune*, Aug. 19, 1914.
75. *Cincinnati Enquirer*, Aug. 19, 1914.
76. *Ibid.*

Chapter 25

1. Alfred H. Spink, *The National Game*, Second Edition, Southern Illinois University Press (2000).
2. *The St. Louis Sporting News*, April 18, 1912.
3. *Topeka Journal*, March 3, 1915.
4. *Arkansas Democrat*, March 21, 1916.
5. *Dubuque Telegraph-Herald*, April 30, 1915.
6. *Topeka State Journal*, March 18, 1915.

7. *El Paso Herald*, May 15, 1922.
8. *Ibid.*
9. *Chicago Examiner*, Jan. 31, 1915.
10. *New York Evening World*, Oct. 20, 1915.
11. *Washington Times*, Dec. 31, 1915.
12. *Bridgeport (CT) Evening Farmer*, Jan. 1, 1916.
13. *Washington Evening Star*, Dec. 30, 1915.
14. *Chicago Examiner*, March 16, 1914.
15. *Washington Times*, Feb. 24, 1921.

Chapter 26

1. *Chicago Tribune*, March 22, 1908.
2. *Brooklyn (NY) Eagle*, July 15, 1917.
3. *Memphis News-Scimitar*, Jan. 10, 1919.
4. *The Sporting News*, Jan. 2, 1919.
5. *Cincinnati Enquirer*, Aug. 1, 1918.
6. *Washington Times*, Nov. 7, 1918.
7. *Charlotte Observer*, Jan. 26, 1919.
8. *Charlotte Observer*, Jan. 30, 1919.
9. *Washington Post*, Nov. 10, 1919.
10. J.V. Fitz Gerald, reprinted in *Washington Post*, Nov. 10, 1919.
11. *New York Times*, Oct. 9, 2019.
12. J.V. Fitz Gerald, reprinted in *Washington Post*, Nov. 10, 1919.
13. *Dubuque Telegraph-Herald*, Dec. 11, 1921.

Chapter 27

1. *Reno Gazette-Journal*, July 7, 1919.
2. *Winston-Salem Journal*, March 9, 1921.
3. *Washington Times*, Feb. 15, 1922.
4. *The Sporting News*, April 27, 1922.
5. *New York Herald*, May 23, 1922.
6. *Washington Herald*, June 20, 1922.
7. *Washington Times*, April 16, 1922.
8. *Washington Herald*, June 20, 1922.
9. *Collier's Eye (Chicago)*, June 17, 1922.
10. *Nashville Times*, Feb. 15, 1922.
11. *Dubuque Times Journal*, July 8, 1923.
12. *Reno Evening Gazette*, Aug. 18, 1920.
13. *The Chicago Examiner*, Aug. 25, 1917.
14. *The Sporting News*, May 28, 1925.
15. *Washington Post*, Oct. 4, 1924.
16. *Washington Post*, Nov. 10, 1924.
17. *The Sporting News*, Dec. 12, 1918.

18. *Dubuque Telegraph-Herald* July 8, 1923.

19. *The Sporting News,* Dec. 6, 1926.

20. *Washington Herald*, Feb. 22, 1921.

21. *The Sporting News*, Dec. 12, 1918.

22. *Bloomington (IL) Pantograph*, June 16, 1923.

23. *Richmond (VA) Times-Dispatch*, Sept. 25, 1920.

24. *Baltimore Evening Sun*, March 28, 1921.

25. John B. Foster, *Rock Island Argus*, Jan. 26, 1932.

26. *Spink Sports Stories*, 213–214.

Chapter 28

1. *Liberator (Tralee)*, Nov. 9, 1926.

2. *Liberator*, April 10, 1926.

3. *Kerry Reporter*, Dec. 11, 1926.

4. Richard McElligot, *Forging a Kingdom: The GAA in Kerry, 1884–1934*, The Collins Press, Cork, Ireland (2013), 324.

5. *Kerry News*, May 14, 1927.

6. *Kerryman*, June 18, 1927.

7. *Irish Examiner*, June 13, 1927.

8. *Kerry News*, Sept. 5, 1927.

9. *Kerryman*, Aug. 27, 1927.

10. *Kerryman*, June 24, 1927.

11. *Kerry Reporter*, Sept. 20, 1927.

12. *Kerry Reporter*, Sept. 24, 1927.

13. *Irish Independent*, Aug. 23, 1927.

14. Tom Mahon and James J. Gillogly, *Decoding the IRA*, Mercier Press, Cork, Ireland (2008), 212.

15. *Kerry Reporter*, July 23, 1927.

16. *Ibid.*

17. Mahon and Gillogly, 216.

18. *Kerry Reporter*, Sept. 23, 1927.

19. *Kerry Reporter*, Aug. 27, 1927.

20. *Ibid.*

21. *Kerryman*, September 10, 1927.

22. *Ibid.*

23. *Ibid.*

24. *Ibid.*

Chapter 29

1. *St. Joseph (MO) News-Press-Gazette*, April 16, 1909.

2. *Brooklyn (NY) Citizen*, Feb. 19, 1929.

3. *Washington Post*, Feb. 18, 1929.

4. *Brazil (IN) Daily Times*, April 13, 1929.

5. *Washington Post*, Feb. 18, 1929.

6. *Ibid.*

7. *Milwaukee Sentinel*, July 6, 1929.

8. *Milwaukee Journal*, July 6, 1929.

9. *Humorous Stories*, 186.

10. *San Francisco Exasminer* July 11, 1929.

11. Timothy Paul Sullivan's Last Will and Testament, signed April 16, 1929, and filed July 10, 1929, in Washington, D.C. Copy in authors' possession.

Bibliography

Achorn, Edward. *The Summer of Beer and Whiskey: How Brewers, Barkeeps, Rowdies, Immigrants, and a Wild Pennant Fight Made Baseball America's Game.* New York: Public Affairs Publishing, 2014.

Axelson, Gustaf W. *Commy: The Life Story of Charles A. Comiskey.* Chicago: Reilly & Lee, 1919.

Casway, Jerrold I. "Baseball: The Early Years." *The Encyclopedia of the Irish in America.* University of Notre Dame Press, 1999.

_____. *The Culture and Ethnicity of Nineteenth Century Baseball.* Jefferson, NC: McFarland, 2017.

Cey, Monte. "Major League Spring Training, Early Twentieth-Century Baseball Took Center Stage in Central Texas." *The Marlin Democrat,* February 5, 2008.

Clavin, Tom. "The Inside Story of Baseball's Grand World Tour of 1914." Smithsonian.com. March 21, 2014.

Cooper, Brian E. *Ray Schalk: A Baseball Biography.* Jefferson, NC: McFarland, 2009.

Crowley, John, William J. Smythe, and Mike Murphy, eds. *The Atlas of the Great Irish Famine 1845–5.* Ireland: Cork University Press, 2012.

Dellinger, Harold. *Nineteenth Century Stars.* Robert L. Tiemann, and Mark Rucker, Eds. Published by The Society for American Baseball Research, 2012.

Dellinger, H.L. *From Dust to Dust: An Account of the 1885 Western League.* Kansas City: Two Rivers Press, 1977.

Dickson, Paul. *The Dickson Baseball Dictionary.* New York: W.W. Norton, 2009.

Elfers, James. *The Tour to End all Tours: The Story of Major League Baseball World Tour, 1913–1914.* Lincoln: University of Nebraska Press, 2003.

Elias, Robert. *The Empire Strikes Out: How Baseball Sold U.S. Foreign Policy and Promoted the American Way Abroad.* New York: The New Press 2010.

Fleitz, David. *The Irish in Baseball: An Early History.* Jefferson, NC: McFarland, 2009.

Gray, Timothy M. *Tris Speaker: The Rough-and-Tumble Life of a Baseball Legend.* Lincoln: University of Nebraska Press, 2005.

Gurda, John. *Milwaukee: City of Neighborhoods.* Milwaukee: Historic Milwaukee, 2015.

Honig, Donald. *Baseball America.* New York: Macmillan, 1985.

Hornbaker, Tim. *Turning the Black Sox White.* New York: Simon and Schuster, 2014.

James, Bill. *The New Bill James Baseball Historical Abstract,* New York: Free Press, 2001.

Light, Thomas Fraser. *The Cultural Encyclopedia of Baseball,* 2nd ed. Jefferson, NC: McFarland, 2005.

Mack, Connie. *My 66 Years in the Big Leagues.* Philadelphia: John C. Winston, 1960.

Mahon, Tom, and Gillogly, James J. *Decoding the IRA.* Cork, Ireland: Mercier Press, 2008.

Margalas, Jim. "Introducing: The White Sox Around the World, 100 Years Later." SB Nation, Nov. 1, 2013.

Mathewson, Christy. *Pitching in a Pinch: Or, Baseball from the Inside.* New York: Gossett & Dunlap, 1912.

McElligot, Richard. *Forging a Kingdom: The GAA in Kerry, 1884–1934*. Cork, Ireland: Collins Press, 2013.

McGraw, John Joseph. *My Thirty Years in Baseball*. New York: Boni & Liveright, 1923.

Mills, Dorothy Seymour, and Harold Seymour. *Baseball: The People's Game*. New York: Oxford University Press, 1990.

Montgomery, Rick, and Shirl Kasper. *Kansas City: An American Story*. Kansas City: Kansas City Star Books, 1999.

Morris, Peter. *A Game of Inches: The Game Behind the Scenes*, Vol 2. Chicago: Ivan R. Dee, 2006.

Nemec, David. *The Beer & Whiskey League: The Illustrated History of the American Association—Baseball's Renegade Major League*. New York: Lyons Press, 2004.

_____. *The Great Encyclopedia of Nineteenth Century Major League Baseball*, 2nd ed. Tuscaloosa: University of Alabama Press, 2006.

_____. *The Rank and File of 19th Century Major League Baseball*. Jefferson, NC: McFarland, 2012.

Nicholls, Rochelle Llewelyn. *Joe Quinn Among the Rowdies: The Life of Baseball's Honest Australian*. Jefferson, NC: McFarland, 2014.

Podoll, Brian A. *The Minor League Milwaukee Brewers, 1859–1952*. Jefferson, NC: McFarland, 2003.

Reisler, Jim, ed. *Guys, Dolls and Curveballs: Damon Runyon on Baseball*. New York: Carroll & Graf, 2005.

Rielly, Edward J. *Baseball: An Encyclopedia of Popular Culture*. Lincoln: University of Nebraska Press, 2005.

Riess, Steven A., ed. *Encyclopedia of Major League Baseball Clubs*, Vol. 1. Westport, CT: Greenwood, 2006.

Ritter, Lawrence S., ed. *The Glory of Their Times*. New York: Macmillan, 1966.

Rosen, Charley. *The Emerald Diamond: How the Irish Transformed America's Greatest Pastime*. New York: HarperCollins, 2012.

Rutherford, Kris. *Baseball on the Prairie: How Seven Small-Town Teams Shaped Texas League History*. Charleston, S.C.: The History Press, 2014.

Sackmann, Jeff. "The Summer of Jeff," https://summerofjeff.wordpress.com/2011/08/08/ted-sullivan-humorous-stories-of-the-ball-field/.

Shulman, David. "On the Early Use of Fan in Baseball." *American Speech*, Vol. 71, No. 3, Duke University Press, 1996.

Silverman, Jeff, ed. *Great American Baseball Stories*. Lanham, MD: Lyons Press Classics, 2019.

Spink, Al. *One Thousand Sport Stories*. Chicago: Spink Brothers, 1921.

Spink, Alfred H. *The National Game*. Carbondale: Southern Illinois University Press, 2000. First published 1910 by The National Game Publishing Co.

Sullivan, Neil J. *The Minors: The Struggles and the Triumph of Baseball's Poor Relation from 1876 to the Present*. New York: St. Martin's Press 1991.

Sullivan, Ted. *History of World's Tour—Chicago White Sox and New York Giants*. Chicago: M.A. Donohue, 1914.

_____. *Humorous Stories of the Ball Field*. Chicago: M.A. Donohue & Co., 1903.

Sutter, L.M. *Arlie Latham: A Baseball Biography of The Freshest Man on Earth*. Jefferson, NC: McFarland, 2012.

Thorn, John. *Baseball in the Garden of Eden: The Secret History of the Early Game*. New York: Simon & Schuster, 2011.

Tiemann, Robert L., and Martin Rucker, eds. *Nineteenth Century Stars*. The Society of American Baseball Research, 1989.

Weisberger, Bernard. *When Chicago Ruled Baseball: The Cubs–White Sox World Series of 1906*. New York: Harper, 2006.

Wildman, Edwin. *Famous Leaders of Industry: The Life Stories of Boys Who Have Succeeded*, Vol. 2. Boston: Boston Company, 1922.

Witt, Brian, and Bob Buege. "The Founding of the American League by Five Irish American Milwaukeeans." CelticMKE.com, CelticMKE-Blog, 2017, https://celticmke.com/CelticMKE-Blog/Founding-American-League-Five-Irish-Americans.htm.

Websites

www.baseball-almanac.com
www.baseballhistorydaily.com
www.baseball-reference.com
www.clareherald.com
www.clarelibrary.ie
www.encyclopediadubuque.org
www.ripbaseball.com
www.sharockclubwis.com
www.thedeadballera.com
www.thenextbaseballcountrywillbefrance.
  blogspot.com
www.thisgameofgames.com

Newspapers

Alaska Daily Empire
Anaconda (MT) Standard
Arizona Republican
Arkansas Democrat
Athens (GA) Daily Banner
Atlanta Constitution
Atlanta Georgian and News
Austin American-Statesman
Baltimore Sun
Bloomington Pantograph
Boston Daily Globe
Boston Sunday Post
Bridgeport Evening Farmer (CT)
Brooklyn Daily Eagle
Bryan Daily Eagle
Buffalo Courier
Buffalo Enquirer
Buffalo Times
Burlington (IA) Gazette
Butte (MT) Miner
Cairo (IL) Bulletin
Calumet (IL) News
Charlotte Observer
Chattanooga Daily Times
Chattanooga News
Chester (PA) Times
Chicago Daily News
Chicago Examiner
(Chicago) Inter Ocean
Chicago Journal
Chicago Tribune
Cincinnati Commercial-Tribune
Cincinnati Enquirer
Clinton Herald (IA)
Council Bluffs Nonpareil
Daily Arkansas (Little Rock) Gazette
Daily Gate City (Keokuk, IA)
Daily Gazette (Wilmington, DE)
Daily Journal (Kankakee, IA)

Daily Morning Journal and Courier (New Haven)
Daily Nebraska State Journal (Lincoln)
Daily Press (Newport News)
Davenport (IA) Daily Times
Dayton Herald
Deaf-Mutes Journal
Decatur Herald
Des Moines Register
Deseret News
Detroit Free Press
Dubuque Daily Times
Dubuque Telegraph-Herald
El Paso Herald
El Paso Morning Times
Escabana (MI) Daily Press
Evening Star (Washington, D.C.)
Evening Times-Republican (Marshalltown, IA)
Evening World (NY)
Fairmont West Virginian
Fort Worth Gazette
Galveston Daily News
Hartford Courant
Herald Democrat (Sherman, TX)
Houston Post
Indianapolis Journal
Indianapolis News
Indianapolis Sun
Irish Independent
Irish Times
Jersey City News
Kansas City Daily Journal
Kansas City Daily Times
Kansas City Evening Star
Kerry Examiner
Kerry News
Kerry Reporter
Kerryman
Key West Citizen
Lake County (IN) Times
Lawrence (KS) Daily Journal
Leadville (CO) Herald-Democrat
Lewiston (ME) Daily Sun
Liberator (Tralee)
Lincoln (NE) Star
Los Angeles Herald
Louisville Courier Times-Journal
Macon Telegraph
Memphis Appeal
Milan Exchange (Gibson County, TN)
Milwaukee Journal
Milwaukee Sentinel
Minneapolis Tribune
Montgomery (AL) Advertiser
Monticello (IA) Express
Morning Record (Meriden, CT)

Muscatine (IA) Journal
Nashville Tennessean
Nashville Times
New Castle (PA) News
New Haven Morning Journal-Courier
New York Clipper
New York Evening World
New York Herald
New York Sun
New York Times
New York Tribune
News Scimitar (Memphis, TN)
Norfolk Virginian
Ogden Standard
Omaha Daily Bee
Paris (TX) News
Philadelphia Times
Phillipsburg (KS) Herald
Pittsburgh Daily Post
Pittsburgh Dispatch
Pittsburgh Gazette Times
Pittsburgh Herald
Pittsburgh Press
Post and Courier (Charleston, SC)
Racine (WI) Journal
Reno Gazette-Journal
Richmond (MO) Democrat
Richmond (VA) Dispatch
Richmond (VA) Times
Rochester (NY) Democrat
Rock Island (IL) Argus
Roswell (NM) Daily Record
St. Bernard (Arabi, LA) Voice
St. John Daily Sun (New Brunswick)
St. Joseph (MO) Gazette
St. Louis Globe-Democrat
St. Louis Post-Dispatch
St. Louis Republic
St. Louis Star and Times
St. Paul Daily Globe
Salem (OR) Capitol Journal
Salt Lake Herald
Salt Lake Tribune

San Antonio Gazette
San Antonio Sunday Light
San Francisco Examiner
Saskatoon Star Phoenix
Savannah Morning News
Scranton Republican
Seattle Star
Sheboygan Press-Telegram
Sioux City (IA) Herald
Spokane (WA) Daily Chronicle
Spokesman Review (Spokane, WA)
Sporting Life
Sporting News
Sunday Herald & Weekly National
    Intelligencer
Sunday Oregonian
Syracuse Herald
Times-Democrat (New Orleans)
Times Dispatch (Richmond, VA)
Times-Picayune (New Orleans)
Topeka Capital Journal
Topeka Daily Capital
Topeka Daily Herald
Topeka State Journal
Traverse City (MI) Evening Record
Trenton (NJ) Evening Times
Vancouver Sun
Warren County (VA) Democrat
Washington Evening Star
Washington Herald
Washington Post
Washington Sunday Star
Washington Times
Waterbury (CT) Evening Democrat
Watertown (NY) News
Watertown (WI) Republican
Waxahachie Daily Light
Wichita Eagle
Wilkes-Barre Record
Winnipeg Tribune
Winston-Salem Journal
Wisconsin (Madison) State Journal

Index

Adams, James Barton 37
Agnew, John "Admiral" 196
Alexander, Grover 226
Allison, Senator William 23
Altoona Mountain Cities 45, 46, 53
Altrock, Nick 220, 180, 182, 220
Alverreta, Henry 25
American Baseball Agency 185
American League 92, 139, 141–147, 166, 197, 214, 230, 231, 246
American Soccer League 111
Andrews, T.S. 71
Anson, Adrian "Cap" 28, 140, 142, 173, 174, 247
Arundel, Tug 66, 67
Atlanta Firecrackers 102
Aulick, W.W. 89
Axelson, Gustaf (G.W.) 14, 201, 203

Baker, Newton 226
Baker, Phil "Old Reliable" 78
Baltimore Monumentals 49, 53
Baltimore Orioles 46, 74, 111, 126, 146, 163, 205
Bancroft, Dave 2
Barney, William 140
Barnum, P.T. 1, 79
Bastain, Charlie 53
Baum, A.T. 249
Beaten, Ed 52
Bennett, Charlie 52
Birmingham Grays 74
Black Sox 28, 229, 235, 249
Blackburn Rovers 112
Blakeney, Mary 7
Boston Americans 46
Boston Beaneaters 87, 88
Boston Reds/Red Stockings 25, 53
Bracketlegs Charlie 115
Broadway Central Hotel (NY) 36
Brooklyn Grays 74

Brooklyn Superbas 124, 143
Brotherhood of Professional Base Ball Players 95, 214
Buckley, Frank 142
Buffalo Bisons 31, 144
Bulger, Bozeman 16, 231
Burch, Ernie 65
Burns, James D. 144, 145
Burns, Tom 67
Burtis House Hotel 23

Callahan, Jimmy 235
Carroll, Cliff 43
Casway, Jerrold I. 3, 4
Catholic University, D.C. 220
Chadwick, Henry 9, 184
Charles Hotel (St. Joseph, MO) 155
Chattanooga Chatts 102, 103
Chicago Browns 53
Chicago Orphans 103, 123, 144
Chicago Unions 48
Chicago White Sox 4, 181, 188, 223, 229
Chicago White Stockings 11, 28, 83, 144
Cincinnati Outlaw Reds 53
Cincinnati Red Stockings 10
Clarke, J. Justin 92, 150
Clarkson, Jim 5, 191
Cleveland Blues 146
Cleveland Forest Cities 59, 63
Cleveland Lake Shores 145
Clinton Teddies 187, 189
Cobb, Ty 3, 174, 226
Cody, William "Buffalo Bill" 93, 94
Cogan, Dick 96
Colgan, William 59
Collins, Eddie 224, 226
Collins, Scott "Bright Eyes" 111, 121
Collins, Shano 2
Colquitt, Governor Oscar 116
Comiskey, Ann "Nan" Kelly 32, 33
Comiskey, Charlie 1–249

Comiskey, "Honest John" 14, 20, 142
Comiskey, Jim 15, 110
Commodore Hotel, NY 240
Congress Hotel, Chicago 214
Corbett, James J. 103, 110, 117, 127, 142, 187
Corsicana Oil City 92, 149–151
Crawford, Sam 118
Cream Citys 10, 11, 71
Cresco, IA 27, 28
Croke Park, Ireland 233
Cuban Giants 85, 96, 122, 124

Daily, Con 4
Daily, Hugh "One Arm" 48, 68, 69, 70
Dallas Steers 114–120, 137, 174
Davis, "Big Jim" 37
Deasley, Tom "Sneak" 77, 78, 79
Decatur Commodores 190
Decker, Harry 59, 61
Decorah, IA 27, 28
Delahanty, "Big Ed" 173
Dempsey, Michael 92
Detroit Tigers 144, 161
Diaz, President Porfirio 127, 180, 181
Dickson, Paul 49
Dixon, Thomas 170
Donlin, "Turkey Mike" 174, 197
Dougherty, Charlie 71
Doyle, Cornelius 59
Doyle "Dirty Jack" 110, 127, 235
Doyle, Mrs. Larry 201
Dubuque Rabbits 23–28, 31, 32, 39, 155, 237
Dugan, Bill 49
Dugan, Ed 59, 65
Dunlap, Fred 46

Eisenfelder, Charles 150
Elfers, James E. 195
Elgin Kittens 190
Elgin Watch Factory team 17
Empress of Japan 201, 202, 205
Evans, Steve 199, 211
Everett House Hotel 32
Evers, Johnny 162, 175
Ewing, William "Buck" 43, 173, 235

Faber, Urban "Red" 197, 224, 226
Farrell, Joe "Rooter" 193, 202, 214
Feist, Albert "Hotspur" 212
Ferdinand, Archduke Franz 215
Fitzgerald, Dick 238
Fitzgerald, the Rev. Edward 238–240, 244, 250
Fitzgerald, J.J. 229, 230
Fitzsimmons, Bob 117, 127, 138
Fogarty, Jim 173

Foley, Patrick 241, 243
Forepaugh's Circus 96
Forest Citys 59, 63
Fort Worth Panthers 119, 150
Fournier, Jack 2
Fullerton, Hugh S. 220, 228

Gaelic Football 238–244
Gaffney, John 79
Gallinger Hospital (D.C.) 247
Gandil, Arnold "Chick" 229, 248, 249
Gardner, Charles 21
Garvin "Bullet-Proof-Ned" 118, 123, 124
Gay, Timothy M. 215
Gilman, Jimmy 116
Gleason, John "Jack" 23, 31–34, 37
Gleason, William 23, 31–34
Great Northern Hotel, St. Louis 140, 143
Green, Hetty "Witch of Wall Street" 121
Green, Ned "Colonel" 121
Griffith, Clark "The Old Fox" 134, 145, 232
Griffith Field 4

Hamilton, Billy 2
Hanlon, Ned 111, 112, 124, 138, 143, 165
Hart, James A. 143, 162, 204
Hartnett, Leo "Gabby" 234
Havana, Cuba 132
Havenor, C.S. 142, 177
Henderson, David 23
Hepworth, W.F. "Billy" 120
Hermann, Garry 177, 178, 183
Hewitt, Robert 77, 86
Hewitt, Walter 86, 95
Higgins, Bob 83
Hinton, Charles "Bull" 133
History of World's Tour—Chicago White Sox and New York Giants 4, 208, 210, 216
Hogan, Joe 14
Hogan, Paul 188
Hough, Frank 142
Hoy, William "Dummy" 2, 77, 81, 82 86, 89, 173
Hutchison, Bill 53

Indianapolis Hoosiers 55, 59, 144
Irish Greenstockings 90
Irish Republican Army (IRA) 4, 239, 242, 243
Isbell, Frank "Baldy" 162

Jackson, Joe S. 192
Jacksonville Jacks 190
James, Bill 54
Jeffries, James J. 138
Jennings, Hughie 173, 235

Johnson, Byron Bancroft "Ban" 37, 139–146, 197, 200, 212, 218, 231
Johnson, Walter "Big Train" 235

Kaiser Bill 222
Kankakee Kays 190
Kansas City Blues 144, 190
Kansas City Cowboys 46–51, 53–59, 61–65
Keefe, Tim 235
Keeler, William "Wee Willie" 145, 173
Keio University 205
Kelly, Joe 235
Kelly, Mike "King" 75, 87, 161, 173, 235
Keokuk Hawkeyes 55
Kerry Gaelic GAA Footballers 238–243
Killilea, Henry 139, 140, 143, 144
Killilea, Matt 144
King George V 212, 213
Kirby House Hotel (Milwaukee) 61
Kittridge, Malachi 188
Kling, Johnny 2, 144
Knickerbocker Rules 55

Lajoie, Napoleon "Nap" 173, 178
Landis, Kenesaw Mountain 234
Lapham, W.B. 25
Lapp, Jack 224
Lardner, R.W. "Ring" 211, 217
Latham, Arlie 2, 35, 173, 211
Lee, General Fitzhugh 132
Lehigh College 96
Leibold, Nemo 224
Lipton, Sir Thomas J. 207
Lobert, Hans 200, 206, 211
Loftus, Tom 23, 31–35, 64, 67, 139, 140, 142, 143
Lucas, Henry V. 44–48
Lucas, W.H. 72, 138
Lynch, Jim (umpire) 115
Lynch, Tom 204, 206, 207

Mackey, Gus (Wolf-Eating Bear) 122
Macon Central City 102
Manchesters (soccer team) 112
Manning, James 143
Marquard, Rube 226
Marsans, Armando 134
Mathewson, Christy 83, 173, 174, 178, 197, 212, 226
McCarthy, Tom 235
McCloskey, John J. 135
McGarr, Chippy 54
McGillicuddy, Cornelius "Connie Mack" 2, 78, 79, 80–84, 87, 88, 142–144, 173, 235
McGinnis, George "Jumbo" 35–37, 42, 43

McGinnity, Joe "Iron Man" 145
McGlynn, Frank 216
McGraw, John J. "Muggsy" 127, 132, 138, 140, 146, 173, 174, 195–199, 203, 205, 207, 209–212, 215, 221, 235
McKee, Jim 23
McKim, Americus 47, 48, 53, 54
McMullin, Fred 224
McNair, H.C. 43
McNealus, J.C. 114
McSorley, John "Trick" 94
Memphis Fever Germs 104
Memphis Giants 102
Memphis Reds 65
Merchant Hotel (Dubuque) 130
Merkle, Fred 175, 209, 211, 216
Meyers, John Tortes "Chief" 174
Mike Corbett's Saloon – Chicago 195
Miller Park Milwaukee 247
Milwaukee Brewers 53, 144, 177, 247
Milwaukee Home for the Friendless 71
Minneapolis Millers 144
Mobile Blackbirds 102
Montgomery Lambs 102
Montgomery Senators 136–138
Mulford, Ren, Jr. 38, 39, 103
Mullane, Tony "The Count" 35, 36, 42, 101
Murnane, Tim 121, 154, 161
Muscatine Pearl Finders 190
Mutrie, Jim 82

Nashville Tigers 104, 105, 106
Nation, Carrie 146
Neenan, Connie 242
New Haven Steers 121–126
New Orleans Pelicans 102
New York Giants 4, 82, 88, 110, 134, 175, 178, 195–198, 202, 211, 212, 219, 232, 234, 235
New York Highlanders 134
New York Metropolitans 36, 121
Newark Colts 121
Nichols, Charles "Kid" 50
Nolan, Jim 122
Norfolk Clams 121
Northwestern League 23–26, 68, 72, 73

O'Brien, Billy 49, 54, 59, 62, 65, 67, 76
O'Brien, Thomas 59
O'Connor, Jack 235
O'Connor, Mike 117, 118
O'Day, Hank 2, 16, 77, 86, 87, 175
O'Doul, Lefty 95
O'Dwyer, Bill 241
O'Leary, Dan 64
Omaha Omahogs 55
Overall, Orval "Orrie" 2, 177

Paris Exhibition 91
Paris Homeseekers 150
Paris Parasites 151, 152
Paterson Silk Weavers 121, 126
Pathe Eclectic Film Company 215, 216, 220
Peoria Reds 21, 23
Philadelphia Athletics 84
Philadelphia Keystones 53
Phillips, Bill 100
Pittsburgh Stogies 53
Players' League 85
Plessy v. Ferguson 4
Poincare, French President Raymond 211
Pond, Arlie 205
Pope Pius X 209, 210
Prairie du Chien College 25
Prickly Ash Bitters 57

Quille, Rev. C.J. 193
Quinn, H.D. 142
Quinn, Joe 46

Radbourn, Charles "Hoss" 2, 21, 25–28, 31, 173
Reck, Alfred P. 245
Record (Mexican baseball team) 182
Reis, Lawrence P. "Laurie" 25
Republican House (Milwaukee) 139, 143, 144
Ritter, Lawrence 200
Robbins, George 14, 15
Roberts, J. Doak 150, 152
Rockford White Stockings 23, 25–27
Roosevelt, Teddy 172, 184
Ross Castle (Ireland) 92
Rowe, David 2, 46
Runyon, Damon 1, 211, 221
Rusie, Amos 134
Ruth, George Herman "Babe" 232
Ryan, Paddy 15, 109

St. Gall's School Milwaukee 8
St. James Hotel Kansas City 57
St. Joe Saints 130
St. John's Cathedral Milwaukee 248
St. Louis Brown Stockings 30, 31, 35
St. Louis Browns 29, 31–37, 41, 43, 57, 247
St. Louis Red Stockings 30, 40
St. Louis Unions 45
St. Louis University 219
St. Marys, KS 9, 11–13, 90, 223
St. Mary's College 12–17, 223–225, 250
St. Mary's Saints 15, 223, 224
St. Paul White Caps 53
Say, Lou 53
Scanlon, Michael B. "Cap" 163

Schaefer, Herman A. "Germany" 197, 199, 203–205, 207, 209, 211
Schalk, Ray "Cracker" 2, 192, 248, 249
Seery, Emmett 49, 54, 59, 65
Seward, George (umpire) 51, 52
Seymour, Cy 163
Seys, John O. 202
Shafer, George "Orator" 46
Shaughnessy, Thomas 16
Sheehy, John Joe 242, 243
Sheridan, Jack (umpire) 201
Sheridan, John B. 165, 234
Sherman, Sadie 175
Sherman-Denison Students 150
Sisters of Charity 42
soccer 4, 100–113, 147, 231, 239
Southern League 65–68, 87, 102–106 , 108, 113, 115, 116, 135, 138, 174
Spalding, Albert Goodwill 61, 93, 102, 195
Speaker, Tris 197, 209, 213, 226
Spink, Al 3, 31–34, 48, 51, 112, 138–140, 142, 171, 218, 219, 230, 234, 246
Spink, C.C. 37
Sportsman's Park and Sportsman's Park Club Association 30, 36, 41
Stallings, George 144
Stars of Milwaukee 11
Stovall, George 2
Stovey, George Washington 83, 148
Street, Charles "Old Sarge" 177
Sullivan, Detective Dennis 90
Sullivan, Eugene 8, 90
Sullivan, Fleury 59
Sullivan, John "Chub" 173
Sullivan, John L. 15, 40, 42, 43, 109, 110, 188
Sullivan, Pat 53
Sullivan, Thomas "Sleeper" 25, 31, 34, 37, 237
Sullivan, Timothy, Sr. 8, 90
Sullivan's Baseball Freaks 122
Swampdoodle Park 86
Sweeney, Charlie 46

Taub, Sam 120
Taylor, William "Billy" 25–28, 46
Texarkana Casketmakers 150
Texas League 92, 113, 120, 121, 127, 135, 149, 150–152, 158, 191
Texas Southern League 116, 119
Thorpe, Jim 197, 201, 209, 210, 216
Thorpe, Mrs. Jim 201
Tinker, Joe 174, 175
Toledo Avengers 55, 64
Troy Trojans (New York) 78, 84, 86, 89–91

Unglaub, Bob 163
University of Alabama 104
University of Pennsylvania 193

Vanderbeck, George A. "Count" 161
Veach, William Walter "Peek-a-Boo" 50,
  51, 53, 59, 60, 62, 65, 73
Veeck, Bill 166
Veeck, Bill, Jr. 166
Visner, Joe 62
Von der Ahe, Chris 30–38, 46, 101, 140, 235

Waco Tigers 152
Waddell, Rube 178
Wagner, Johannes Peter "Honus" 126
Wake Forest 231
Walker, Fleet 83
Walker, Weldy 83
Walsh, "Big Ed" 193
Ward, Billy 119
Warhop, Jack "Warhoop" 162
Waseda University 205
Washington and Lee University 128
Washington Nationals 53
Washington Senators 67, 77–79, 83–91, 93,
  95–99, 124, 146, 163, 167, 188, 196, 235

Weaver, Buck 2
Welch, Mickey 235
Western Association 131
Western League 39, 61, 65, 117, 139, 140, 183
White, Sol 83
Whitney, Jim "Grasshopper" 86
Whitney, William C. 142
Williamson, Ned 83
Wilmington Peaches 121
Wilmington Quicksteps 53
Wilmot, Walt 2, 79, 144
Wilson, Woodrow 212, 221
Wingo, Ivey 202
Wolcott, "Barbados Joe" 111
Wolf-Eating-Bear (Gus Mackey) 122
World's Tour of Baseball 1913–1914 195–217
Wright, George 9, 10, 172

York, Tom 55
Young, Ben (umpire) 65
Young, Cy 145